THE
DARK AGES

Life in the
United States 1945-1960

by Marty Jezer

SOUTH END PRESS   BOSTON

Library of Congress Catalog Card Number: 81-51391

ISBN 0-89608-127-3 paperback
ISBN 0-89608-128-1 casebound

Design, typesetting, paste-up done by the South End Press collective.
Cover design by Michael Prokosch

South End Press/ 302 Columbus Ave./ Boston MA 02116

In memory of my sister, Ruth

TABLE OF CONTENTS

INTRODUCTION

I began this book in 1973 at a time when American society, polarized by the Vietnam War, seemed to be coming apart. I was inspired to write it because there was then no comprehensive history that adequately discussed the root causes of our follies abroad and our difficulties at home.

Revisionist historians (William Appleman Williams, Gabriel Kolko, Lloyd Gardner, David Horowitz, Walter Lafeber, and others) were already reinterpreting the origins of the Cold War to show that the United States was not entirely an innocent party. Their writings exploded the myth that the Soviet Union had been to blame for all the troubles of the postwar world. The main expansionist power, in fact, had been the United States.

But there seemed to be no reliable histories that dealt with what had happened in the United States itself during the period from 1945 to 1960.* True, we did have the excellent contemporary writings of such social and political critics as Paul Goodman, C. Wright Mills, I.F. Stone, Jane Jacobs, Lewis Mumford, Paul Sweezy, Dwight MacDonald and Murray Kempton. But no one had tried to put this commentary into a historical format, or even to integrate it into a broader discussion of American foreign policy goals.

So, besides wanting to explore the causes of the social and political disintegration I was seeing all around me, I wanted to make connections: first, between the recent past and the present (that is, between the crisis of the 1970s and 1980s and the events of the postwar period); and second, between issues and problems that are usually perceived as separate in themselves.

The connections between present and past ought to be obvious. For instance, the energy "shortage" and our "crisis" with Iran are both results of decisions made during the 1950s. Likewise, our "difficulties" in Central America are products of policies chosen during that same time. In Central America and

---

*Lawrence Wittner's *Cold War America* (Prager, 1974) and Howard Zinn's *Postwar America* (Bobbs Merrill, 1973) have since filled this gap.

the Persian Gulf, as in the Mississippi Delta and the industrial cities of the North, we are reaping what we have sown. Policies that seemed benign and even successful during the postwar period come back to haunt us later.

As for the connectedness of all things, most texts describe the various aspects of foreign and domestic policy as separate from one another. Foreign policy has nothing to do with domestic economics; policies for energy, housing, land use, transportation, urban affairs and rural life are all arrived at pragmatically, independent of each other. The issue of agribusiness and concentration in agriculture, for example, is usually discussed solely as a parcel of overall farm policy. But I treat it in the context of monopolistic tendencies endemic to American capitalism as a whole, and I link it to over-crowded and over-burdened cities. In this analysis, urban and rural problems are intertwined; they cannot be understood as distinct or separate. And similar contextual relationships are apparent with most other issues of our time.

This book is not intended as a thorough history of the period. It ignores many important subjects (religion, leisure, elections, the growth of bureaucracy—public and corporate—for example), and makes no attempt at chronological order. Rather, it deals with broad social themes and with crucial patterns of decision-making and policy. Its value, such as it has, is to provide historic background for some of the important issues that involve us today.

When I began writing this book, our domestic problems seemed mainly cultural (alienation of the young, the fracturing of the nuclear family, the on-the-job ennui of working people, discrimination against blacks and other minorities, oppression of women, etc.). Today our problems are also economic (high unemployment, double-digit inflation, declining productivity, high energy costs, serious environmental problems). Whatever our troubles—cultural, social, economic or political—their source can be traced directly back to the postwar years (if not before), to ideological assumptions, choices perceived and decisions made in the period between 1945 and 1960.

Limiting the postwar period to these fifteen years is admittedly arbitrary. Some historians extend the postwar period up through the 1970s. Others ignore World War II as a guide-mark and treat the period from 1933 as one self-defined era. For me, 1960 marks the definitive end of the repressive Dark Ages, and the beginning of a more hopeful and democratic period. This activist era began in 1960 and lasted, I would say, until the early 1970s when the movement that gave it definition was destroyed by the Nixonian reaction and its own inherent flaws.

Some might suggest that the Reagan Administration is likely to introduce repressive elements of a new dark age. But the lessons of the 1960s have not all been forgotten. Whatever policies the right wing has in store, Americans will not be as acquiescent in their own suppression as they were during the postwar years. The same can also be said, even more so, of other peoples in the world.

The book is divided into three parts. Part One provides the political backdrop against which life within the United States unfolds. The first three chapters deal with foreign policy from a revisionist perspective. I have tried, in as short a space as possible, to synthesize the research of the afore-mentioned historians. Chapter four, which concludes the first part, deals with political repression at home as the domestic aspect of our Cold War foreign policy.

Since hostility towards the Soviet Union is a premise out of which so much of American politics flows, it behooves an author, who writes from an American vantage and argues that the Cold War is primarily an American invention, to say something about Soviet complicity. Until the Soviet archives are open (which will take a domestic upheaval within the Soviet Union, i.e., an authentic socialist revolution), we can only guess at Soviet motives. But this much is certain: until the late 1960s, the United States was by far the most powerful country in the world and the Soviets were in no position—militarily or economically—to challenge our supremacy. Moreover, U.S. foreign policy, though always obfuscated in moralistic rhetoric, has concrete imperial goals. Investment in foreign countries is a necessary prop for domestic prosperity and an essential source of profit for many large corporations. An open door for overseas investment (as is explained in part one) is the cornerstone of our foreign policy. However repugnant Soviet totalitarianism is, the Soviet Union has never represented a threat to the United States, except insofar as it aids socialist revolutions that threaten American overseas corporate investment.

But revolutionary, socialistic currents, especially in the Third World, are inevitable with or without Soviet assistance. By insisting that the Soviet Union is a threat to our own security and that the Kremlin is the sinister behind-the-scenes mastermind of Third World unrest, the United States justifies its support of counter-revolution under the guise of stopping Soviet expansionism all over the world.

In short, the Cold War is a ballet of two clumsy giants locked in a dance of death. The United States—openly expansive, confident, brash, masking its imperial ambitions with self-righteous propaganda, believing competition inherent in human affairs—perceives every Soviet action as a challenge to itself. Through the prism of our capitalist gestalt we expect the Soviets to act aggressively in the competition for global dominance. And the Soviet Union—believing, with some historic justification, that the capitalist west is its enemy, its ruling class blinded by the paranoia typical of all dictatorships, and assuming, therefore, the defensive position of a cornered bear, snarling and lashing out in self protection—confirms for Americans their own perception that the Soviet Union is an irrational, aggressive, violent society, therefore a danger to their own security. As President Truman once said, the Soviets "are like bulls in a china shop." But it doesn't necessary follow, as Truman insisted it did, that "we've got to teach them a lesson."

The seven chapters of Part Two cover life within the United States: the economy, customs, and social mores of the country. Chapter five deals with the economy and its various components: military spending, advertising and easy-credit, artificial consumption. Chapter six shows the effects of monopoly on the brewery business and in the transportation and energy sectors. Chapter seven talks about agriculture and land use. Chapter eight is about housing, the deterioration of urban neighborhoods and the evolution of suburban living and culture. Chapter nine explores the plight of the working class. Chapter ten discusses family life, the myth of togetherness and the prevailing anti-feminist ideology. Chapter eleven is about growing up as part of the postwar baby boom generation. A unifying theme of this entire section concerns how the large corporations used their wealth, power and influence to shape the quality of life in virtually every social sphere.

Part Three represents an eccentric departure from the direction of the text. Instead of discussing the mainstream politics of American life, I go off on a tangent to describe the postwar roots of the civil rights movement, the peace movement, the counter-culture and the new left—those participatory and democratic currents that marked the 1960s and the early 1970s. Because political repression was prevalent through much of the postwar period, radicalism was expressed culturally and artistically more so than through political action. I emphasize cultural rather than political radicalism, not out of personal preference, but in order to accurately depict dominant trends of the time.

I have two reasons for discussing the seeds of sixties radicalism rather than the direction of mainstream politics. First, the history of the Democratic and Republican parties, including their dominant personalities and their liberal and conservative tendencies, is readily available. And this history, to be frank, is not very interesting. The differences between the leading political players of the time were more of style than of substance. Dean Acheson, for example, fancied himself a realist; John Foster Dulles spoke in moral absolutes. As secretaries of state, both men pursued a similar and rather hysterical anti-Soviet policy. As President, Harry Truman was admirable for his plain-speaking honesty. Where Truman was combative, President Eisenhower seemed more genial and grandfatherly. His great popularity as a wartime hero transcended partisan politics. Yet, other than allowing big business a free hand, Ike followed the same overall policies, both domestic and foreign, as President Truman.

Adlai E. Stevenson, Governor of Illinois and twice Democratic candidate for President, was, for many, the most attractive political figure of the time. I cut my political teeth in Youth for Stevenson during the 1956 campaign and even got to shake the great man's hand. Stevenson was rational, witty and always articulate. After losing an election to Eisenhower he said, "I'd rather be right than President." Alas, he ended up neither. As our delegate to the United Nations in the Kennedy and Johnson administrations, he closed his career defending the Bay of Pigs invasion of Cuba, the landing of U.S. Marines in the Dominican

Republic, and the intervention in Vietnam. Supporters of
Stevenson, who were passionate in their faith, persist in
believing that he died a weak and broken man. But if nothing
else, the Governor had integrity; one has to assume that he
supported the policies he so eloquently defended.

Corporate liberals, like Stevenson, no matter how well-
intentioned, have been wedded to the demands of the corporate
economy that sustained them in power. Two options for change
remain: the right and the left. A genuine conservative movement does not exist in the U.S. Those, as in the Reagan
Administration, who call themselves "conservative" are actually
reactionaries intent upon expanding their own economic and
social privilege no matter what the cost to society. True
conservatives take a prudent, cautionary approach to change.
Reactionaries, of the American kind, use conservative rhetoric
but in fact are bent on destroying any fragment of the past that
stands in their way. Those who preach conservative solutions
support corporate enterprise even as it despoils the very fabric of
our social and cultural life, the preservation of which is the
premise of true conservative thought. A gaggle of honking
hypocrites, the right serves to catalogue every native strain of
prejudice and greed. Racism is masked by states' rights; though
when it comes to foreign affairs, states' righters want their
central government aggressive and strong. The right speaks
boldly for individual freedom but is the first to unleash the police
on political dissenters and social nonconformists. Rightists
abhor government spending but will give the armed forces
everything they ask. They want to curb the power of government; yet they would use the power of government, as with the
abortion issue, to interfere with a most precious human right,
the right to control one's own body. The right enters stage center
with President Reagan. The one positive achievement of his
administration ought to be a revival of the political left.

As flawed, confused and misdirected as it so often is, the left
remains the fragile, humane hope. The radical tradition in
America is a proud one. Virtually every useful reform in
American life—from the abolition of slavery, to woman's
suffrage, to desegregation, to the right of working people to
organize unions—is a result of ideas and agitation emanating
from the left. But you'll rarely read anything of its influence in

the standard history texts. Thus, the need for the three chapters (two cultural and one political) that make up Part Three. If history is useful it is because people, actively participating in the processes of self-rule, can and do learn from the past. The failures (and the weaknesses) of the left are embedded in recent times: its ignorance of history, its sexist attitudes, its estrangement from working people and alienation from the mainstream culture are all outgrowths of the postwar experience. And the left's achievements as well—its courage and its success in mobilizing people for civil rights, against the bomb, against war, poverty, injustice and repression—all come out of the cauldron of that time.

I mean this book to be an activist tool. If my analysis of U.S. foreign policy and domestic programs makes sense to you; that is, if you can place yourself in the historical context that I describe, then you have no choice but to participate in the movement for change and to seek solutions to our problems that are radical, that go directly to the core. Political issues, in these frightening times, cut close to the bone. Let's understand our history, or we will doom ourselves to a treadmill of past mistakes.

ACKNOWLEDGEMENTS

Jeffrey Weiss first encouraged me to write this history; I thank him.

John Schall and Mary Lea, my editors at South End Press, guided the book from rough draft to production. They, like the other members of the South End Collective, are committed to the books they publish. As an author, I benefited from their criticisms and their encouragement.

Jim O'Brien edited what I hoped would be my final draft. He challenged many of my interpretations, tightened the text, and pressed me into yet another revision. The book is vastly improved thanks to his good effort. I, alas, am responsible for any of its failings.

I majored in American history, graduating from college in 1961. Given the climate of the times it is not exceptional that I was shielded from dissenting and radical views, from non-orthodox historical interpretations. My intellectual awakening came after I graduated from college, from my friends and, beginning in the mid-sixties, my comrades in The Movement. But I'm also grateful to Arthur Church, my editor on the staff of the Merit Student Encyclopedia, for encouraging me to write history and to question hand-me-down historical assumptions.

The writing of history is shaped by the political perspectives individual historians bring to the task. My co-editors at *Win* magazine and my comrades in the War Resisters League greatly fostered my writing career and shaped my political thinking. Special thanks to Paul Johnson, Maris Cakars, Susan Kent Cakars and David McReynolds—among many others—for their friendship and tutelage.

A brief stint on the editorial board of *Liberation* magazine, then under the editorial direction of Dave Dellinger, Barbara Deming, Paul Goodman, Staughton Lynd and Sid Lens, was my graduate seminar in political theory and action. They, and many of the other contributors to that magazine, have had a profound and ongoing influence on my ideas.

Between completion of the first draft and the final

manuscript I benefited from participating in a political study group. My cohorts in Brattleboro, especially Shoshana Rihn, Bobby Payne, Judy Ashkenaz, David Ershun, and Virginia Page greatly enhanced my understanding of history.

Martin S. Mitchell, Kathryn Kilgore, Gilbert Ruff, Judy Ruff, Virginia Page, Harold Crooks, Suzanne Peters and Paul Johnson commented upon various drafts and chapters. Their criticisms were invariably valuable.

Allison Hannan typed the first draft, Virginia Page the final. Thanks to both for their assistance.

Thanks to my friends at Packer Corner, and to Alain and Mardi Ratheau at Solar Applications for enabling me to find time to complete the book. Carol Bernstein and W.H. Ferry gave timely assistance. My mother, Blanche, and my father, Meyer, who died in 1975, were very supportive.

Last and first, thanks to Mimi Morton for a sturdy oak desk, a room off the kitchen, and the best possible writing environment a few months of each year.

—Marty Jezer

PART ONE:
Repression at Home and Abroad

The problem is not how to get rid of the enemy, but rather how to get rid of the last victor. For what is a victor but one who has learned that violence works. Who will teach him a lesson?"
— *Niccolo Tucci in* Politics *Magazine,*
July 1945.

Prologue:
Blues for a Triumphant America

> Moppin' up soda pop rickeys
> To our hearts' delight
> Dancin' to swingeroo quickies,
> Jukebox Saturday Night.
> —The Glenn Miller Orchestra with the
> Modernaires.*

> Oo bop sh'bam a cooga mop.
> —standard bebop riff.**

*Words and music by Al Stillman and Paul McGrane, copyright 1942 by Mutual Music Society, Inc.
**"Oo Bop Sh'Bam" recorded by Dizzy Gillespie sextet with Gil Fuller, vocal, May 25, 1946, is available on a number of albums, including *Dizzy Gillespie: The Small Groups (1945-1946)* Phoenix LP-2, which includes many of the classic bop sides with Charlie Parker and others.

13

Bandleader Glenn Miller died in December 1944 when his plane was lost over the English Channel during a flight from London into France. The liberation of France was all but completed when his plane went down and Allied forces were preparing for the invasion of Germany. Victory was less than six months away and Miller was en route to the war zone to prepare for the arrival of his Army Air Force Band, which was going to entertain American troops at the front.

Although over-age and exempt from the draft, Miller had accepted a commission in the Army Air Force in 1942, at the peak of his musical career. "I, like every American, have an obligation to fulfill," he said at the time of his enlistment."That obligation is to lend as much support as I can to winning the war." Miller's idea of duty went beyond selling war bonds or recording air-checks for use on the armed forces radio network, which is what the government asked of most draft-exempt musicians and entertainers. He wanted to play for the troops personally, to raise their morale, and to bring his band where its playing would mean the most: at the front, as close to the combat as his superior officers would allow. "Glenn Miller's enlistment," piped one fan magazine, "was as great a boon to the morale of the men in the army as his music was to the folks back home."[1]

Between 1939 and his death, Glenn Miller had the most popular dance band in America. He dominated the Hit Parade the way Elvis Presley would in the 1950s and the Beatles a decade later. In 1940, it was estimated that one out of every four jukebox nickels went to spin a Miller tune. His music was confident and lighthearted, with a gentle jazz-infected beat and a disciplined sense of ease that was lacking in most other jazz-influenced white swing bands. His music had a cohesive, inner strength as well, an assurance that transcended the horror of war and recalled the way life was in the peaceful prewar days, at the height of the big band sound. His music spoke to an innocent America, to bobby-soxers and jitterbuggers, to drugstore cowboys, young people in love, and lovers going off to war. The smooth, professional competence of his band expressed optimism of ultimate victory and good days to come. Because of his popularity, especially with the servicemen and women overseas, he became an authentic wartime hero and his music took on added meaning from its association with the wartime years.

After the war, and despite the decline of the big dance bands, the Glenn Miller Orchestra was resurrected under the directorship of its original drummer, Ray McKinley. The band remained popular throughout the 1950s playing old Miller favorites like *Tuxedo Junction, In the Mood, String of Pearls, Chattanooga Choo Choo, Kalamazoo,* and *Jukebox Saturday Night.* But its audience was growing old and the music old with it. From an expression of vital, youthful exuberance that described the essence of wartime America, the music of Glenn Miller became a stagnant, sad-eyed remembrance of a rapidly fading past.

World War II produced a second music, a music that articulated a different perception of the American dream. Bebop was black music. Its roots were in the ghettos and rural poverty of black America and it was nourished in obscure nightspots that few people, even the most dedicated afficionados of cafe society, knew existed. Bebop was a deliberate and self-conscious musical rebellion, an attempt by black musicians to reclaim jazz as their own cultural expression. The popularity of big band swing during the 1930s had made jazz marketable to a white audience for the first time. Although swing had developed in black jazz bands (especially those led by Fletcher Henderson, Jimmy Lunceford, Duke Ellington, and Count Basie), it was white bandleaders, copying the style of the black innovators, who gained commercial success. Some white bandleaders, notably Benny Goodman, opposed segregation, hired black musicians, and retained the spontaneity of authentic jazz. But most white bandleaders chose to appeal to the mass white audience, and the creative excitement of jazz was sacrificed in the process.

Young black jazz musicians, coming up through the ranks of the swing bands, wanted to create a music that the popular white bands could not copy. Bebop was developed during the early forties at jam sessions at such Harlem nightspots as Minton's Playhouse and Monroe's Uptown House. Among the pioneers of the new music were alto saxophonist Charlie "Bird" Parker, trumpet player Dizzy Gillespie, pianist Thelonious Monk, and drummers Kenny Clarke and Max Roach. The art of bop was to take the chord progressions of traditional blues and standard popular tunes and stand them on their head, metamorphizing them in the process into complex, jagged, multi-noted improvisations often played at breakneck tempos with furious intensity. Bop was a music like nothing that had come before: psychosis in blue, a nightmarish experience that, at first hearing, assaulted the listener's ear, offering no point of commercial compromise. It was too fast to dance to and few could hum the tunes; the riffs and improvisations, powered as they were by a raw and raging energy, sounded as if they were composed by madmen. Yet, for those who would dig this strange new music, that is, those who could march to the unevenly accented onomatopoeic polyrythms of a bebop drummer, the music was beautiful, almost classical in the perfection of its own inner logic. If the music of Glenn Miller reflected a yearning for order and things familiar, bebop based itself on a perception of reality gone askew, a society run amuck. In a world engulfed by violence and war a Charlie Parker saxophone solo or a Dizzy Gillespie scat chorus, like "oo bop sh'bam," seemed therapeutic, even sane.[2]

The night the war ended, 9 August 1945, Charlie Parker, the most influential of all bop musicians, the one cat the hipsters dug most, had a gig at a small, cavernous cellar joint on 52nd Street called the Three Deuces.[3] That night and into the early morning, while millions of New Yorkers were celebrating V-J Day in a triumphant outpouring of long-contained emotion at Times Square, Bird was playing his brilliant music ten blocks to the north. Bird lived. Glenn Miller was dead. Who, on that most wonderful of all summer nights, would have imagined that this black bopster genius (and not the celebrants dancing, cheering, singing, kissing, hugging, and winding their way through tons of confetti in long, exuberant conga lines) was attuned to the future, and that his apocalyptic nightmare vision of the American dream was a vision of a world to come.

Chapter One

> The conjunction of an immense military establishment and a large arms industry is new in the American experience. The total influence—economic, political, even spiritual—is felt in every office of the federal government. We recognize the imperative need for this development. Yet we must not fail to comprehend its grave implications. Our toil, resources and livelihood are all involved; so is the very structure of our society.
>
> —President Dwight D. Eisenhower, Farewell Address, 17 January 1961.

At the end of World War II, the United States was the richest, most powerful nation on earth. War production had ended the Depression and, for the first time in more than fifteen years, the economy was booming. Industrial and agricultural profits were at record highs. Unemployment was at a low, pre-Depression level; personal savings were two and a half times higher than they were before the war; and corporate profits, estimated by the *Wall Street Journal* at $55 billion for the wartime years, represented a healthy nest-egg to finance reconversion to peacetime production.[1] At war's end, *Business Week* looked to the future and reported a "wholesome optimism about industry's ability to get back speedily into normal civilian production."[2] A few months later, *Life* surveyed business prospects along the narrow financial canyons of Wall Street and announced that "the sunny radiance of money-making is brightening the citadel of U.S. capitalism."[3]

It was not hard to be bullish about America. The American dream of material well-being, of a chicken in every pot and two cars in every garage—a nasty joke during the Depression—now seemed likely to come true. "Americans have come through depression and war to a new pinnacle of self-confidence," wrote John Chamberlain in November 1946. "The future is as bright as they can make it."[4] And *Fortune* magazine, discussing the prospects of American capitalism, promised, "Practically everybody seems sure that the U.S., once it hurdles reconversion, cannot avoid the most wonderful time in world history."[5]

In 1941, Henry Luce, publisher of *Life, Fortune,* and *Time* magazines, and one of the most influential leaders of the mass media, had predicted the coming of what he called "The American Century." The time has come, he said "to accept wholeheartedly our duty and our opportunity as the most powerful and vital nation in the world and in consequence to assert upon the world the full impact of our influence, for such means as we see fit." "Duty" and "opportunity," for Luce, lay principally with world trade. "The vision of America as the dynamic leader of world trade, has within it the possibility of such enormous human progress as to stagger the imagination. Let us not be staggered by it. Let us rise to its tremendous possibilities."[6] With victory, Luce's dream of planetary manifest destiny seemed assured. The American victory opened the world to American corporate expansion. The coming century would belong to the American capitalist.

The United States, alone of the major powers, emerged from the war physically unscathed. Although German U-boats torpedoed U.S. merchant ships and oil tankers within sight of the Atlantic coast, and the debris of destruction—oil slicks, cargo, corpses—often washed ashore, the mainland itself was never threatened. The surrounding oceans served, as the Isolationists had argued they would, as impenetrable moats. Neither Germany nor Japan had the capability of attacking the North American continent by air; nor, given that the Nazis had been unable to invade Britain across the narrow English Channel, was there any danger of an enemy landing on North American shores. It was "for the sake of the righteous," one minister said in a V-E Day sermon, that "God has preserved our cities and kept them from harm."[7]

Europe, Japan and much of Asia, by contrast, were in rubble. Practically all of the European landmass, from Brittany to the suburbs of Moscow and from the North Sea to Sicily, had felt the advance and retreat of opposing armies. In many areas, local government had broken down and resistance groups were skirmishing among themselves for postwar political advantage. Agriculture was a mess, industry destroyed, and millions of refugees were roaming the continent looking for food, housing, and work. Many of Europe's largest and oldest cities had been virtually blown off the map. Both sides, particularly the Allies once they gained superiority in the air war, had indulged in the carpet-bombing of entire cities.*

---

*In 1943, President Roosevelt had insisted that the United States was "not bombing tenements for the sadistic pleasure of killing as the Nazis did, but blowing to bits carefully selected targets—factories, shipyards, munitions dumps" (*The Decision to Drop the Bomb* by Len Giovannetti and Fred Freed, Coward, McCann 1965, p. 37). This was a lie. During World War II, in Germany and later Japan, the Allies perfected the technique of strategic bombing based on indiscriminate attacks on civilian populations. On one night alone, Allied bombers killed 125,000 people in Dresden, Germany, a city that had no significant military targets at the time.

After the fall of Germany, the U.S. Air Force turned to the Pacific and reduced Japan's cities to ashes. B-29 Superfortresses, sometimes number-ing 1,000 in formation, made nightly raids. Napalm-like jellied gasoline

The Soviet Union was the country hit hardest in World War II. From June 1941, to the Allied invasion of Normandy three years later, the war in Europe was fought primarily on the eastern front, and the Soviet Union, alone, bore the burden of fighting Nazi Germany. While the Allies, in Churchill's words, were "playing about" with six German divisions in North Africa during 1942-43 (in a campaign that had the strategic purpose of protecting the British Empire), the Soviet Union was facing 185 German divisions in a fight for its survival.[8] Germany attacked Russia in 1941 along a front 800 miles wide and eventually penetrated 1000 miles into the Russian interior, reaching a line from Leningrad south past Moscow to Stalingrad and the Caucasus Mountains. It was as if the Germans had landed on the Atlantic coast of the United States and attacked inland to a front between Chicago and New Orleans, killing and destroying everything in their path.

Only Poland lost a greater percentage of its population in the war than the Soviet Union. The Soviet losses were staggering: more than 20 million dead, 25 million homeless, over 70,000 towns and villages destroyed. By contrast, the United States suffered fewer than 300,000 battlefield deaths.[9] In the U.S.S.R., unlike the U.S., the war traumatically affected almost every citizen. As one American historian has put it, "No people besides the Jews had suffered more from Nazi atrocities; none of the Western Allies had sacrificed as much as the Russians in the fighting itself."[10]

Roosevelt's Legacy I: The New Deal

As victory in World War II approached, the United States began to find itself in the unaccustomed role of the world's strongest power. Accordingly, there were crucial decisions to be made as to how the country would use its new position. Broadly

and incendiary bombs killed an estimated 500,000 civilians in Tokyo, and 100,000 or so died in the nuclear attacks on Hiroshima and Nagasaki. As Lewis Mumford has written, "in principle, the extermination camps where the Nazis incinerated over six million helpless Jews were no different from the urban crematoriums our Air Force improvised in its attacks by napalm bombs on Tokyo." (*Atlantic Monthly*, October 1959, p. 39).

speaking, there were two competing visions that offered themselves. Each of them could lay claim to a part of the legacy of President Roosevelt, whose death in April 1945 at the start of his fourth term stunned the nation and left a yawning gap in the decision-making apparatus of Washington.

The first vision was one propounded most eloquently by Henry A. Wallace, Vice-President during Roosevelt's third term before being sacrificed to the Democratic Party bosses who pushed forward for vice-president the little-known Missouri senator, Harry S. Truman, at the 1944 Democratic convention.* Wallace, who made his mark as Secretary of Agriculture in the 1930s, embodied the reform impulses of the New Deal. Against Henry Luce's American Century, with its vision of American capitalism triumphant over the world, Wallace championed the idea of "The Century of the Common Man."[11] "Some have spoken of the 'American Century'," Wallace responded to Luce in 1942, "But I say that the century on which we are entering—the century which will come out of this war—can and must be the century of the common man." Returning to this theme in 1944, the Vice President said, "the people are on the march all over the world and there is nothing the reactionary forces in the United States can do to stop it—but we can, if we are sympathetic, channel those revolutionary forces for the constructive welfare of the whole world."[12]

Throughout the war, Wallace spoke of postwar reconstruction in New Deal terms. He promised the expansion of the Tennessee Valley Authority concept not only to the Columbia and Missouri River basins at home, but to the Danube and the Yangstze River basins in Europe and Asia. U.S. money, funneled through an international agency, like the U.N., would finance public works projects throughout the world. Soviet cooperation would be encouraged through respect for Russian sovereignty and an understanding of Russian fears; more concretely, the Soviet economy would be bound to our own economy through expanded trade. After the war, the Russians would need foodstuffs, consumer products, and heavy machinery

---

*Truman kept Wallace on as Secretary of Commerce. Wallace believed that in this post he could further the ideal of free trade as a basis for postwar peace with the Soviet Union.

to convert their industrial plants to peacetime production. The U.S. alone had the capacity to supply the Soviet Union with essential goods. As financier Bernard Baruch reminded President Truman shortly after Roosevelt's death, "Let us not forget that it is on the productive capacity of America that all countries must rely for comforts—even the necessities—that a modern world will demand. We have the mass production and the know how. Without us the rest of the world cannot recuperate; it cannot rebuild, feed, house, or clothe itself."[13]

Henry Wallace appreciated the strategic importance of the United States' economic primacy in international affairs. But his agricultural background guided him to promote trade rather than investment. There was a mixture of national self-interest and idealism in the way that he tried to carry the New Deal legacy into postwar foreign policy. All during the Depression, as Secretary of Agriculture, Wallace had worked with Roosevelt and Secretary of State, Cordell Hull, to remove barriers to international trade. According to Hull, protective tariffs were barriers to prosperity; free trade would provide us an outlet for our surplus products and, because of our dominant economic position, bind other countries to our own industrial and market specifications. Peaceful coexistence with the Soviet Union, Wallace thought, would be encouraged by free trade. As a Christian who believed in the social gospel, and as an Iowa born farmer and a Jeffersonian democrat, Wallace had no illusions about the nature of the Stalinist regime. But, he believed, "under friendly competition, the Russian world and the American world will grow more alike. The Russians will be forced to grant more and more personal freedom; and we shall become more absorbed with the problems of social-economic justice."[14]

Wallace's approach to foreign policy was grounded not only in the spirit of the New Deal but in FDR's notable pragmatism in dealing with the Soviet Union. When Roosevelt took office in 1933 he inherited a policy of unremitting hostility to the USSR. The Wilson administration had sent American troops to join those of other Allied nations in trying to crush the young Bolshevik regime at the end of World War I. As Secretary of State Robert Lansing had written at the time, "Absolutism and Bolshevism" were "the two great evils at work today;" of the two, Bolshevism was worse since it was the "most hideous and

monstrous thing that the human mind has ever conceived."[15]
Even after American troops were withdrawn in 1920, the U.S.
refused diplomatic recognition until Roosevelt extended it in
1933. FDR shattered precedent by accepting that the Soviet
Union was a sovereign state, with unique interests of its own
that the U.S. was bound to recognize.

In fighting the war, Roosevelt also accepted the USSR as a
full ally. Basic to his understanding of Russia's postwar needs
was his realization that Stalin would insist on having secure
borders in eastern Europe. As Bernard Baruch suggested to
Roosevelt in 1945, after the Red Army had liberated most of
eastern Europe from the Nazis, it would be futile "to demand of
Russia what she thinks she needs and most of which she now
possesses.[16]

Stalin had good reason to insist upon friendly neighbors.
Unlike the U.S., Russia had no oceans to protect it from
aggression. Twice during the twentieth century, Russia had been
invaded by Germany, once by Poland, and after its Civil War by
most of the Allied nations. Napoleonic France had invaded
Russia through Germany and Poland a century earlier, and Japan
had invaded Siberia in 1906. During the Second World War the
neighboring countries of Hungary, Rumania, and Bulgaria were
German allies and invaded Russia from the Balkans. In the
Ukraine, they carried out a scorched earth policy of death and
destruction. Stalin had cause to insist upon secure borders.

Roosevelt and the British wartime leader Winston Churchill were alike in their attitudes toward relations with the
Soviets. Though militantly anti-Communist and a fervent
imperialist, Churchill tempered his hatred of the USSR with his
practical shrewdness as a political horsetrader. In 1944 he sat
down with Stalin and offered the Soviets dominant interest in
Rumania, Bulgaria, and Hungary in exchange for the free hand
in Greece that was so vital to Britain's imperial interest,
especially its access to the Suez Canal and Middle East oil. As the
Red Army was then occupying these Balkan countries, Churchill
gave away nothing. Stalin, for his part, faithfully carried out his
end of the bargain. During the winter of 1944-45, 70,000 British
troops who could otherwise have been fighting the Germans,
were hunting down anti-fascist Greek forces in the streets of
Athens. Though the Greek communists, who were leaders of the

anti-fascist resistance, were the principal targets of the British offensive, the Soviet Union did nothing to protest. After the war, the British installed a right-wing monarchy subservient to its interests and continued to battle the communist-led popular forces, who, as even the British admitted, had the support of three-quarters of the population. Stalin, as always, was less interested in spreading communism than he was in protecting Russia. As Churchill later acknowledged, "Stalin adhered strictly and faithfully to our agreement...and during the long weeks of fighting the Communists in the streets of Athens, not one word of reproach came from *Pravda* and *Izvestia*."[17]

Roosevelt's Legacy II: The Triumph of the Corporate Liberals

To speak of Wallace as Roosevelt's heir, however, would be much too simple. Roosevelt's conduct of the war gave almost a free rein to the leaders of the largest American corporations— men whose indifference to domestic reforms was matched by a zeal for using American power to advance the worldwide interests of American business. FDR himself, in a radio speech in 1940, had told the nation that he was abandoning the role of "Dr. New Deal" to become "Dr. Win-the-War." In this new capacity he had opened his arms to the same corporate leaders who had fought the New Deal and whom he had earlier denounced as "economic royalists." As Republican Henry L. Stimson, a Wall Street lawyer whom FDR appointed Secretary of War, expressed it, "if you are going to...go to war...in a capitalist country, you had better let business make money out of the process or business won't work."[18]*

Organized labor, which was ideologically opposed to fascism and generally supported Roosevelt's preparations for war, wanted to share in wartime economic planning. Indeed, the first plan for economic mobilization had come from Walter Reuther of the United Auto Workers and President Philip Murray of the Congress of Industrial Organizations (CIO). The Reuther-Murray plan called for business and labor to work as equals with the federal government in coordinating war production. But

---

*Stimson had previously served President Taft as Secretary of War and President Hoover as Secretary of State.

Roosevelt ignored this plan. The unions had to settle for a voice on boards that dealt narrowly with labor relations not on war production or economic priorities; in this compromise, existing union membership was guaranteed (so that membership swelled with wartime full employment) in return for a no-strike agreement. Despite thousands of brief wildcat strikes over immediate workplace greivances, there were no national strikes (except for a series held by the militant United Mine Workers, whose president John L. Lewis was aloof from both the CIO and the AFL). Real wages actually declined during the war despite the clout that a tight labor market would normally have given to the workers. But plentiful overtime more than made up the differences.

Big business participated in the war effort under no such restraint. Corporate officials got the most crucial planning jobs. Many of them came to work for the government as "dollar-a-year men," maintaining their corporate affiliations and their executive salaries, which generally were higher than the government could legally pay. Conversion to military production meant producing for a customer (the U.S. government) that guaranteed to buy the entire product at a price above cost, lent business money, gave it tax write-offs for expansion and capital investment, and even built factories for it. (U.S. Steel, for instance, bought the Geneva steel plant, which cost the taxpayers $202.4 million to build, for $47.5 million—a sweet deal.[19]) In the words of Bruce Catton, the Civil War historian who served as an information specialist on the War Production Board, "the most striking thing about the whole war production program was not that there were so many controls, but that all of them fell within the established pattern of industry."[20]

When the mobilization began in 1940, the hundred largest American corporations were responsible for about 30% of the country's manufactured products. Within three years this share had jumped to 70%.[21]* At the other end of the spectrum, half a

*Besides the direct impact of government war contracts (80% of which went to the hundred biggest firms by 1945), there was also the matter of federal research spending. According to economist Elliot Janeway, "World War II, more than any other war in history up to that point, had created limitless new technological openings for capital investment." (The Econo-

million small businesses went out of business during the war, and countless others were in such precarious positions after the war that it was easy for the larger corporations, rolling in money, to buy them out and further consolidate their economic power.[22]

Roosevelt's appointments to key positions in the area of foreign policy during the war reflected his wartime catering to big corporations. Many of these officials outlived FDR and remained influential in the administrations of Truman, Eisenhower, Kennedy and Johnson. Serving under Henry Stimson as Undersecretary of War, for example, was James V. Forrestal, head of the powerful Wall Street investment house of Dillon, Read. Forrestal, who became the first secretary of the reorganized Department of Defense in 1947, was described by historian Lloyd D. Gardner as "a conservative Democrat" who "was extremely uncomfortable around 'New Dealers'." Even more than other conservatives, Forrestal thought that world capitalism was under siege, and throughout the war he kept large files on individuals, organizations and publications he suspected of being under communist influence."[23]*

Stimson's other assistants at the War Department included Harvey Bundy, Robert Lovett, and John J. McCloy. Bundy was the father of McGeorge and William Bundy, both prominent hawks during the Kennedy/Johnson administrations and advocates of the U.S. intervention in Vietnam. Lovett was an investment banker with Brown Brothers, Harriman, a Wall Street firm founded by Averill Harriman, who, in various government posts during the Roosevelt and Truman administrations counseled a harsh, anti-Soviet line. Lovett served in the War Department from 1941 to 1945, in the State Department

mies of Crisis, Weybridge & Talley, 1968, p. 199). The 68 largest recipients got two-thirds of all government funds for scientific research. This meant, according to Maury Maverick, the head of the Small Business Administration and one of the few federal administrators who fought the corporate takeover of the economy, that the large corporations had "control, through patents, of the commercial applications of that research" and thus had a competitive advantage when the technological advances of the war were transformed for peacetime use. (Quoted in *Warlords of Washington* by Bruce Catton, Harcourt Brace, 1945, p. 121).

*Forrestal's anti-Communism eventually became an obsession. In 1949 he committed suicide, frustrated by the country's supposed inability to stem what he perceived to be an ever-increasing communist tide.

from 1947 to 1949, and as Secretary of Defense from 1951 to 1953. During the Second World War, he was responsible for luring Robert McNamara away from the Harvard Business School and into the War Department, where together they helped create the Army Air Corps. McNamara went on to become President of Ford Motors until 1961, when he returned to Washington to become Secretary of Defense for Kennedy and Johnson and an early partisan of the Vietnam War. Resigning in 1967, he became president of the World Bank, responsible for the administration of long term loans to Third World countries.

Lovett, meanwhile, remained influential in Washington politics while serving on a number of corporate boards, including the Union Pacific Railroad, founded by Harriman's father. When John F. Kennedy was elected president in 1960, Lovett was his first choice for Secretary of State.*

John J. McCloy served with Stimson from 1941 to 1945, during which time he supervised the imprisonment of American citizens of Japanese extraction in wartime concentration camps in California. McCloy was first President of the World Bank, from 1947 to 1949; and from 1949 to 1952 he was U.S. Military Governor and High Commissioner of the American occupation of Germany, responsible for restructuring the German economy and integrating non-communist Germany into a bastion for the defense of the "free world." In this position, McCloy was influential in rehabilitating German industrialists, returning them to their corporate positions, in spite of their Nazi pasts. During the Kennedy/Johnson years he performed numerous diplomatic tasks, including that of coordinator of U.S. disarmament activity. When the Internal Revenue Service moved to

---

*Turning it down, he suggested Dean Rusk in his stead. Rusk was another veteran of the War and State Departments. At State, during the Truman Administration, he became an "expert" on Asian affairs and a champion of the Nationalist cause in China and of French colonialism in Indochina. As a result, he became a protege of John Foster Dulles, Eisenhower's Secretary of State and a corporate lawyer who, before the war, had counted as his clients some of the largest corporations in the Third Reich. As Chairman of the Rockefeller Foundation, Dulles secured for Rusk the office of President of that foundation during the Eisenhower years. As Secretary of State for Kennedy and Johnson, Rusk presided over the Bay of Pigs invasion of Cuba, the U.S. intervention in Santo Domingo, and the war in Vietnam.

force American oil companies to start paying taxes on their tax-exempt foreign royalties, it was McCloy whom the oil companies called in for advice. Besides working for the big oil companies, McCloy held corporate directorships with Allied Chemical, Westinghouse, AT&T, Metropolitan Life, United Fruit, and the Rockefeller Brothers' Chase Manhattan Bank, of which he was chairman of the board from 1955 to 1961.[24]

Of the governing elite that these men typified, it could easily be said that never have men of so limited perspective been so unsuited to administer so grand a task. At a time when the traditional world structure was crumbling and the Soviet Union and the United States were superseding France, Great Britain, and Germany as superpowers, and during a revolutionary era when Third World countries were struggling against their colonial pasts, these businessmen, corporate lawyers, investment bankers, and "gentlemen of the old school" were in an unchallenged position to rule. Their worldview reflected their own parochial interests and they responded to politics within the context of their upper-class backgrounds. To a man, they lived in a safe, enclosed world, with their own shared vision of America. During the Depression, when many of the brightest and most politically sensitive young people were involved in the domestic crisis (those few of the upper class who had a social conscience had already rallied to the idealism of FDR's New Deal administration), the men who came to dominate the Pentagon and the foreign service had remained in their clubs and banking houses worrying only about their personal fortunes. Unlike the New Deal reformers, soon to be eased out of influence, they didn't walk picket lines, protest racial discrimination, take part in anti-fascist demonstrations, or agonize over the war in Spain. While thousands of Americans were protesting immigration policies that prevented refugees from Nazi Germany from entering the United States, these men of privilege were silent or, as in the case of the Dulles Brothers and the executives of General Motors, Ford and ITT, actually doing business with the Nazi leaders.

Besides, public activism was not their style. Born to power, they rightfully assumed that the country was an inheritance safe in their hands. Democracy, for them, was an illusion. The public might respond to this or that particular issue, but because they and men like them controlled the media, the grounds of debate could easily be manipulated to support the ultimate decisions that they would make in their own private settings. World War II, as it destroyed the old order, sent forth revolutionary currents that these distinguished patriarchs were congenitally unable to understand. What could they make of bearded revolutionaries, poet-warriors, or rag-tag guerrilla armies steeled with a sense of their own historic destiny? No wonder that in the postwar years, American leaders would find it easier to deal with corrupt right-wing dictators than with political revolutionaries who could not be tempted with American money. Chiang Kai-shek of China, Rhee of South Korea, Batista of Cuba, the Shah of Iran, Trujillo of the Dominican Republic, Salazar of Portugal, Franco of Spain, Somoza of Nicaragua, Jimenez of Venezuela, Castillo Armas of Guatemala—whatever else their failings, these men knew the value of a dollar.

The Importance of the Open Door

Both sides in the debate over American postwar policy recognized the importance of foreign trade. The United States, in historian Daniel Boorstin's phrase, is a "go-getting" nation. When capitalism stops growing, when markets shrink and profits fall, the result is depression, mass unemployment, and often social rebellion. Throughout its history, the United States had consistently produced more goods than it could itself consume; with sometimes disastrous consequences. For example, our agricultural bounty forced prices down and farmers into bankruptcy. And when industry cyclically produced more products than it could sell, the result was depression. Until the 1890s, westward expansion provided jobs for a growing population, and the construction of railroads, cities and other capital projects absorbed surplus wealth. In Lloyd Gardner's words, the U.S. until the 1890s "had its own internal empire where the problems of ruling over an alien race were minimal, where raw materials and mineral resources were abundant. And as the leading edge of civilization pushed into the West, behind it grew up a single unified nation with needs to be filled and resources to be developed."[25]

But during the 1890s, construction of the intercontinental

railroads was completed and the frontier settled. Correspond-
ingly, the country found itself in the throes of one of its periodic
economic depressions. At this very same time, the U.S. began to
look across the waters for new investment opportunities, a new
frontier for surplus goods and capital. The Spanish-American
War, the suppression of the Filipino resistance to American
colonial rule in 1902, and the American demand, stated three
years earlier, for an Open Door for American business in China,
each reflected the importance of the global trade to the domestic
economy.[26]

Now that World War II was ending, there was agreement
that overseas economic expansion was more crucial than ever if
the United States were to avoid another depression. The war had
ended unemployment. But with the coming of peace, the
economy would have to absorb more than 11 million returning
servicemen. Would there be enough jobs? In the summer of
1945, John W. Snyder, director of the Office of War Mobilization
and Conversion, predicted that there would be 8 million
unemployed by the spring of 1946, compared to a wartime low of
610,000.[27] A poll in January 1945 showed that nearly half of the
public fully expected a serious depression within ten years.[28]
Assistant Secretary of State Dean Acheson testified in 1944 that
"So far as I know, no group which has studied the problem, and
there have been many as you know, has ever believed that our
domestic markets could absorb our entire production under our
present system." Ruling out the option of a socialized, planned
economy, Acheson continued, "You could probably fix it so that
everything produced here would be consumed here. That would
completely change our Constitution, our relations to property,
human liberty, our very conception of law. And nobody contem-
plates that. Therefore, you find you must look to other markets
and those markets are abroad."[29]

Though there was consensus on the importance of trade,
for most leading capitalists the issue went beyond trade to
investment. For them, the open door meant opportunity to
invest surplus capital in overseas markets. It was possible, after
the war, for the United States to trade manufactured goods and
agricultural commodities with the Soviet Union (or with any
other socialist country for that matter). But socialism, with its
state-owned enterprise, is, by definition, inhospitable to private

investment. And that was the crux. Private capitalists could sell wheat and steel to the Soviet Union, but they could not invest their surplus capital or build their own factories there. Whereas trade represents, in Harry Magdoff's words, a *flow* of commodities, investment represents an *accumulation* of capital stock, and as this stock grows it leads to ownership and economic control which translates into political influence and more investment opportunities, an ever widening international arena for power and profit.[30] It was in the capitalists' interest to keep the world open to foreign investment. And as socialism represented a barrier to this investment, it had to be opposed. As presidential advisor William C. Bullitt wrote in 1945, "Everytime the Soviet Union extends its power over another area or state, the United States and Great Britain lose another normal market."[31]

Rise of the Military-Industrial Complex

Closely related to this view of a world made safe for American investors was a corporate recognition of the advantages of military spending. By 1944, according to historian Gabriel Kolko, "many big business leaders temporarily in government increasingly saw postwar cooperation among industry, government and the military as the key to prosperity."[32] Military spending was the pot of gold at the end of the corporate rainbow and even with the coming of peace corporate leaders were loathe to give it up. In January 1944, General Electric's Charles E. Wilson, speaking before the Army Ordinance Association, issued a call for a "permanent war economy." In little more than two years of war, business hostility toward government spending had vanished. Wilson's idea, which anticipated the defense program to come, was:

> First of all, such a program must be the responsibility of the federal government. It must be initiated and administered by the executive branch—by the President as Commander-in-Chief and by the War and Navy Department. Of equal importance is the fact that this must be, once and for all, a continuing program and not the creature of an emergency. In fact, one of its objects will be to eliminate emergencies as far as possible. The role of Congress is limited to voting the needed funds...[33]

Charles Wilson found willing allies in the military. At war's end, defense planners were looking forward to an army capable of mobilizing 4.5 million men in a year; a navy with 600,000 men, 371 major combat ships, 500 auxiliary vessels, and an air force of 8,000 planes. The air force also wanted to become an independent arm of the military with 400,000 men.[34] No sooner had peace come than high-ranking military officials were planting stories in the press about the military needs of future wars. In November 1945, General Henry (Hap) Arnold, commanding officer of the Army Air Corps, reported to the Secretary of War that "enemy airpower can, without warning...deliver devastating blows at our population centers and our industrial, economic and governmental heart even before forces can be deployed." *Life* magazine summarized this report with a picture showing rockets emanating from an unnamed country on the back side of the globe raining down on major American cities. A map showed the United States "as it might appear a few years from now, with a great shower of enemy rockets falling on thirteen key U.S. centers." "In the cities, more than ten million people have been instantly killed by the bombs," *Life* predicted. The most effective defense against such an attack, *Life* quoted Arnold as saying, would be "our ability to take immediate offensive action with overwhelming force. It must be apparent to a potential aggressor that an attack on the United States would be immediately followed by an immensely devastating air-atomic attack on him."[35]

Who would the potential aggressor be? General Arnold and *Life* were not saying, but the attack, as shown on *Life*'s map, was coming from the proximity of the Soviet Union. But the Soviet Union, theoretically still our ally, possessed neither the rockets nor the air power to mount such an invasion. Besides, devastated by the Second World War, the Soviet people were in no condition to embark on a third one. Yet, even before the German surrender, the United States and the Soviet Union were at loggerheads over the future of Eastern Europe. In 1945, even as the world welcomed peace, the stage was set for a new global confrontation: socialist Russia, on the one hand, a world power for the first time, but still licking its wounds, and capitalist America, rich, powerful, and at the height of its military strength and world influence.

Chapter Two

"Force is the only thing the Russians understand."
— Harry S. Truman

"Truman's opposition to Soviet expansion and aggression after World War II is the proudest period in American history."
—Clark Clifford

President Franklin Delano Roosevelt died 12 April 1945, having just begun his fourth consecutive term in office. The fall of Nazi Germany was less than a month away, and American forces were advancing island by island in the Pacific, building air bases in preparation for the nuclear bombing and final defeat of Japan. Harry S. Truman, Roosevelt's successor, was totally unprepared to assume the responsibilities of office. As a senator and as vice president for less than three months, he had had little to do with planning for either the war or postwar reconstruction. As to the discussions and decisions about the atomic bomb, economic planning, and relations with the Soviet Union, he knew almost nothing. But his hostility toward the Soviet Union was public record. Commenting upon the German invasion of the Soviet Union in 1941, he said that "if we see that Germany is winning, we ought to help Russia, and if Russia is winning we ought to help Germany and that way let them kill as many as possible, although I don't want to see Hitler victorious under any circumstance."[1]

Truman, upon assuming the presidency, lacked Roosevelt's knowledge, his experience and his charismatic self-confidence. The corporate leaders who had become influential during the war years could advise, but under Roosevelt they did not decide. With Roosevelt gone, these corporate liberals now came to the fore. Truman had to listen; new at the job, he had no other choice. Historian Martin J. Sherwin writes:

> The suddenness of Roosevelt's passing thus effectively left policy making in the hands of his inherited advisors, who, for the most part, viewed Soviet intentions in a more sinister light than Roosevelt had. Under these circumstances, they easily persuaded Truman to adopt a harsher, less conciliatory stance than his predecessor had pursued. The result was a serious crisis in American-Soviet diplomacy—within two weeks rapport between the allies had declined precipitously.[2]

Washington reporter Howard K. Smith put the change in another light. With the coming of Truman to power, "the effective locus of government seemed to shift from Washington to someplace equidistant from Wall Street and West Point."[3]

As the stale wind of reaction blew through Foggy Bottom, Roosevelt's attempt at cooperation with the Soviet Union came to an end.

Harry Truman Gets Tough

As a politician, Truman was most comfortable with the self-image of an embattled little man. Roosevelt, with his usual touch of grandeur, once had said, "We have nothing to fear but fear itself." But under Truman, fear became a motif, and his attitude toward the Soviets seemed at times to be based upon proving his manliness, showing that he was tough. As I. F. Stone has pointed out, Truman started to gain respect for himself only after he announced his "get tough" policy with the Russians. "Toughness," Stone explained, "became a mask for weakness, and stubbornness for strength."[4] Presenting himself as the blunt-speaking common man may have helped him defeat a pompous Governor Dewey in the Presidential election of 1948, but such a posture was hardly appropriate for the President of the most powerful nation on earth. Personally, he may have felt like David contesting Stalin's Goliath; but the United States was hardly a beleaguered underdog fighting against impossible odds. True, his forthrightness and willingness to accept full responsibility for his actions were admirable characteristics, and he was the last president not to hide behind public relations techniques. But his decisiveness was often a shield for his ignorance. Distrustful of the subtleties of diplomacy and impatient with compromise, he was prone, too prone, to confrontation. In the days immediately after Truman assumed office, Henry Wallace, the Secretary of Commerce, observed that "everything he said was decisive. It almost seemed as though he was eager to decide in advance of thinking."[5]

A president's personality often shapes the mood of the country. Roosevelt's confidence stiffened the American people during the Depression and war. His faith in himself gave the American people faith in themselves. But Truman's sense of himself as just an average Joe holding the fort against the communist hordes gave Americans the feeling of being on the defensive, of being losers of a peace despite a war they had just won. As historian D. F. Fleming has written, "After 1945 we ourselves at once assumed the position of a loser. Though we were the mightiest nation which had ever stood upon this planet, and though our undamaged strength had increased prodigiously as a result of World War II, we said that we had 'lost' Eastern Europe and China, and we rebelled against these two main consequences of the war."[6]

One cannot lose what one doesn't have. To feel that we had lost Eastern Europe and China had to mean we had assumed that we had once possessed these areas in the first place. The idea of a manifest destiny conditioned us to believe that we had a sacred right to rule magnanimously over the world; thus we could not tolerate any nation's going its own way or becoming part of some other country's sphere of influence. Nationalism, or simply a show of independence by any nation, was to the American mind a sign of anti-Americanism, an act of aggression against our divine and righteous mission. The New York *Herald Tribune* accurately described this illusion in an editorial on 5 March 1947: "We expected, in short, that most of the world would make itself over in our image and that it would be relatively simple, from such a position, to deal with the local aberrations of the Soviet Union."[7] Hence, when other countries, most especially the Soviet Union, insisted on defining their own interests and acted independently of us, we responded defensively and began to believe that we were losing a position in the world that we had never had, a position that was real only in our own mythology of manifest destiny.

A Bomb in Our Pocket

Truman's second meeting with Soviet Foreign Secretary V. M. Molotov, one week after taking office, set the tone for the impending Cold War. Before the meeting, Truman told his advisors that up until now all the agreements with the Soviets had been a one-way street, but that would now end. If the Russians didn't like it, Truman blustered, "they can go to hell." Truman carried this attitude into the talk with Molotov. He berated the Russian about Soviet activity in Poland and about its intentions in Eastern Europe. Molotov, according to the President, was taken aback. "I have never been talked to like that in my life," he said. To which Truman supposedly answered, "Carry out your agreements and you won't get talked to like that." When Republican Senator Arthur Vandenberg, a leading critic of Roosevelt's foreign policy but Truman's most cooperative Republican ally, heard of this confrontation, he said, good— "FDR's appeasement of Russia is over." Truman, too, was pleased with his showing. "I gave it to him straight, one-two to the jaw," he boasted later.[8]

With the atomic bomb, Truman had a devastating knockout punch, and wartime cooperation began to disintegrate from this point onward. President Roosevelt had ordered a crash program for building the bomb—the Manhattan Project—in response to news that the Nazis were working to develop an atomic bomb themselves. By 1945, the cream of American, British and refugee scientists were hard at work developing the bomb and over $800 million had been spent. But the Manhattan Project was so secret that, as Vice President, Harry Truman didn't know of its existence.

Not even the atomic scientists were positive that the bomb would actually explode. By the time the first prototype was ready for testing, the Germans had surrendered. Truman, on assuming the Presidency, had been briefed on its potential power. In Potsdam, Germany, in July 1945, while discussing European postwar reconstruction with Stalin and Churchill, Truman waited for word of the first test. "If it explodes...I'll certainly have a hammer on those boys," he told members of the American delegation.[9] The news arrived shortly thereafter: "At 0530, 16 July 1945, in a remote section of the Alamogordo Air Base, New Mexico," the message began, "the first full scale test was made of the implosion type atomic fission bomb...The test was successful beyond the most optimistic expectations..."[10] At once, the tenor of the Potsdam Conference changed. Churchill was struck by the difference. "When [Truman] got to the meeting after having read the report" of the successful test, "he was a changed man," Churchill noted. "He told the Russians just where they got on and off and generally bossed the whole meeting."[11]

With Germany defeated, many of the scientists working on the Manhattan Project wanted to scrap the idea. Japan was on the edge of defeat anyway; and the strategic bombing campaign, in its aggregate, was as destructive as any one atomic bomb would be. But American policy-makers understood the importance of the bomb for postwar diplomatic strategy. Its use would signify American power. By hastening the fall of Japan it would keep the Russians out of the war in Asia. And with "the bomb in our pocket," as Truman's new Secretary of State James Brynes put it, the United States would be in the position "to dictate our own terms at the end of the war."[12]* After the Alamogordo test, the U.S. had just two bombs ready for use. The first was dropped on Hiroshima, August 6th, and the second on Nagasaki three days later.

Besides the gambit of atomic diplomacy, Truman also attempted economic gamesmanship, reneging on Roosevelt's promise to extend credit to the Soviet Union. The loan was an American idea first broached to the Soviets in 1943, when advocates of the New Deal still had influence within the administration. One of its proponents, chairman of the War Production Board, Donald Nelson, a former Sears, Roebuck executive whose views on many issues reflected those of Henry Wallace, pressed the idea on a visit with Stalin.** The U.S. has "great surplus capacity for producing the goods that you need," he told the Russian leader. "We can find a way to do business together."[13] Treasury Secretary Henry Morganthau who, like Wallace, would be fired by Truman also was a proponent. A departmental report, endorsed by Morganthau, concluded that trade with Russia "could make an important contribution to the maintenance of full employment during our transition to a peace economy."[14] Such trade would also bind the two economies together in a precedent for further cooperation. But so much of Russia was destroyed during the war, it would need some credit to get its industry rolling. By the time of Roosevelt's death, Harriman, then ambassador to Russia, was viewing the promise

---

*As General Leslie Groves, the highest ranking military officer involved in the nuclear program, put it, "There was never from about two weeks from the time I took charge of the project any illusion on my part that Russia was our enemy, and the project was conducted on that basis." (Quoted in *Lawrence and Oppenheimer* by Niel Pharr Davis, Simon & Schuster 1968, p. 151).

**As a merchant, Nelson was interested more in trade (i.e., the flow of goods) than investment and capital accumulation.

of credit as a way of gaining "leverage" on Soviet conduct. And the idea of using the loan as a carrot to influence Soviet behavior gained currency within the Truman Administration. Two weeks after V-J Day, the Soviets formally asked for $6 billion in credit, at 2.5 percent interest. The Truman Administration procrastinated until the following year, then piled conditions onto the loan, in effect demanding that the Soviets accept the American dollar as the standard of international currency and open Eastern Europe to American private investment. By May 1946 most of the money appropriated by Congress as credit for the Soviet Union had been given to France, but by this time U.S.-Soviet relations had so deteriorated that the loan, which the Soviets ultimately refused, was no longer a big issue. Eastern Europe, especially Russian intentions in Poland, had by now become the major source of conflict. Truman saw Poland as the symbol of Stalin's intentions. Stalin saw Poland as a vital buffer state to protect Russia from an anti-communist pro-American Western Europe. In 1946, the Red Army began liquidating the pro-Western Polish forces and in 1947 the supporters of Stalin were in absolute control.

Another hotspot in 1946 was oil-rich Iran, where the British monopolized the oil concession. During the war, the Red Army occupied Azerbaijan, a province bordering Russia. After the war, the Russians refused to leave and began organizing an opposition to the Shah and his feudal society. The U.S. protested. Russian activity in Iran, Truman said, was "another outrage if I ever saw one," proof, he claimed, that "Russia intends an invasion of Turkey and the seizure of the Black Sea Straits to the Mediterranean."[15] But the Soviets withdrew, and U.S. military advisors accompanied the Iranian troops who reasserted the Shah's control of the northern province.

Though the Soviets pulled out of Iran, it was obvious they were in Eastern Europe to stay. Rumania, Bulgaria, and Hungary had each joined Nazi Germany in its Russian invasion. When the Red Army moved into Rumania, after the German offense had been broken, it liquidated the conservative, pro-Nazi ruling class and set up a government friendly to its interests. The takeover of Bulgaria was equally thorough and encountered little opposition except from the pro-Nazi minority that ruled the country and owned the land. In Hungary, the Soviets moved more slowly, allowing the election of a friendly but non-communist regime. Nothing the Soviets did in Eastern Europe immediately after the war indicated aggressive plans to compete with the U.S. on a global scale.

Containment and the Iron Curtain

Six months after the war had ended, each side was perceiving in the other warlike ambitions. On 2 February 1946, Stalin addressed his people, warning them of future conflict. World War II had not destroyed the "capitalist-imperialist monopoly," and the same aggressive anti-Soviet forces that had caused the world war were still "in control abroad," he said. The Russian people would have to stand firm despite the prospects of hardship; a future war with capitalism was inevitable. The U.S. seized upon this speech as proof of Stalin's warmongering. Dean Acheson later pointed to it as the beginning of the Cold War, and *Time* described it as "the most warlike pronouncement uttered by any top ranking statesman since V-J Day."[16]

The beating that the Russian people had taken in their struggle against the Germans left them in no condition, physically or psychologically, to wage a major offensive war, but, to some Americans, Stalin's speech was a Soviet version of Hitler's *Mein Kampf*, proof positive that Russia was bent on world conquest. In Moscow, diplomat George Kennan was inspired to send Washington an 8,000 word cable which, misinterpreted within the State Department and the White House, became the ideological basis for Truman's policy of containment. Kennan's view was historical, that Russia had a traditional and instinctive sense of insecurity. Stalin's foreign policy, Kennan argued, was based not on external reality, but on the internal needs of an autocratic government; nothing the U.S. could do would change the aggressive thrust of Soviet policy, seeking to secure its borders. Rewriting this cable with the encouragement of Defense Secretary Forrestal for the magazine *Foreign Affairs*, Kennan concluded that the U.S. response must be "a long-term, patient but firm and vigilant containment of Russian expansive tendencies."[17]

The view that world peace rested on the ability of the U.S. to contain communism was encouraged by Winston Churchill, who had been voted out of office in 1945 and was in the U.S. lobbying to win American support for Britain's intervention in Greece and a hardline anti-Soviet policy. After a visit in the White House, he and Truman journeyed to Fulton, Missouri, where on 5 March 1946 he gave one of his most brilliant orations. "From Stettin in the Baltic to Trieste in the Adriatic an Iron Curtain has descended across the continent of Europe. The Dark Ages may return, the Stone Age," he said. Communism was on the move worldwide, and no one could know what Russia and its "Communist international organization intends to do in the future, or what are the limits, if any to their expansive and proselytizing tendencies."[18] Churchill's speech, with Truman sitting on the dais behind him, was a master stroke by a crafty politician. At once, it confirmed the anti-Soviet direction of American foreign policy without any American leader having to defend it. And, by allowing Roosevelt's wartime partner to make the statement, Truman was effectively linking the Roosevelt era to his own and making it seem that he was continuing a policy originated by Roosevelt and Churchill before Roosevelt's death.

That Roosevelt's policy of peaceful coexistence had been reversed became clear in September 1946 when Henry Wallace made a speech to a Soviet-American friendship rally in Madison Square Garden, New York. While criticizing Stalinist tactics and British imperial ambitions and calling also for an open door for American trade, Wallace insisted that "we should recognize that we have no more business in the political affairs of Eastern Europe than Russia has in the political affairs of Latin America, Western Europe, and the United States."[19] This was not the first time that Wallace had used his position as Secretary of Commerce to further his own ideas about foreign policy.

Truman, who had approved the draft of Wallace's Madison Square Garden re-statement of Roosevelt's foreign policy principles, now came under pressure from his advisors and fired Wallace. Dean Acheson, then on the rise in Truman's inner circle, summed up the break with precision: Wallace's mistake was in believing that "Russia was entitled to its sphere of interest."[20] But the Truman Administration wasn't buying this. Here, spelled out, was the crux of the American Cold War attitude. Under Truman, the U.S. would not recognize that the Soviet Union had any legitimate rights anywhere in the world;

therefore any action that Stalin took for his own security would be perceived by the United States as an act of aggression against itself.

The Truman Doctrine

U.S. economic needs and the failure of the British to defeat the Greek partisans brought matters quickly to a head. The harsh winter of 1946-47 devastated much of Europe, hindering plans for reconstruction. A U.N. task force reported that emergency aid was needed to avert mass starvation in Austria, Greece, Hungary, Italy, Poland, and Yugoslavia. The Communist parties in France and Italy (which had played leading roles in the anit-fascist resistance) were growing in strength and had powerful influence within the labor movements there. The Truman Administration was in trouble at home. The Republicans had won big in the 1946 election and were moving toward a neo-isolationist policy as they had done after the First World War. Truman's economic plans were threatened by this call for retrenchment. The GOP policy of high tariffs, low taxes, and isolationism had struck a responsive public chord. The Republicans even wanted to cut the military budget, which the Keynesians among the Democrats feared would wreck the domestic economy. Though reconversion was moving along comfortably, there was no saying how long postwar prosperity would last. European recovery was too slow to support the rate of American exports needed to sustain the American boom. Taking a cue from New Deal economics, the U.S. decided to prime the pump by financing European recovery with American money. This idea of foreign aid was a two-edged sword sheathed in charity. European countries would have the necessary resources to buy American goods and thus help American business. At the same time, foreign aid of this kind would tie Europe into the American economy.

The one hitch was that this kind of internationalism was not popular with large sectors of the public, as evidenced by the Democratic congressional defeat in 1946. The Truman Administration had but one ace up its sleeve to rally public support: anti-Communism. By orchestrating a Cold War and inventing crises where none existed, by calling every diplomatic move that the Soviets made evidence of Soviet expansionism, and by posing the U.S.S.R. as a military threat—which for many years it was not—the Administration could win support for its economic policies under the guise of militant anti-Communism.

The crisis in Britain was especially serious. The cost of supporting the pro-British, right-wing monarchists in Greece, as well as a share of the German occupation, put a severe strain on the British budget. As early as autumn 1946, the U.S. understood that it would have to take over the British commitment in Greece or else allow the Greeks to run their affairs in a way that would not necessarily be in the Anglo-American interest. But the domestic situation was not favorable to intervention, nor was it favorable to passage of other potential foreign aid bills. To intervene in Greece and to provide financing for the European economy would require a crisis situation. To win Congressional approval for his foreign policy, Senator Vandenberg told President Truman, he would have "to scare hell out of the country."[21]

Despite Stalin's hands-off policy, the Greek National Liberation Front (or EAM) had been giving the British a difficult time, and early in 1947 Britain officially asked the U.S. for military assistance. This gave Truman the chance to take a decisive step long in the planning. The Truman Doctrine, delivered in a special message to Congress on 7 March 1947, called for direct military aid to Greece and to Turkey. Because it was designed to frighten both the Republican opposition and the Soviet Union and to create a precedent for future foreign aid bills, the doctrine vastly exaggerated the issue at hand in a way that established the U.S. in the role of policeman of the world. As Truman specified, it was now American policy "to support free peoples who are resisting attempted subjugation by armed minorities around the world." The word "free" was left ambiguous. The U.S. would decide its definition.

The anti-Communist rhetoric of the Truman Doctrine shocked even its own supporters. Charles Bohlen of the State Department was with Secretary of State George C. Marshall, en route home from a conference in Moscow, when the doctrine was announced. As Bohlen recalled, "When we received the text of the President's message we were somewhat startled to see the extent to which the anti-Communist element of this speech was stressed. Marshall sent back a telegram questioning the wisdom of this presentation, saying he thought the doctrine was overstating the case a bit."[22] Kennan, too, considered the speech overly militaristic. And to Bernard Baruch, it was "tantamount to a declaration of...an ideological or religious war."[23] But the fantasy of Greek Communists taking orders directly from the Kremlin—and threatening to cut off access to the Suez and to Mideast oil—was irresistible, and Congress enthusiastically voted support. In Congressional testimony, Acheson drew a picture of the Soviet Union on the march around the world.

> Like apples in a barrel infected by one rotten one, the corruption of Greece would infect Iran and all to the East. It would also carry infection to Africa through Asia Minor and Egypt, and to Europe through Italy and France, already threatened by the strongest domestic Communist parties in Western Europe. The Soviet Union was playing one of the greatest gambles in history at minimal cost. It did not need to win all the possibilities. Even one or two offered immense gains. We and we alone were in a position to break up the plan.[24]

Acheson's rotten apple theory would later be reincarnated as the "domino theory," used to justify U.S. aggression in Vietnam.

The Truman Doctrine was a hoax. The Greek rebels battling the British and American-backed rightists were our former allies in the anti-fascist resistance. The Communists, who made up the bulk of their forces, enjoyed, at least at this point, popular support. An investigative team from the Twentieth Century Fund found that "no monopoly of EAM existed, and it won broad support among the peasants by inviting their participation in resistance activities."[25] The rebels got aid from Yugoslavia, Albania, and Bulgaria; but the Soviet Union, concerned primarily with its own security, sold the rebels out. The Yugoslavian patriot Milovan Djilas, among others, has pointed out that Stalin neither instigated the uprising nor supported it. Djilas quotes Stalin as saying to him in February 1948, "What do you think? That Great Britain and the United States—the United States, the most powerful state in the world—will permit you to break their line of communication in the Mediterranean? Nonsense. And we have no navy. The uprising in Greece must be stopped, and as quickly as possible."[26]

In later testimony before the Senate Foreign Relations Committee, Acheson admitted that the crisis situation in Greece was overstated and that there was no direct evidence of Russia's presence. On their part, the Senators expressed concern about by-passing the U.N., giving the President a blank check to intervene anywhere, and supporting non-democratic regimes such as the one propped up by the British in Greece. But, as an indication of the tide to come, these questions brought forth no response. As Chairman Vandenberg said, not without a touch of resignation, "Here we sit, not as free agents, because we have no power to initiate foreign policy. It is like, or almost like, a Presidential request for a Declaration of War. When that reaches us there is precious little we can do except say 'yes.'"[27]

The European Recovery (Marshall) Plan

Aid to Greece and Turkey was followed by the European Recovery Plan (ERP) or Marshall Plan, the grand design to isolate the Soviet bloc and turn Europe into an economic partner of the United States. Conditions in Europe had continued to deteriorate. In May 1942 the State Department's Will Clayton warned that, "Without further prompt and substantial aid from the United States, economic, social and political disruption will overwhelm Europe. Aside from the awful implications which this would have for the future peace and security of the world, the immediate effects on our domestic economy could be disastrous; markets for our surplus products gone, unemployment, depression, a heavily imbalanced budget on the background of a monstrous war debt. These things must not happen."[28]

A State Department Policy Committee led by Kennan was already planning for that contingency. The ERP, announced by Secretary of State Marshall (hence the name Marshall Plan) at Harvard University on 5 June 1947, was the master stroke of American diplomacy. Disguising economic imperialism as anti-Communism, the ERP solidified Western Europe under the American economic umbrella and isolated the Soviet Union and its East European satellite states. The crux of the plan was that the European countries, including the Allied occupied zones of Germany, would meet to discuss their overall economic needs and that the U.S. would supply them billions of dollars in credit for reconstruction. This would make the American dollar the standard unit of international trade, integrate all of Europe into the American industrial system, and supply the U.S. with the markets it so desperately needed—all this in language that made the U.S. seem like samaritans. "Our policy," explained Marshall at Harvard, "is directed not against any country or doctrine but against hunger, poverty, desperation, and chaos. Its purpose should be the revival of a working economy in the world so as to permit the emergence of political and social conditions in which free institutions can exist." "But," he added, "governments, political parties or groups which seek to perpetuate human misery in order to profit therefrom politically or otherwise will encounter the opposition of the United States."[29]

Speak softly and carry a big stick: ERP was designed with a Machiavellian genius to isolate the Soviet bloc without making that intention clear. The hooker was that Russia and the Eastern European countries were invited to join the Plan and share in the American largess. But, as Kennan admitted, the plan was so structured "that East European countries would either exclude themselves by unwillingness to accept the proposed conditions or agree to abandon the exclusive [i.e., non-capitalist] orientation of their economies."[30] As for the Soviet Union, the U.S. was so sure that Stalin would reject the plan that in figuring a budget it did not include Soviet needs. Indeed, the terms of Soviet participation assured Soviet rejection. To join, the Soviets would have had to accept U.S. influence in its own economic affairs and American dominance in Eastern Europe.

The ERP faced an uphill battle in Congress, where a sizeable bloc of isolationists were opposed to foreign aid in principle. "Isolation has reappeared on the public scene," noted the New York Times in August 1947, and in October it seemed to the Washington Times-Herald that "from all the evidence it looks as if the celebrated Marshall Plan is out the window."[31] Meanwhile, the promise of foreign aid was having a chilling effect on European politics. In France and Italy, the influential Communist parties, which had been part of popular front coalition governments, now moved into opposition, describing the proposed plan as a means of integrating Europe in an America-dominated anti-Soviet bloc. In the fall, the Communists led labor strikes in these two countries and the U.S., viewing this as yet another instance of Kremlin mischief-making, gave covert assistance to the anti-Communist opposition.

The delay in the passage of ERP and the continued deterioration of the economy of Western Europe led Truman to call a special session of Congress in November 1947 to introduce an Interim Aid bill to tide Europe over until the Marshall Plan money could be sent. Again, Truman spoke not in terms of domestic economic needs, but in terms of "totalitarian pressures" and the threat of another hard winter that the Communists would exploit for nefarious ends. To enhance this point, Averill Harriman issued a report in November predicting that if the U.S. refused Europe aid, all of the continent would go Communist and so would the Middle East and North Africa. In the House of Representatives, Republican Everett Dirksen, of Illinois, one of the last of the old-fashioned silver-tongued orators, warned of "this red tide...like some vile creeping thing which is spreading its web westward..."[32] The Interim Aid bill passed.

ERP was next on the agenda. Marshall, Clayton, Acheson, Forrestal, and Attorney General Tom Clark took to the stump to drum up support. The propaganda was incessant. The Soviet Union was a threat to Western Europe and the only defense, short of war, was economic aid. As if to fulfill this prophecy, the Soviet Union gave the administration the crisis it needed to pass the ERP. In February 1948, Stalinists within Czechoslovakia overthrew the democratic government. Passage of ERP was assured.

The Communist takeover of Czechoslovakia was Russia's reaction to the ERP, especially with regard to the American program to rebuild Germany as a key ally in the anti-Communist bloc. A hostile Germany was something the Soviets would not tolerate; therefore, in order to secure their borders as tightly as possible, they moved for absolute control in Czechoslovakia. This did not come as a surprise to U.S. policymakers. In the fall of 1947, Kennan had predicted that the ERP would force the Russians to consolidate their position in Czechoslovakia, an opinion that he reiterated when the coup did indeed take place.[33] Until this time, the Czech government had included Communists in its cabinet and had followed a social democratic policy, sympathetic but independent of Russia's foreign policy. The Communist Party was strong in Czechoslovakia but, as nowhere else in Eastern Europe, the democratic tradition was entrenched, socialism had a strong following, and Stalinist tactics were resisted by a popular movement. But the winter of 1947-48 brought the country to the economic brink, and the Czech leaders, believing themselves to be independent of the Kremlin in fact as well as in theory, accepted the American invitation to participate in the ERP. This led the Communist leaders of the police and the labor unions to provoke mass strikes and the arrest of anti-Stalinist political figures. On 25 February 1948 the democratic government fell and Stalinist repression blanketed Czechoslovakia. The Truman Administration moved to exploit this for all it was worth. The memory of Munich—where the Western Allies abandoned Czechoslovakia to Hitler without a fight—was brought to mind. That Czechoslovakia had a long tradition of political democracy contributed to the emotional impact of the event.

In Congress, opposition to the ERP evaporated. What had been scheduled as a long drawn-out debate over the concept of foreign aid was telescoped into a steam roller of approval. The vote itself, at the end of March, was described this way in the *Washington Post*: "As the roll call went on in a seething and excited house, shouts of 'aye' came from one Republican after another who had seldom, if ever, voted for any international legislation."[34] Eventually, some $12 billion would be spent for the ERP over a four year period, but the principle of foreign aid would continue into the next two decades.

Reconstruction of Germany

The U.S. effort to reconstruct Germany was the most provocative anti-Soviet aspect of American foreign policy. Twice, in thirty years, German armies had invaded Russia. Roosevelt himself was sympathetic to Russian fears of a resurgent German state. He was also on record in support of a plan for German reconstruction set forth by his Treasury Secretary, Henry Morgenthau, that would strip Germany of its industrial potential and turn it into a decentralized agrarian state, a guarantee that it could never make war again. The

Potsdam Agreement, negotiated in the summer of 1945 by Truman, Stalin, and Churchill's successor, Clement Atlee of the British Labor Party, was based in part on the spirit of the Morgenthau Plan. It called for the decentralization of the German economy under rigid Allied controls, division of the German nation under four occupied zones, denazification, and democratic social reform. According to I. F. Stone, Potsdam signified "a blow at the industrial and financial circles that twice supported and profited by German aggression."[35]

Potsdam was never carried out. In East Germany, the Russians dismantled German industry, purged Nazi leadership, and set up a pro-Russian puppet regime. The French who, like the Russians, had suffered directly from the Nazis, also took a harsh view of German reconstruction and attempted to thwart German industrialization. In the British and American zones, however, industrialization was encouraged under the guidance of occupation authorities, many of whom as corporate executives and Wall Street lawyers before the war had close ties with German corporations.

Truman rejected the Morgenthau Plan and Morgenthau resigned from the Cabinet. By September 1946, the U.S. was hinting at the creation of an independent Germany, an idea that it knew the Russians could not accept. In that month, Secretary of State James Byrnes announced a policy designed to prevent Germany from becoming a poorhouse. Rather, he said, the U.S. favors economic unification and "giving the German people primary responsibility for running their own affairs."[36] The denazification process necessary for Germany to resume its role in world affairs was highlighted by the Nuremberg War Crimes Tribunal that began taking evidence of Nazi crimes against humanity in November 1945. The cream of the Nazi heirarchy was here found guilty and a few of its leaders sentenced to death or to life imprisonment. For the U.S., this seemed to have a cathartic effect. With the leadership guilty, it was as if the burden of Nazism was lifted from Germany's shoulders, at least in the eyes of American officials. In January 1950, John J. McCloy, the American High Commissioner to Occupied Germany, admitted to Congress that former Nazi schoolteachers were returning to their jobs, a situation he shrugged off as inevitable because, he said, they were all Nazis anyway. Nor was McCloy bothered that former Nazis were gaining prominence in German industry. "The top figures, generally speaking, in all lines, are not Nazi today," he said, "but on the lower levels, and in important positions, there are people who certainly are prepared to affiliate themselves with the Nazi Party, who are getting back into positions of substance in the community..."[37]

A prosperous Germany was essential to European reconstruction. In May 1947 the U.S. and Britain, against the objections of France and the Soviet Union, merged their zones of occupation into one zone called Bizonia, with headquarters in Bonn. About the same time, and just before the official announcement of the ERP, Acheson spoke in favor of "reconstruction of those two great workshops of Europe and Asia—Germany and Japan—upon which the ultimate recovery of the two continents so largely depends."[38] In November, a reluctant France reversed its hardline position and West Germany became a unified Trizonia aligned against the Soviet occupied zone. The ERP was the cement that sealed West Germany into the American orbit. Two years after the German surrender, the German people—or at least those of them living in the Western zones—were considered rehabilitated, members in good standing of what the U.S. called "the free world."

German integration into the Western bloc increased rapidly despite Soviet protests and over frequent French objections. In May 1948 the West hurled a challenge at the socialist economy of East Germany by granting West Germany its own currency. When, in June, this monetary system was extended into the Western sector of occupied Berlin, a city that was a capitalist island in socialist East Germany, the Russians began a land blockade of the city. An announcement at the beginning of this crisis that the U.S. intended to set up a West German government with "the minimum requirements of occupation and control" confirmed Soviet fears about an independent West Germany; and, indeed a year later, Acheson was speaking of extending "the Bonn constitution to the whole country," which, in effect, meant reuniting East and West Germany as an anti-Soviet Western ally.[39]

The Berlin Blockade lasted from June 1948 to May 1949 during which time West Berlin was supplied by a round-the clock allied airlift that sustained the Berlin economy. The Soviets continued to protest against U.S. plans for Germany, but did not interfere with the airlift. But as West Germany moved towards economic and political independence, Soviet opposition continued to feed the fire of American Cold War rhetoric and support the American fantasy of Russia as a ruthless, aggressor state. To this was added fear of nuclear destruction that became a reality in September 1949 when the Soviet Union successfully tested its first nuclear bomb.

In response to the changing European situation, the State Department drafted a new foreign policy statement, entitled NSC-68, that contained all the familiar Cold War anti-Soviet cliches that the Administration had developed since World War II as a cover for its own imperial ambitions. The U.S., however, was judged to be on the side of the angels. "While our society felt no compulsion to bring all societies into conformity with it," the document said, "the Kremlin hierarchy was not content merely to entrench its regime but wished to expand its control directly and indirectly over other people within its reach." NSC-68 recommended rearmament as the best means of meeting Soviet threats. "In dealing with the Soviet Union," Acheson said, "the most useful negotiation was by acts rather than words...from repairing weaknesses and creating situations of strength."[40]Increased military spending would also have a salutary effect on the domestic economy. In 1949 the postwar boom came to an end and the economy began to take a downward turn towards recession. In the spring of 1950, *Business Week* reported, "Pressure for more government spending is mounting. And the prospect is that Congress will give a little more now, then more by next year. The reason is a combination of concern over tense Russian relations and a growing fear of a rising level of unemployment here at home."[41]

The domestic economy and foreign policy always went hand in hand. In April 1949 the North Atlantic Treaty Organization (NATO) was created as a military alliance against Communist aggression. Its price tag the first year was over $1 billion in federal spending for military equipment, plus aid to Greece, Turkey, and Iran, which the administration continued to view as eventual targets for Russian expansion. NATO turned the American military presence in Europe into a permanent force and assured a permanent market for American-made weapons.

Meanwhile an independent anti-Communist Germany was becoming a reality. By 1952 the Bonn government was granted virtual sovereignty and all economic controls were lifted. In 1954 remilitarization was begun and the next year West Germany was admitted into NATO. The Soviets responded by tightening their control over East Europe, coming down particularly hard on East Germany which, having been stripped of its industrial potential after the war, suffered economically in contrast to the capitalist West. In 1955, the Soviet Union created its own equivalent of NATO, the Warsaw Pact, and the two super powers took up positions on each side of the Iron Curtain parading their military strength, rattling their nuclear weapons, and accusing each other of aggressive intentions.

Chapter Three

At the apex of its power, the United States found itself progressively thwarted in its efforts to inspire, lead, and reform the world. This supreme paradox of American history becomes comprehensible when viewed as a direct result of the nation's conception of itself and the world in terms of open-door expansion. For America's weakness in strength was the product of its ideological definition of the world. The United States not only misunderstood the revolutions in economics, politics, color and anticolonial nationalism, it asserted that they were wrong or wrong-headed and that they should be ignored or opposed in favor of the emulation of American expansion.

William Appleman Williams in The Tragedy of American Diplomany, *1959.*

The Truman Administration had more difficulty containing communism in Asia than it did in Europe. Obstinate in its world view no matter what the facts, the U.S. imagined the Soviet Union to be behind every nationalist movement. In Europe, the Soviets had to impose their system on their satellite bloc. But in Asia, communism had authentic roots in the anti-imperialist struggles of China and Indochina. In 1949, Chinese communists gained complete control of China, ending a civil war that had started in the 1920s. The corrupt "Nationalist" regime of Chiang Kai-shek fled the mainland to take refuge on the island of Taiwan (Formosa). The U.S. had supported Chiang during World War II, although it was the communist armies, using guerrilla tactics, that had been most persistent in fighting the Japanese. After the war, the U.S. Air Force helped the Nationalists seize strategic points throughout China. The U.S. also provided Chiang with more than $1 billion worth of military aid. Much of this money was pocketed by Nationalist officials, while an estimated 75 percent of the material ultimately ended up in communist hands as Chiang's armies disintegrated.[1]

Truman, at first, tried to prop up the Nationalists and then, as Mao's army gained ground, attempted to unite the two sides in a coalition government. But Chiang's armies continued to collapse; as American reporters and State Department officials reported from the scene, the Nationalists were detested by the Chinese. But in the U.S. the Republican Party had long championed Chaing's regime. A powerful China Lobby was organized to press for a hardline anti-communist policy in Asia to match the tough stance that Truman had taken in Greece and Western Europe. The principal propaganda organs of the China Lobby were the Luce publications, *Time, Life,* and *Fortune.* Luce, who had been born in China to a missionary family bringing Christianity to the heathen Chinese, was reluctant to let reality impinge upon his support for Chiang's regime. When his own foreign correspondent, Theodore White, reported from China that the Nationalists were being beaten, Luce had his dispatches rewritten in New York to show them doing well.[2] The Red Chinese are on the run, *Life* insisted in October 1946 and frequently thereafter. "American hopes take a turn for the better."[3]

In 1949 the Democrats bowed to the inevitable and abandoned the Nationalist cause. But the Republicans remained faithful, blaming the Democrats for Chiang's defeat. In defense, the State Department issued a lengthy "white paper," documenting the reasons for the communist victory. Arguing from two contradictory standpoints, the White Paper concluded that China "fell" because of internal factors—but the Russians were also to blame.

Testifying before Congress in October 1949, Acheson reiterated the theme of Russian responsibility. Speaking of the new Communist regime, he said, "This Chinese government is really a tool of Russian imperialism in China." This fact "gives us our fundamental starting point in regard to our relations with China."4 Dean Rusk, Assistant Secretary of State for Far Eastern Affairs, even denied that the leaders of the Chinese revolution were Chinese. "We do not recognize the authorities in Peiping* for what they pretend to be," he told Congress in 1951. "The Peiping regime may be a colonial Russian government—a Slavik Manchuko on a larger scale. It is not the government of China. It does not pass the first test. It is not Chinese...."5

In Indochina, the Truman Administration viewed the Vietnamese Civil War the same way. Under Roosevelt, the United States attempted to promote itself as the champion of the anti-colonial cause; thus, the Vietnamese nationalist leader, Ho Chi Minh, looked to the United States to persuade France to end its colonial rule and to accord Vietnam, in Ho's words, "the same status as the Philippines." But Ho's request for American support was ignored. "Keep in mind Ho's clear record as agent international communism," Acheson cabled an American diplomat in Hanoi in December 1946. True, Ho was a communist. But this didn't mean, as Acheson and others believed, that he was an "agent" of the Kremlin. As the leader of the nationalist Viet Minh movement leading the fight against the French, he had overwhelming popular support. For the U.S., however, as Acheson emphasized in 1950, Ho Chi Minh was nothing more than a Soviet puppet, "the mortal enemy of national independence in Indochina."6

As with the British in Greece, the U.S. sided with the old

*Even as Secretary of State in the 1960s, Rusk would insist on using "Peiping," the old Western imperialist name for China's capital, instead of "Peking."

colonial regime and eventually had to assume the entire colonial burden. In part, U.S. aid to the French in Indochina was a by-product of American support for a strong West German nation in Europe. France was never happy with the rapid reconstruction of its traditional enemy and went along only after exacting American aid for its colonial war in Vietnam. To the American leaders the issue, as usual, was Soviet expansionism. As the State Department explained in 1950, since "neither national independence nor democratic evolution can exist in any area dominated by Soviet imperialism," U.S. aid was warranted to help the French "in restoring stability and permitting these states to pursue their peaceful and democratic development."[7] A month after this statement was made, in June 1950, a civil war broke out in Korea, and the U.S., with United Nations support, intervened on the side of the anti-communist South. The Cold War in Europe had become a hot war in Asia and some officials in the United States, especially Republicans, began to look beyond containment towards an all-out effort to "roll back" communism and free the so-called captive nations.

The Korean War

The attack by the North Korean army across the 38th parallel into South Korea came at a time of mutual provocation when both sides were threatening war in order to force reunification. Korea, according to the Joint Chiefs of Staff in 1945, was "indefensible and of little strategic value to the United States"— an opinion that was verified shortly before the outbreak of war when Korea (along with Formosa) was deliberately left outside the announced Pacific Defense Perimeter of areas that would come under U.S. protection in case of war. But with the invasion, Korea was instantaneously transformed into an area of strategic importance to American democracy. American policymakers assumed that the North Koreans were acting under orders from the Kremlin, and later from the Chinese as well. On the day of the invasion, Acheson concluded that "the attack had been mounted, supplied and instigated by the Soviet Union and that it would not be stopped by anything short of force."[8] Testifying about Korea before the Senate Foreign Relations Committee in December 1950, Acheson reiterated "that the real center of opposition to us, the real heart of the problem we face, is the Soviet Union. We must never allow that to be obscured at all. All these moves by the North Koreans and of the Chinese and of anyone else who is opposing the United Nations and the free world go back to that point."[9] Acheson had no concrete evidence of Soviet complicity, and in testimony before Congress he made no attempt to offer any. Yet his view became the orthodox position; to this day, it has rarely been challenged.[10]

For the Democrats, pressed by the Republicans as being "soft on communism," Korea was a chance to prove their anti-communist mettle in what promised to be a short war and an easy victory. After Truman announced the decision to intervene militarily, Acheson received a phone call from Averill Harriman in Paris which indicated the way the liberal Cold Warriors jumped into the war in Korea as an opportunity to show their stuff. In Acheson's description, Harriman was "carried away with enthusiasm about the President's action." He wanted to come to Washington immediately to get in on the planning. "He could not stand delaying his return another hour while Washington was electrifying the world."[11]

At the time of the Korean invasion, the Russians were boycotting the UN in protest of its refusal to seat the new communist regime in China. Because they were absent, they could not argue the case for the North Koreans or veto the Security Council resolution making the UN the official sponsor of the American-led intervention. Emotionally, the U.S. decision to go to war in Korea did electrify the nation and our anti-communist allies. The analogy to Munich was again on everybody's lips. In 1938 the allies had refused to stand up to Hitler in Czechoslovakia and this led to further German aggression and World War II. Now in Korea, Truman was standing firm. As Truman told Congress, "The attack upon Korea makes it plain beyond all doubt that Communism has passed beyond the use of subversion to conquer independent nations and will now use armed invasion and war."[12]

The U.S., controlling the air and seas, turned the North Korean attack at the Pusan perimeter and rapidly drove past the 38th parallel into the heart of North Korea, bombarding North Korean cities and towns from land and by sea. The stated objective of the American intervention of repulsing North Korea had been achieved. But to the north of Korea lay China. To the American commander, General Douglas MacArthur, this was an opportune time to spread the war to China and wipe Communism off the Asian map. China had made no effort to aid North Korea but had continuously warned that it would protect its Yalu River border. Nevertheless, MacArthur drove north to the Yalu, bombing power stations along the river and (in violation of Truman's orders) engaging Chinese troops in battle. Finally, in November 1950, China responded with a massive counter-attack that sent the UN forces in a headlong retreat back into South Korea. From his Tokyo headquarters. MacArthur fought a war of press releases, portraying the Chinese advance as an invasion of the Yellow Peril bent on taking over all of Korea. The only solution, he insisted, was all-out war with China, utilizing Chiang's army in a land invasion and a strategic bombing campaign, including nuclear weapons, on the mainland. This violated Truman's policy of limited war and when MacArthur attempted to raise the call for all-out war in public, he was fired.

Under General Matthew Ridgeway, the retreat ended and positions were stabilized in an area around the 38th parallel. Meanwhile, the U.S. continued to terrorize North Korea with daily bombing raids and offshore naval bombardments. In February and March 1951, U.S. naval forces bombarded the northern port city of Wonson for 41 days and nights. According to Rear Admiral Allen E. Smith, this was "the longest sustained naval or air bombardment of a city in history." Describing its effect on the city's 35,000 inhabitants, Smith said, "you cannot walk in the street. You cannot sleep anywhere in the twenty-four hours, unless it is the sleep of death."[13]

The Korean War was never a popular war among the American people. Accustomed to unconditional victory, many could not understand the reasons for sending troops thousands of miles across the Pacific to fight a war that we seemingly did not want to win. Even the pervasive ideology of anti-communism did not encourage enthusiasm for the war as much as it discouraged public protest against it. Indeed, to criticize American intervention was taken as proof of communist sympathy. The only dissent allowed came from the right: not that the war was wrong, but that limited war was wrong and that American troops, with the help of the Strategic Air Command and the atom bomb, should "liberate" all of Asia.

As the stalemate continued and casualties mounted, there was a groundswell of opinion in favor of a negotiated settlement. In General Dwight D. Eisenhower, the Republicans had a presidential candidate with the military prestige to end American participation in the war without making it seem like surrender. In the presidential campaign of 1952, Eisenhower promised to go to the front as the first step in bringing "our boys home from Korea." He also promised to balance the budget and end Democratic "appeasement" of the Soviet Union. After twenty years of Democratic rule, Republicans said, it was "time for a change." In November, Eisenhower won a resounding victory over the Democratic candidate, the liberal governor of Illinois, Adlai E. Stevenson.

The Eisenhower Administration

Under Eisenhower's leadership, a new group of businessmen entered government service and the rhetoric of anti-communism took a more militant turn. The most influential member of the Eisenhower Administration was the Secretary of State, John Foster Dulles, a nephew of President Wilson's anti-Bolshevik Secretary of State, Robert Lansing, and the head of Sullivan and Cromwell, a Wall Street law firm whose clients included Standard Oil of New Jersey, United Fruit, and, before the war, a number of large corporations in the Third Reich. Dulles shared his uncle's distaste for communism but was rather soft on authoritarianism from the right, insisting that Sullivan and Cromwell's Berlin office be kept open long after Hitler's persecution of the Jews had become public knowledge, and opposing Roosevelt's interventionist policy in Europe until Pearl Harbor and America's entry into the war.[14]

Like the Democrats before him, Eisenhower turned to the corporate world for leadership of the Pentagon. When Charles E. Wilson, the head of General Motors (known as "Engine Charlie," to distinguish him from General Electric's "Electric Charlie") was nominated for Secretary of Defense, Democratic senators refused to confirm his nomination until he sold off $7 million worth of personal stock, including $2.5 million worth of GM's holdings. Protesting this "pushing around," Wilson argued that his corporate holdings represented no conflict of interest. "What is good for our country," Engine Charlie insisted, "is good for General Motors and vice versa."[15]

Also appointed to top Pentagon positions were textile king Robert Stevens, (his company, J. P. Stevens, was notorious for its anti-labor practices) Secretary of the Army; Texas oilman Robert Anderson, Secretary of the Navy; and Harold Talbott, an old corporate hand whose affiliations included Chrysler and North American Aviation, Secretary of the Air Force. Corporate leaders dominated Eisenhower's cabinet and administrative staff as well. The one misfit was Plumbers union leader Martin Durkin, who served briefly as Secretary of Labor before realizing that he was powerless to advance labor's positions in this businessman's administration. Next to Dulles, Eisenhower's most important advisor was Treasury Secretary George Humphrey, head of the Mark Hanna Company, a conglomerate with interest in coal, copper, iron, steel, gas, plastics, synthetic fibers, shipping, and banking. Humphrey was a proponent of the balanced budget and old-fashioned laissez-faire capitalism. During Eisenhower's administration, the regulatory powers of the federal government were left to wither and business was allowed to do anything it wanted in the marketplace.

The Republicans rejected Truman's policy of containment for a more aggressive rhetorical stance. To Dulles, containment was "negative, futile and immoral."[16] Instead, he offered the hope of rolling back communism and liberating the "captive nations" of Eastern Europe and Asia from Soviet dominance. On television, Dulles pointed to a map that showed the areas of the world under Communist control and said, "Our nation must stand as a solid rock in a storm-tossed world. To all those suffering under Communist slavery, to the timid and the intimidated peoples of the world, let us say this: you can count upon us."[17] Eisenhower, in his State of the Union message, reiterated this theme, promising that the U.S. would "never acquiesce in the enslavement of any people."[18]

Another component of Eisenhower's foreign policy was the concept of "massive retaliation." Instead of relying on conventional weapons and an expensive standing army, Eisenhower chose to build up the strategic arm of the Air Force so that it could strike with nuclear weapons anywhere in the world. No longer would the U.S. fight localized wars with limited objectives. Nuclear annihilation would greet the Soviet Union anywhere it tried aggression. To budget-minded Republicans, this "new look" military represented "more bang for the buck."

Stalemate in Europe

Republican bombast appeased the anti-communist right wing, but it was ill-suited to the political conditions of a rapidly changing world. No sooner had Eisenhower taken office than, on 6 March 1951, Soviet premier Joseph Stalin died. The new Soviet leadership, first headed by Georgi Malenkov, called for a new era of "peaceful coexistence" and promised the Russian people a reversal of economic priorities from military spending to consumer goods. In Moscow, Malenkov told party leaders that there were no outstanding disputes with the West that could not "be decided by peaceful means, on the basis of mutual understanding by interested countries."[19] Malenkov's successor, Nikita Khruschev, also emphasized peaceful co-existence and greatly reduced the size of the Soviet military. In 1956, Khruschev startled the Communist world by publicly acknowledging and then denouncing Stalin's crimes against the Russian people.

The U.S. interpreted this thaw in the Cold War as a sign of Soviet weakness, proof that its own hardline anti-communism was wearing the Russians down. In April 1953, Eisenhower responded to Malenkov's peace overtures by demanding that the Soviets match words with deeds. Specifically, Eisenhower called for a "free and united Germany, with a government based on free and secret elections," full independence for Eastern Europe, a peace treaty for Austria, then under Allied and Soviet occupation, and a settlement of the Korean War.[20]

In June 1953, negotiations ended the war in Korea with the country divided much as before. During the next summer, negotiations involving France, Great Britain, the U.S.S.R., Vietnam, and China brought an end to the Indochina War with Vietnam divided into Communist and non-Communist sectors, and free elections promised as a step towards unification. The U.S., however, refused to become a signatory to this settlement. Also in 1955, an Austrian Peace Treaty was signed with the Soviets guaranteeing Austrian neutrality but allowing it to develop its own capitalist economy. Only on the status of

Germany and the Eastern European countries did the Soviets refuse concessions. In Great Britain, Winston Churchill chastised Eisenhower for making demands on the Russians that he knew they would not accept. "It would, I think, be a mistake to assume that nothing can be settled," Churchill said. "It would be a pity to impede any evolution which may be taking place inside Russia...Russia has the right to feel assured [that] the real events of the Hitler invasion will never be repeated."[21]

Despite U.S. mistrust of Soviet intentions and Dulles' militant anti-communist rhetoric, the Cold War in Europe fizzled into a mutually accepted stalemate. In 1954, following the U.S. by one year, the Soviets tested their first hydrogen bomb, thus upping the ante of nuclear terror at the same time they kept the arms race in balance. In the summer of 1955, over Dulles' objections, Eisenhower met with Soviet leaders in a "summit conference" in Geneva—the first such meeting since the wartime alliance. At Geneva, Eisenhower advanced his "Open Skies" proposal for nuclear disarmament that was meant to top the earlier Soviet proposal of mutual inspection. Open Skies called for an exchange of all military blueprints and complete access to each country's airspace for aerial inspection. Later, Eisenhower would admit that the proposal was a propaganda ploy. "We knew the Soviets wouldn't accept it," he recalled in 1965. "We were sure of that."[22] Nothing concrete resulted from the Geneva Summit meeting; but the fact that Eisenhower and the Soviet leaders were talking to one another engendered an optimistic "spirit of Geneva" which raised hopes everywhere.

In the meantime, Khruschev's anti-Stalinist policies began to have serious ramifications in the Communist world. In Poland, during the spring and summer of 1956, demonstrations and a general strike led to the overthrow of the unpopular Stalinist regime. Khruschev negotiated a settlement with the Poles that allowed the new Communist government of Wladyslaw Gomulka to chart a more independent course. The winds of change then hit Hungary. A popular uprising during the autumn demanded similar reform. Khruschev responded this time by sending the Red Army into Hungary, but the Hungarians would not give in. Bending to popular will, as he did in Poland, Khrushchev withdrew his forces and allowed an independent Communist regime, led by Imre Nagy, to assume power. But anti-Soviet sentiment in Hungary could not be so easily curbed. Popular agitation for democratic reforms and for Hungarian withdrawal from the Warsaw Pact continued to grow. The U.S. welcomed the uprising as proof that its policy of rolling back communism was a success. From Munich, Germany, the CIA's Radio Free Europe urged the rebels forward. Now the Soviets became scared. If the Hungarian agitation was allowed to continue it might spread to other satellite countries. Khruschev changed course. The Red Army moved back into Hungary and put down the uprising with brutal force. Nagy and other independent-minded Communists were arrested and later shot. A hand-picked pro-Soviet government was installed. The U.S. protested but did nothing. For all of Dulles' promiscuous rhetoric, he was powerless to assist the anti-Soviet resistance.

The events in Hungary certified the stalemate in Europe. Although the U.S. and the Soviets continued their battle of words, and the situation in Germany occasionally reached crisis proportion, the Cold War in Europe had become institutionalized; each side knew what to expect from the other. Indeed, the U.S. began to have as much trouble with allies as it was having with the Soviet Union. The European countries, rebuilt with American money but restless under American economic domination, began to assert their own independence—especially in the Third World where, before the war, they had been so economically prominent.

Intervention in Vietnam

The Korean War, after the Chinese intervention, gave the discredited dictatorship of Chiang Kai-shek a new lease on life on its embattled fortress of Formosa. From 1949 to 1961 the U.S. spent $5 billion to keep Chiang's exiled government solvent, much of it going into military aid to put muscle behind the China Lobby's promise to "unleash Chiang" and win back China. While pouring money into Formosa, the U.S. studiously sought to ignore the growing strength of the legitimate Communist government on the mainland. Besides withholding diplomatic recognition from the Peoples' Republic of China, the U.S. sent CIA saboteurs to the mainland to stir up internal disorders; supported, again through the CIA, the remnants of a Nationalist

Army along the China-Burmese border, an army which spent most of its time supplying the American heroin trade; and in 1958 seriously considered a nuclear strike against Chinese cities in the event that a dispute with the exiled government in Formosa over the offshore islands of Quemoy and Matsu erupted into war. In addition, the U.S. established an economic boycott of all Chinese goods, but failed to pressure its allies into doing the same. Finally, in the mid-fifties, when evidence of an ideological split between China and the Soviet Union became evident to analysts within the CIA, Secretary of State Dulles rejected the theory and his brother Allen, who directed the CIA, ordered an end to that kind of thinking.[23] As John Foster Dulles explained, "The Communist Party is running both governments. International communism is in effect a single party...The Chinese are dependent on the Soviet Union. Their regime couldn't control China if it were not for Russia."[24]

After the Korean War, the U.S. also turned its attention back on Indochina where the French colonials were being pressured by the Viet Minh. Peace in Korea enabled the United States to increase its logistical support of the French. In September 1953, the American Ambassador to Indochina, Donald Heath, told the American people that France was "fighting the good fight" and that "given continued financial support of the U.S....final victory, I am convinced, is possible."[25] Less than a year after this optimistic report, the French suffered a demoralizing defeat at Dienbienphu, despite efforts by the CIA to fly in aid.

After Dienbienphu, the French people lost their will to fight in Vietnam. Still, Eisenhower tried to impose an imperial solution, calling on the French to remain in the battle and Britain to join with the United States in a tripartite intervention. Southeast Asia, Eisenhower explained at a press conference, was rich in tin, tungsten, and rubber. In Vietnam, he said, you have "what you would call the 'falling domino' principle. You have a row of dominos set up, you knock over the first one, and what will happen to the last one is the certainty that it will go over very quickly. So you could have the beginning of a disintegration that would have the most profound influences."[26] but Britain refused to commit troops and France was exhausted, so if the U.S. were to intervene in Vietnam it would have to go it alone—

an idea Eisenhower rejected. The U.S. did preserve its options, however. When the new French government sued for peace, the United States refused to be a part of the resulting Geneva Accords. To bolster its position in Indochina, the U.S. created SEATO, an alliance of anti-communist nations in Southeast Asia, and set about building up an anti-communist regime in South Vietnam. Ngo Dinh Diem was plucked out of a Catholic seminary in New Jersey in 1954 and chosen, by the Americans, to head the government. An autocrat who placed members of his family in high office, Diem antagonized the peasantry by reversing the agrarian reforms won by the Viet Minh during the war. The Vietnamese Communists, expecting victory in the elections called for by the peace treaty, did not fight back. But in 1956 the elections were cancelled because Diem, with American support, refused to take part. In his *Memoirs*, Eisenhower admitted that had the election been held, Ho Chi Minh would have received 80 percent of the vote, and Vietnam would have been unified under Viet Minh rule.[27] Rather than allow this to happen, the U.S. poured more money, weapons, and advisors into South Vietnam.

Diem's repressive rule provoked uprisings throughout the country. At first, these were spontaneous uprisings of peasants, Buddhists, students, and non-Communist politicians. Diem responded by throwing all of his opponents in jail. In 1958, Viet Minh cadre, many of them Southerners by birth who had moved North after the Geneva Accords, began to filter back into the South to coordinate the opposition. In 1960, the National Liberation front (NLF) of South Vietnam was formed to carry out the anti-Diem resistance.[28] A guerrilla war, organized by the same people who had defeated the French, now broke out against Diem and his American advisors.

The U.S. and the Third World

The commitment to stop communism in Vietnam was a natural outgrowth of U.S. economic requirements. With the example of China, Third World countries now had an alternative model for economic development, one that did not depend upon capital accumulation through investments by foreign corporations or by such quasi-public institutions as the World Bank, with its stringent regulations and its capitalist bias.

The American capitalist scenario for Third World development included certain advantages for underdeveloped countries. Private investment offered these countries the capital and business expertise that they usually lacked. Moreover, it promised the ruling elite and the small class of educated civil servants a standard of living far above the accustomed poverty. But the capitalist model also came with strings. Corporations investing in the Third World produce goods for their own marketing purposes, without regard to the needs of the population of the host countries. In addition, private investors skim off a share of the profit and take it out of the country. Some of this profit may be re-invested, of course; but this only furthers foreign domination of native industry and resources.[29]

In the words of economist Harvey O'Connor, this pattern of foreign investment results in "the formal control over local resources in a manner advantageous to the metropolitan power (i.e., the United States) at the expense of the local (i.e., the Third World) economy." As O'Connor writes, "production goals and techniques, investment policies, labor relations, prices, profit allocations, purchasing, distribution and marketing policies are all decided from the standpoint of the goals of the international corporation whether or not these goals are consistent with local economic developments."[30] In other words, corporations have a vested interest in destroying indigenous cultures and societies and forcing Third World countries to adapt, as much as possible, to consumption patterns dictated by the corporate patterns of production and investment.

Until the Chinese revolution, the capitalist scenario was the only development model Third World countries could follow, the only way impoverished Asian, African, and Latin American countries could accumulate capital for internal reconstruction. In China, capital was developed through public control of all industry, agriculture, and natural resources, and a planned economy with controlled consumption in order to generate capital for the public sector and achieve relative self-sufficiency as geophysical conditions allowed. Such a model promised (at best) a slow but steady increase in living standards. Individual wealth (and the freedoms that money can buy) would be sacrificed for the benefits of the overall society. No one would get rich, but people would share the burden of underdevelopment with relative equality.

The ability to control Third World economic development was one that the United States could not afford to lose. Not only must the United States insist that other countries be hospitable to American investors, but it must also combat the example of China—and socialism in general—as a viable model for the emerging nations of Asia, Africa, and Latin America. The competition for Third World influence was highlighted in 1955 when Khruschev, for the first time, offered Soviet economic assistance to non-Communist nations, and China took a leadership position in the Bandung Conference of non-aligned nations, at which delegates from 29 Third World nations declared that "colonialism in all its manifestations is an evil which should speedily be brought to an end."[31] The United States responded to the self-proclaimed neutrality of many of the newly independent nations with suspicion and hostility. To Dulles, in 1953, "the Soviet leaders in mapping their strategy for world conquest hit on nationalism as a device for absorbing the colonial peoples." Three years later, responding to the principles of non-alignment articulated at the Bandung meeting, Dulles described neutralism as an "obsolete" and "an immoral and shortsighted conception."[32]

The Importance of Oil

Complicating the economic picture of the postwar years was the awareness that the U.S. was running low on critical natural resources. A 1952 report of the President's Commission on Foreign Economic Policy, described World War II as a time of "transition" for the United States "from a position of relative self-sufficiency to one of increasing dependence upon foreign sources of supply."[33] Surveying the domestic supply of strategic raw material, the report found that only in coal, sulfur, potash, magnesium, and molybdenum was the U.S. "fully self-sufficient." But advanced technology demanded sophisticated use of a wide spectrum of raw materials. Critical materials for a jet engine, for example, included not only molybdenum but also tungsten, columbium, nickel, chromium, and cobalt.[34] Of even greater importance was the availability of gasoline to get the jet off the ground.

World War II had stimulated research into the industrial use of oil and petrochemicals. Before the war, coal was the basic raw material used in the generation of electricity, in home heating, and in many chemicals and synthetic products. But coal mining was dangerous work and destructive to the environment. Coal miners were organized, militant, and, as history showed, not easily controlled by either the mining corporations or the state and federal government. Besides, converting coal into chemical by-products was difficult. Oil, on the other hand, once discovered was easy to extract. Being a purer form of energy, it was easier to refine into other products. The number of petroleum-based products grew astronomically after World War II to include chemical fertilizer, biocides, lubricants, synthetic rubber, synthetic fibers, pharmaceuticals, many plastics, artifical food flavorings and additives, building materials, paints, industrial chemicals, detergents, synthetic vitamins—ultimately, by the 1970s, more than 6,000 individual products. Domestic consumption of gasoline alone jumped from 22,303 million gallons in 1945 to 63,714 million in 1960. Before the war, the U.S. was self-sufficient in crude oil production. In 1945 it was even able to export 4 percent of its supply. But five years later, 10 percent of domestic consumption had to be met by foreign imports. Between 1950 and 1960 petroleum imports jumped from 592 million barrels to 1,544 million and until the "energy crisis" of the 1970s continued to rise rapidly. In 1970, the U.S. was importing one-third of its supply; estimated imports in 1980 reached almost one-half.[35]

Where was this oil to come from? In March 1954, a *Reader's Digest* reporter, Wolfgang Langeweische, asked why the United States was not running out of oil. "Here we are," he said, "using the stuff like mad—more and more oceans of it every year (a jet engine burns up a gallon of fuel every five seconds)—and there is only so much in the ground." Langeweische toured the oil fields, spoke with petroleum executives and noted that new oil fields, like the ones in Iran, were just now being exploited by American oil companies. "The end of oil is like the end of the rainbow," he concluded. "Approach it, it recedes." Experts insisted the supply was unlimited, and Langeweische was confident that the U.S. would never run out. "It's sort of a miracle," he said, "The more we use, the more we find."[36]

This optimism resulted from the success of American foreign policy and its ability to provide the political climate for American control of Third World supplies. Before the war, American oil companies controlled Venezuela's oil production, but owned only 13% of the Middle East's supply.[37] At this time, Iran was the Middle East's main supplier and British oil interests, with the favor of the Shah, monopolized production. Saudi Arabia looked very promising, but its vast resources were as yet untapped. In 1933, Standard Oil of California gave King Ibn Saud $250,000 in gold for a sixty-year concession to Saudi oil. Explorations during the next few years proved promising and Standard sold a half-share of its holdings to Texaco for $3 million down and $18 million to be paid out of future profits. When Saudi Arabian oil reserves proved greater than anyone had imagined, Mobil and Standard Oil of New Jersey were brought in as partners and the Arabian-American Oil Co. (Aramco) was created. In 1950, taking its cue from Venezuela, the Saudi leaders insisted that Aramco share its profits with the royal family on a 50-50 basis. As became government practice, the U.S. allowed the oil companies to subtract these royalty payments from their U.S. taxes.[38]*

During the 1950s, the five leading American oil companies, Standard Oil of New Jersey (now Exxon), Texaco, Standard of California, Gulf, and Mobil, plus a number of small ones like Getty, extended their oil holdings all over the world. By 1959, American companies controlled 64 percent of the Middle East's proven reserves, 68 percent of Venezuela's, and 70 percent of Canada's.[39] U.S. foreign policy assisted the American oil companies in this advance. Up until 1949, for example, the British

---

*In effect, the American taxpayer was subsidizing foreign countries to the profit of the big oil companies. For money paid out by the oil companies in royalties was subtracted from their tax bill to the U.S. Treasury. Between 1950 and 1951, for instance, Aramco's royalty payments to the Saudi government almost doubled from $66 million to $110 million. As this was credited to its federal taxes, its payments into the treasury decreased from $50 million to $6 million. By 1955, the U.S. was losing about $150 million a year because of the tax credits. (*The Control of Oil* by John M. Blair, Pantheon, 1976, pp. 193-203; *Seven Sisters* by Anthony Sampson, Pantheon, 1976, p. 76).

Petroleum Company monopolized Iranian oil. The Shah and the small Iranian ruling class siphoned off a portion of the profits, but the vast majority of the people lived in wretched poverty with little hope for anything better. In 1949, the Shah was overthrown by a nationalistic left-wing movement led by Mohammed Mossadegh. In order to finance a seven year plan for internal reconstruction and land reform, Mossadegh in 1951 nationalized the oil industry so that the profits could be used to capitalize this development plan. The Western nations established a consumer cartel in retaliation, boycotted Iranian oil, and denied Mossadegh the revenue with which he hoped to develop his country. Though Mossadegh was a charismatic and popular leader in Iran, Eisenhower, in his memoirs, described him as "a semi-invalid who, often clad in pajamas in public, carried on a fanatical campaign, with tears and fainting fits and street mobs of followers, to throw the British out of Iran, come what may."[40] More to the point, Mossadegh was also accused by American officials of being a Communist agent taking orders from the Kremlin. Consequently, in the summer of 1953, the CIA engineered a coup which resulted in the arrest of Mossadegh and the return of the Shah as ruler of the country. As a reward, the Shah gave five American oil companies a combined 40 percent control of Iranian oil to go with a reduced British share. Iran then became integrated into the American economy, its internal development planned on capitalist lines. With the Shah's support, and with his favorites skimming off billions of dollars, U.S. firms invested heavily in Iranian development and superimposed an advanced, high-technology economy on the country's feudalistic, traditional Islamic society. To safeguard his regime from popular discontent, the Shah used his oil profits to purchase billions of dollars of American arms, and with the help of the CIA developed SAVAK, his secret police. In 1979, traditional Iran would assert itself and force the Shah to flee the country. The Iranian people would then turn on their American benefactors whom they would perceive as having fostered the destruction of their traditional society.

Interventions in Latin America

In the year following the counter-revolution in Iran, the CIA overthrew the democratically-elected left-wing government of Jacobo Arbenz Guzman in Guatemala. The U.S. always considered Latin America to be within its own sphere of interest. Indeed, as Henry Wallace and many others pointed out, the U.S. treated Latin America the same way that the Soviet Union treated Eastern Europe. The Monroe Doctrine, a unilateral statement of purpose first enunciated in 1823, warned the European powers that the Western Hemisphere was no longer open to European colonization. Reinterpreted through the years, the Doctrine came to imply the right of the United States to intervene in Latin American affairs to preserve its own interests. Much of the region's natural resources—copper, tin, coffee, oil, rubber, sugar, etc.—were owned by American corporations. Between 1940 and 1964, corporate investment in Latin American manufacturing facilities rose from $210 million to $2,340 million, while mining investments doubled and the value of American oil holdings rose almost 600 percent from $572 million to $3,142 million.[41] Moreover, friendly regimes, low tax requirements and cheap labor made investment in Latin America especially profitable, more profitable even than similar investments within the United States. For obvious reasons, the U.S. could not allow any Latin American government to assert its independence and close itself off to American capital.

Guatemala began to move in this direction in 1944 when a revolutionary movement toppled the U.S.-backed dictatorship of General Jorge Ubico. A popularly elected government, led by President Juan Jose Arevalo, began a program of democratic reforms, including independent labor unions, social security, and a literacy campaign. Between 1945 and 1953 Guatemala had the highest increase in per capita income in all of Latin America.

American corporations did not approve of these reforms. The United Fruit Company (now Standard Brands), the power behind the Ubico dictatorship, was the largest landholder in the country and the principal employer of the rural Indian population. Its control of banana production—Guatemala's principal cash crop—gave it control of the country's economy. In response to a minimum wage law that put an end to rural peonage, the company reduced its banana exports and began shifting production to other Latin American countries. At the same time, the American travel industry downplayed Guatemala's tourist attractions, American oil companies stopped exploring for oil, and the World Bank, at the behest of the U.S. State Department, withheld development loans.[42]

Still, the revolution prospered, and in 1951 a member of Arevalo's cabinet, Jacobo Arbenz Guzman, was elected President by an overwhelming margin. The next year, the Guatemalan Congress passed legislation for agrarian reform and in 1953 the Arbenz Government expropriated 234,000 acres of uncultivated land belonging to United Fruit. Arbenz offered the company $600,000, the full amount that the land was assessed at for tax purposes. But the American corporation, understanding that agrarian reform threatened its access to cheap labor and its near monopoly of banana production, demanded $16 million. Undaunted, and despite rumors of an American-sponsored coup attempt, Arbenz expropriated a second tract of idle land owned by the big banana company. In response, the U.S. began a naval blockade off the Guatemalan coast and sent a new ambassador, John E. Peurifoy, whose qualification for the post was his experience in helping to suppress the left in Greece immediately after the Second World War. After an interview with Arbenz, Peurifoy reported to Dulles that the Guatemalan president "thought like a communist, talked like a communist, and if not actually one, would do until one came along..."[43]

This was all the justification the Eisenhower Administration needed. A military officer, Colonel Carlos Castillo Armas, in exile for his participation in earlier coup attempts was recruited by the CIA to lead an invasion force. The CIA set up bases in Honduras and Nicaragua (then ruled by the pro-American Somoza dictatorship). In June 1954 Castillo Armas invaded Guatemala, but his army got pinned down and a popular uprising, predicted by the CIA, didn't occur. The bombing of Guatemalan cities by American planes flown by American pilots proved decisive, however, and the Arbenz Government fell with its leaders taking refuge in foreign embassies and going into exile.

On television, Dulles explained that Guatemalan "patriots" had risen up "to challenge the communist leadership—and to change it. Thus, the situation is being cured by the Guatemalans themselves."[44] In the United Nations, the U.S. denied involvement in the coup and vetoed Arbenz's demand for an investigation. In Washington, Ambassador Peurifoy assured Congress that "the Arbenz government, beyond any question, was controlled and dominated by communists. These communists," he insisted, "were directed from Moscow."[44]

In power, the Castillo Armas regime murdered thousands of labor leaders, peasant organizers and political activists, destroyed the labor movement, disenfranchised 70% of the voters, including the Indian population, and gave United Fruit not only the uncultivated lands that Arbenz had confiscated, but an additional 800,000 acres under cultivation by independent peasants.[45] Dulles, who before becoming Secretary of State had been on the board of directors of United Fruit, summed up the coup as stopping "communist imperialism" in Latin America.[46]*

Many of the same CIA officials who participated in the Guatemalan coup, including E. Howard Hunt, later imprisoned for his role in Watergate, were called to perform a similar duty in Cuba in 1961. In 1958, the dictatorial regime of Fulgencio Batista was overthrown by a guerrilla movement led by a young Cuban lawyer named Fidel Castro. During Batista's reign, indeed ever since the U.S. gained economic dominance in Cuba after the Spanish-American War, Cuba was an economic fiefdom of American corporations. Under Batista, American investors controlled virtually all of its utilities, its mines and natural resources, and most of its railroads, sugar, and cattle. Sugar was Cuba's principal cash crop and most of its income came from sugar exports to the United States.[47] But sugar necessitated only seasonal labor and, as in Guatemala, the peasants or *campesinos*

---

*Dulles' brother, Allen, head of the C.I.A., previously was president of United Fruit while the Dulles' law firm, Sullivan and Cromwell, was its legal representative. In addition, John Moors Cabot, Assistant Secretary of State for Inter-American Affairs was a principal stockholder of United Fruit and General Walter Bedell Smith, another high State Department official, would become a director of United Fruit after leaving government. It was Bedell Smith who advised President Eisenhower of the "merciless hounding of American companies there by tax and labor demands, strikes, and, in the case of the United Fruit Company, inadequately compensated seizures of land under a Communist-administered Agrarian Reform Law." (*Eisenhower: Portrait of the Hero* by Peter Lyon, Little, Brown & Company, 1974, pp. 591-592).

who worked the crop were landless, illiterate, and also jobless for most of the year. Rural poverty was thus a fact of life on this Caribbean island, called the "pearl of the Antilles" because of its climate and agricultural resources. In the large cities, tourism was the main industry, the U.S.-based Mafia controlled the gambling casinos. In Havana alone there were reportedly 50,000 prostitutes.[48]

Castro's victory was an inspiration to Third World peoples. When he emerged from the mountains in December 1958, Batista's army disintegrated, and the urban population rose in jubilant support. On New Year's Day 1959, Batista fled the country, having already plundered the Cuban treasury and shipped the money abroad. Castro was not the first Cuban revolutionary to overturn a U.S.-backed dictator. But all previous revolutions were compromised because they could not break Cuba's dependence on the United States for development capital. But Castro, upon entering Havana for the first time, promised the Cuban people an authentic social revolution. *"Revolucion, si; golpe militar, no"* he said.[49] As a guerrilla leader, Castro professed no specific ideology; but as leader of the government he had to find a way of developing his country without compromising his revolutionary goals. The choice, which became apparent after his first few months in power, was a socialist revolution to end U.S. economic dominance and, on behalf of the working class and the peasants, to overturn existing social relations.

Once Castro decided to develop Cuba on a socialist basis, a break with the United States became inevitable. To create a more self-sufficient agrarian economy and to give peasants land, Castro nationalized the sugar industry. Asserting his independence, he began to buy oil from the Soviet Union at a price that the American oil companies wouldn't match, leading Eisenhower to denounce Soviet-Cuban trade as an attempt by "international communism to intervene in the affairs of the Western Hemisphere."[50] When the oil companies refused to handle this Russian oil, Castro nationalized the refineries. Gambling casinos were also closed and prostitution outlawed. The U.S., never comfortable with a revolutionary movement it could not control, began planning a counter-revolution. In April 1959, when Castro visited the United States, Eisenhower—who at different times had welcomed such Latin American dictators as Jimenez of Venezuela and the Dominican Republic's Trujillo—went to play golf in Georgia. Vice President Nixon had a three-hour meeting with Castro and afterward urged that the U.S. organize the Batistaites-in-exile and launch an invasion to overthrow Castro.[51] In the winter of 1959-60 the CIA dispatched the first of an unknown number of assasination teams to kill Castro.[52] In March 1960, President Eisenhower ordered that training for an invasion begin, and the CIA began recruiting Cuban exiles and setting up secret training camps in Nicaragua and Guatemala. The actual invasion was ordered by President Kennedy in May 1961. The CIA expected that the landing would touch off an anti-Castro rebellion within Cuba. But, despite U.S. naval and air support, the exiles never got past the beachhead. Instead of the hoped-for uprising, the Cuban people rallied to defend what by now had become an anti-American socialist revolution.

The American Century

The Chinese and Cuban revolutions excepted, the postwar period from 1945 to 1960 was more like Henry Luce's American Century than it was Henry Wallace's Century of the Common Man. U.S. power, prosperity, and influence were at their apex; U.S. corporate interests were sitting on top of the world. Between 1945 and 1957, the value of overseas exports doubled; compared to 1933 and the bleak days of the Depression this represented an increase of 1000 percent. But commodity trade was only a small part of the story. From 1946 to 1959, direct investment in foreign countries rose from $7.2 billion to $29.7 billion, climbing to $49.3 billion in 1965 despite the loss of Cuban investments. This represented, in 1960, 60 percent of the world's total. This investment was dominated by the largest and most powerful U.S. corporations; 43 firms accounted for 57 percent of the total. According to Harry Magdoff, the U.S. overseas empire absorbed 40 percent of the domestic output of mines, factories, and farms, and accounted for 20 percent of the profits of manufacturing corporations. From this outlay, American investors extracted profits worth $13 billion. In Latin America alone, between 1950 and 1966, the U.S. invested $3.8

billion and profited by $11.3 billion.[53] This wealth, translated into the actual ownership of productive property in countries all over the world, represented political and cultural influence as well. The power of American capital to make or break foreign governments, the impact of American products, styles, tastes, and ideas on other societies—attested to the power of Luce's prophecy.

But the Chinese and Cuban revolutions represented a serious break with this imperial pattern. With Cuba as an example—just 90 miles off the Florida coast—the U.S. could no longer automatically assume that Third World countries would automatically fit into its economic orbit: not without resorting to covert political manipulation or overt military intervention, as was going on in Vietnam. Nor, despite its nuclear arsenal and its anti-communist rhetoric, could the U.S. deny the Soviet Union the status of a superpower. From Truman to Eisenhower (and into the Presidential administrations of Kennedy, Johnson, Nixon, Ford, Carter, and Reagan, the American attitude toward the Soviet Union and toward the rest of the world remained unchanged. A foreign policy predicated upon the expansionist needs of the domestic economy continued to be misrepresented as a moral response to Soviet aggression. The virulence of this anti-communist ideology, adhered to by most liberals and conservatives, Republicans and Democrats, meant that domestic issues could not be seriously discussed, existing dogmas could not be challenged. The resultant intellectual and moral stagnation darkened every aspect of American life.

Chapter Four

*I killed more people tonight than I have
fingers on my hands. I shot them in cold
blood and enjoyed every minute of it...They
were Commies, Lee. They were red sons-of-
bitches who should have died long ago...
never thought that there were people like
me in this country. They figured us all to be
soft as horse manure and just as stupid.*
*—Detective Mike Hammer in Mickey Spil-
lane's popular novel* One Lonely Night,
published in 1951.

The corporate liberals who had come to power during the war feared a return to the conditions of the Great Depression. Could the wartime prosperity be maintained through the reconversion to peacetime production? Would the American people support the precepts of the global foreign policy deemed necessary to promote domestic prosperity? Could the reactionaries and the isolationists be kept at bay? A return to Republican rule would bring the protectionist and trickle-down economic theories that had caused the Great Depression. Much was at stake. Should their mission fail and the economy fall, the radical militance of the 1930s would be revived and the future of capitalism would be at stake.

Events immediately following V-J Day gave the new Truman Administration cause for worry. Working people were restless. At war's end, the CIO and AFL had 14 million dues-paying members, their highest ever, and a treasure chest overflowing with money to support strikes and new organizing efforts. Though labor leaders had cooperated with businessmen during the war, rank and file workers, as evidenced by the more than 14,000 wildcat strikes between Pearl Harbor and V-J Day, had not forgotten their 1930s militancy. In June 1944, the *New York Times* predicted "a post-war period of great turmoil in labor relations."[1]

Beginning in the autumn of 1945 and continuing through the following year, the United States experienced more labor strife than in any time in its history. In 1946, four and a half million workers went out on strike at a loss of 113 million work days, four times the number of days lost during 1937, the peak year of the CIO organizing campaigns. And the militant spirit of the 1930s seemed to have been carried over. In December 1945, for example, 3,000 machinists at the Yale and Towne lock manufacturing company in Stamford, Connecticut walked off the job. Workers in other union shops supported them. Ten thousand union members from all across the city marched in solidarity with the machinists. The musicians local supplied a band and there was dancing in the streets, along with songs and speeches. This effectively stopped work throughout the city for the day.

One year later, on the other side of the continent, workers in

Oakland, California, conducted a two-day general strike over the same type of issue. The walkout began with a strike by retail clerks, most of them women, at two downtown department stores. Early in the morning, 3 December 1946, bus and trolley operators, along with their passengers (many of them factory workers going off to the first shift) observed the Oakland police escorting trucks through the picket lines into the loading zones of the department stores. The unionized transport workers stopped their vehicles and went to the assistance of the retail clerks. Many of their passengers went with them. Word spread to other union shops and more workers, without authorization from their leaders, filled Oakland's business district to protest the police action.

Oakland, then, was a notorious right-wing town. Reactionary William Knowland owned the Oakland *Tribune* and the city government reflected his anti-union bias. As the strike spread, the workers organized the city. All stores, except those selling essential goods, were instructed to close. Groups of workers patrolled the streets, and there was no crime or violence. Bars were allowed to stay open, provided that they only sold beer and that they moved their jukeboxes out into the street and supplied the nickels to provide the public free music. That night, Oakland resembled one huge, happy block party. The next day the general strike spread to the influential dockworkers. There was a march, led by veterans, to City Hall to demand the resignation of the anti-union city government, while a picket line was thrown up around the office of Knowland's paper. Still, the union leadership withheld its support. Instead, they negotiated a settlement with the city officials, who promised not to use police to help management break strikes. The retail workers, however, were left to fend for themselves. On the third morning, the AFL Central Labor Council sent soundtrucks into the streets to urge the workers back to work. The CIO was silent. The Oakland general strike, however brief, was warning that rank and file unionists were often more militant than either the CIO or AFL leadership, and that they were prepared to go out on strike for political as well as economic reasons.[2]

Working people were not the only Americans who were restless after the war. After Henry Wallace was fired from the Truman Administration, he continued to speak out against the anti-Soviet drift of its foreign policy. A week after his dimissal, New Deal proponents came together at the Conference of Progressives. Former Interior Secretary Harold Ickes and former Treasury Secretary Henry Morganthau, Jr.—both of them influential members of Roosevelt's cabinet who were also let go by Truman—shared leadership with CIO president Philip Murray, NAACP leader Walter White, and James Patton of the National Farmers Union, the liberal rival of the conservative American Farm Bureau Federation. The conference issued a call for a return to New Deal social and economic priorities and endorsed Wallace's critique of Truman's foreign policy. Another declaration of the conference, addressed specifically to Wallace, urged him to "carry on with confidence that you have the support of the millions upon millions of Americans who believe in the program of Franklin Roosevelt."[3]

In December 1946, many of the same people organized the Progressive Citizens of America (PCA), with talk of starting a third party to run Henry Wallace for President. The Democrats, beaten badly by conservative Republicans in the November congressional elections, were worried about this threat. Touring the country and attacking Truman for betraying Roosevelt's ideals, Wallace attracted large, enthusiastic gatherings. Following his speaking tour in the spring of 1947 a Gallup Poll estimated that 13 percent of the voters would support Wallace on a third-party ticket.[4] As Gael Sullivan, acting chairman of the Democratic Party, warned Truman in June, "There is no question that Wallace has captured the imagination of a large segment of the population."[5]

Corporate liberalism had one main goal: to win public approval for an interventionist foreign policy so that the U.S. economy could fulfill its overseas potential. Henry Wallace, upholding the New Deal banner, might draw liberal strength away from the Democrats and throw the 1948 elections to the Republican conservatives. This, the corporate liberals feared, would mean a return to isolationism with its protective tariffs, reduced trade, economic stagnation, unemployment, reduced productivity, and a new depression. In this context, anti-communism was a two-edged sword: corporate liberals could red-bait and destroy Henry Wallace on the left, while co-opting anti-communism on the right and refuting Republican charges that they were "soft on communism."

Anti-Communism in American Politics

The roots of anti-communism go deep in the United States. In no other Western country has anti-communism or a more generalized form of anti-radicalism assumed the authority of an indigenous ideology. Other Western democracies have strong socialist and communist parties; Marxism and other radical ideas are part of the political dialogue. Only in the United States is radicalism considered incompatible with national identity. The congressional committee that, from 1938 to 1968, kept a continuous watch on radical organizations was called the House Committee on *Un-American* Activities (HUAC). Such a formulation, for reasons other than the obvious, is peculiar to the U.S.

Except for native Indians, the U.S. is populated entirely by immigrants and their descendents. White settlers coming from many different countries had to invent a national identity for themselves as they spread across the continent. America, at least in the nineteenth century, meant the frontier, open land, and economic opportunity. The most successful immigrants were the ones who came to acquire and keep property. Using their economic power to gain political influence and intellectual authority, they generalized their success to promote the concept of "Americanism," which had free enterprise, individualism, competitiveness, private property, and economic opportunity at its ideological core. New immigrants, having to prove their allegiance, were under social pressure to embrace this Americanism and to proclaim its virtues even louder than the immigrants who came before.

The notion of Americanism included a fear of anything foreign. Although the socialist ideal of a cooperative commonwealth had many proponents in early America, conservatives pointed to Marx, a German, as evidence that socialism was a foreign idea. When, during the latter half of the nineteenth century, many immigrants—Germans at first, then Finns, Swedes, and Russian Jews—brought socialist ideas with them, conservatives were able to discredit socialism among a large part of the population as incompatible with being a good American. Anti-radicalism, as the understandable ideology of the business class, became the political veneer of ingrained class, religious, and social fears and hatreds. In this aspect, the anti-Communism of the postwar years was nothing new.

But if anti-Communism was part of a long tradition, it gained new credibility from the demonstrated subservience of the Communist Party, U.S.A. (CP) to the Soviet Union. Memories were still fresh of the CP's sudden twists and turns in foreign policy in the late 1930s and early '40s. When Germany and the Soviet Union had startled the world by signing a non-aggression pact in August 1939, the CP (losing many of its members in the process) had abandoned its Popular Front alliance with New Dealers and socialists and joined the isolationists in opposing Roosevelt's preparations for war. Then, when the Nazis broke the pact and invaded the Soviet Union, the CP reversed itself and enlisted with Dr. Win-the-War for the duration, compromising, at times, its ties with labor by supporting the no-strike pledge throughout the War.

The support of the American Communist Party for the Soviet government was based on its perception of Russia as a socialist oasis surrounded by hostile capitalist countries. The CP viewed the Soviets as upholding the banner of socialist revolution. Thus, the security of Russia was necessary for the successful advance of socialist ideas the world over. Supporting the USSR was not un-American within this perspective, for if Soviet communism were allowed to die, the hope of the U.S. working class for a better life would die with it. Stalin, however, did not share this sentiment. His concern was with Russian security, and he had no qualms about sacrificing the U.S. working class, the U.S. Communist Party, or the worldwide Communist movement in order to secure the borders of his country. Thus, in the United States, the policies of the CP had very little to do with socialism, communism, or any other radical idea; indeed, on most pressing issues, the Party differed little from the New Deal Democrats.[6]

Even without the opposition of an ideological anti-communist movement the CP would have been in trouble. In the CIO, where the Party was strongest, its success had come through an alliance with labor leaders, often at the expense of support from the rank and file. The CP had earned a lot of influence through its organizing achievements in the 1930s and had gained in membership during the war years. Nevertheless, many of its militants had been antagonized by the Party's strong opposition to wildcat strikes, and anti-communist union leaders were able to exploit this after the war. In 1946, the ex-socialist, Walter

Reuther, was elected president of the United Auto Workers (UAW) defeating the incumbent, R. J. Thomas, who had the support of a large CP faction. Other union leaders took this as a sign that as allies, the Communists were expendable. The Transport Workers Union under Mike Quill purged an active Communist faction in 1947, as did Joseph Curran's National Maritime Union.

The CIO was not immune to the rightward drift of national politics. Republican victories in the 1946 Congressional elections encouraged it to trim its sails and move closer to mainstream Truman Democrats. Indeed, the Republican majority was on the offensive in the new Congress. In 1947, over Truman's veto, right-wingers passed the Taft-Hartley Act which severely limited the normal activities of labor unions. Taft-Hartley also mandated political purges within the labor movement by requiring union officers to swear that they were not Communist Party members. Labor leaders denounced Taft-Hartley as the "Slave Labor Act," and at first refused to sign the non-Communist affadavits, but most eventually complied. At a meeting of the CIO executive board, President Murray told the union heads, "If communism is an issue in any of your unions, throw it the hell out...and throw its advocates out along with it."[7] When ten unions refused to conduct such purges, the CIO expelled them.

Anti-Communism as a Political Tactic

For the Truman administration, anti-communism was a way both to ward off Republican attacks and to insure support for its anti-Soviet foreign policies. In March 1947, shortly after announcing the Truman Doctrine, the President issued Executive Order 9835 establishing a federal loyalty program and authorizing the Attorney-General to compile a list of tainted organizations. Association with any group on this list would subject a federal employee to dismissal. Under the Truman loyalty program, 2,000 federal employees were dismissed, 212 resigned, and countless others were intimidated.[8] Few restrictions were placed on the investigators. If an informer had seen books about Marxism on an employee's bookshelf, that could be damning evidence; workers might also find themselves questioned about their support for civil rights, the Loyalist side in the Spanish Civil War, the United Nations, or even Henry Wallace.[9] Truman himself admitted with customary candor that "some reports showed that people were being fired on false evidence."[10] Be that as it may, being fired as a subversive from a federal job was akin to being convicted of a heinous moral crime. "A man is ruined everywhere and forever," Seth Richardson, the chairman of the Loyalty Review Board, said in 1950. "No reputable employer would be likely to take a chance in giving him a job."[11]

The power to investigate alleged subversion gave J. Edgar Hoover's FBI the ability to destroy the reputation of any person it chose to investigate. Much of its work was done by part-time informers who infiltrated the Communist Party and other leftist groups. A number of these people made informing a career: as long as they could continue to come up with names of alleged Communists, they were able to remain on the job. A few, after losing their cover, wrote books and articles on their experience or toured right-wing lecture circuits describing Communist "plans" to overthrow the government. The juicier their exposes, the more lucrative their work. The FBI had so many informers running around in the field that they sometimes ended up informing on each other. In 1950, a coal miner named R. J. Hardin was cited by an FBI informer, Matthew Cvetic, as the CP organizer for Cambria County, Pennsylvania. When this information was made public, Hardin lost his job, the friendship of his neighbors, and—after his house was stoned—his place of residence. Subsequently, Hardin turned up as an informer himself; like Cvetic, he had been in the CP as a paid employee of the FBI.[12]

In 1949, Bernard DeVoto took the public to task for allowing the FBI to trample so easily on its civil liberties. "We find out that the FBI has put at the disposal of this body or that body a hash of gossip, rumor, slander, backbiting, malice and drunken invention, which, when it makes the headlines, shatters the reputations of innocent and harmless people and of people who our laws say are innocent until proven guilty in court," he wrote. "We are shocked. We are scared. Sometimes we are sickened. We know that the thing stinks to heaven, that it is an avalanching danger to our society."[13] On one level, the repression unleashed by the Truman Administration was not particularly brutal. In contrast to other countries, there were no firing squads, forced labor camps, or political prisoners numbering in the thousands or millions. But such was the state of American democracy that the FBI—without resorting to physical force— was able to stifle dissent and create what was in effect a totalitarian society.

Repression became a means of insuring support for Truman's foreign policy. "Since the President called for aid to Greece and Turkey," the FBI Director Hoover noted in 1947, "the Communists opposing the plan had been mobilized, promoting mass meetings, sending telegrams and letters to exert pressures on Congress to oppose the doctrine."[14] All of these activities were common political practices and perfectly legal, hence none of Hoover's business. But the inference was clear: opposition to Truman's foreign policy was Communist-inspired, therefore subversive.

Hoover and Truman's Attorney-General Tom Clark were also responsible for the Freedom Train, a brilliant public relations idea designed, in Clark's words, because the country "needed a Paul Revere that would go around behind a modern machine," to promote an "upsurge in patriotism."[15] The Free-dom Train toured the nation in 1947 and 1948, carrying the Truman Doctrine alongside such documents as the Declaration of Independence and the Constitution. Wherever the train stopped, it was greeted by school children, marching bands, and patriotic speeches. When it reached Washington, D.C., during the debate on the Interim Aid Bill, federal employees were given time off for a mass rally, where they took a "freedom pledge" and sang "God Bless America."

The real targets of Truman's loyalty campaign were Henry Wallace and his progressive following. In January 1947, one month after the founding of the Progressive Citizens of America (PCA), Americans for Democratic Action (ADA) held its organizing conference. Henry Wallace was specifically not invited, but a host of other prominant New Dealers attended, including Eleanor Roosevelt. Other ADA founders included Walter Reuther of the United Auto Workers and such new-comers to national Democratic politics as Mayor Hubert Hum-phrey of Minneapolis and Harvard professors Arthur Schle-singer, Jr., and John Kenneth Galbraith. The ADA, like the PCA, called for a return to domestic New Deal priorities. But, unlike the PCA, it excluded Communists and, after some hesitation, endorsed the anti-Soviet thrust of the Truman foreign policy. With the creation of the ADA, Wallace was no longer the sole keeper of the New Deal flame. The ADA challenged Wallace for the Roosevelt constituency and attempted to secure it for the Truman Democrats.

With the announcement of the Marshall Plan (ERP), and, especially, with the Stalinist takeover of Czechoslovakia, Wallace began to lose his liberal support. Anti-Communist hysteria made it more and more risky to oppose the Administration's foreign policy. Although Wallace stuck to his critique—given the anti-Soviet aggressiveness of the Truman policy, he said, the belligerent Russian response was predictable—his support dwindled. Except for a few unions led by Communists, the CIO lined up alongside the AFL behind President Truman.*

Although his support was evaporating, Wallace announced for the presidency in December 1947 on the Progressive Party ticket. From the beginning, the party had a strong CP influence, although the platform reflected Wallace's Jeffersonian and New Dealish ideals of small business and small family farms prospering in a mixed economy. The party structure itself was open and democratic. But because of their selfless dedication and their willingness to perform the routine duties of a political campaign, CP members assumed an influence in the Progressive Party far beyond their numbers. Moreover, the presence of so many Communists—or Stalinists, as independent leftists called them— kept non-Communist radicals out of the party. Thus by default, and contrary to its intentions, the CP gained control of the Progressive Party.

Despite Wallace's dwindling support, Truman had to take his campaign seriously. The Republicans were on the upswing;

---

*Economic conditions also worked against Wallace's movement. The experts had been wrong: pent-up consumer demand stimulated the economy in the immediate postwar period and sent it hurtling through the problems of postwar reconstruction. Confidence grew. For the first time since before the Depression, working people were able to enjoy the fruits of their labor. Affluence seemed just around the corner, and there was no longer any urgency to the call for a New Deal revival.

in a close election the votes that Wallace took from Truman could cost him the presidency. The presence of so many Communists in the Wallace campaign was a tempting target, and Truman's campaign staff, taking no chances, chose to go for the jugular. From the beginning, Truman ignored Wallace's challenge to his foreign policy and attempted, instead, to link Wallace to the Communist Party wherever possible. The architect of this strategy was Clark Clifford, an up-and-coming corporate lawyer and an influential advisor to Truman (as he later was to Presidents Kennedy, Johnson, and Carter). In a memo outlining his approach, Clifford called upon "prominent liberals and progressives—and no one else—to move publicly into the fray. They must point out that the core of Wallace's backing is made up of Communists and fellow travelers."[16]

The ADA, specifically, was given the job of wielding the hatchet. During the campaign, the ADA took out newspaper ads listing the Communist-front groups that Progressive Party leaders were members of, distributed literature accusing Wallace of racism during his tenure in Roosevelt's cabinet—a particularly dirty trick given Wallace's outstanding civil rights record as head of the Agriculture and Commerce departments—and portrayed the candidate as a confused victim of Communism, or, in a variation, as its disciplined puppet. The CIO also took up the cudgels, initiating a purge of union leaders who stayed faithful to Wallace, and putting the resources of its Political Action Committee behind the Truman candidacy.[17]

The press needed no prodding to go after the Progressive Party with a vengeance. At least eight newspapers, including the Boston *Herald*, the Nashville *Tennessean*, the Birmingham *Post*, and the Pittsburgh *Press*, published the names and addresses of local citizens who signed Wallace petitions, thus deliberately subjecting these people to right-wing harrassment.[18] The Justice Department joined the attack: a few days before the Progressive Party's convention, twelve leaders of the CP, some of whose names were linked with Wallace, were arrested under the Smith Act for conspiring to advocate the overthrow of the government.*

---

*In 1951, when the U.S. Supreme Court upheld the conviction of eleven of them, Justice Hugo Black, in dissent, wrote, "Public opinion being what it

By election day, Clifford's strategy of linking Wallace to the Communists had become a self-fulfilling fact. Faced with intimidation from government and the press, Wallace's non-Communist support all but disappeared. In November he got 1,156,102 votes, or 2.3 percent of the vote, less even than racist States Rights candidate J. Strom Thurmond, who broke with the Democratic Party over its support for civil rights. The Wallace debacle of 1948 represented the final stand of the Old Left. Moreover, it established anti-Communism as an integral part of electoral politics.

With the Left silenced, the Right went on the offensive in all spheres of American life. In foreign policy, right wingers accused Truman of not being aggressive enough. Rather than merely containing Communism, as was Truman's stated goal, some right wingers wanted to go on the offensive and wipe Communism off the map. This was the policy that General MacArthur tried to blackmail Truman into following in Korea. America's options in dealing with the Soviet Union had been narrowed down to two: preventive war or containment. If the first option was a step into nuclear madness, the second option—implying localized non-nuclear wars with limited objectives, as in Korea—seemed reasonable by contrast. Wallace's critique was quickly forgotten as liberals rallied around Truman, who was now portrayed as being tough but moderate.

The Anti-Communist Crusade in the Schools

In 1947 the federal Office of Education introduced the "Zeal for Democracy" program for use by school boards throughout the country. Local school boards had always zealously resisted federal interference, but they generally welcomed federal help in combatting "communist subversion." "The single most important educational frontier of all," Commissioner John Studebaker wrote in a report to Truman, involved the need "to strengthen national security through education."[19] The Zeal for Democracy

is now, few will protest the conviction of these Communist petitioners. There is hope, however, that in calmer times, when the present pressures, passions, and fears subside, this or some later court will restore the First Amendment liberties to the high preferred place where they belong in a free society." (Dennis v. U.S.)

curriculum was designed "to vitalize and improve education in the ideals and benefits of democracy and reveal the character and tactics of totalitarianism."[20] "STUDEBAKER MAPS WAR ON COMMUNISM," was the way the *New York Times* described the program.[21] In general, teachers were ready to go along. The theme of the 1947 national convention of the American Federation of Teachers was "Strengthening Education for National and World Security."[22] Two years later, the rival National Education Association declared that Communists should be prohibited from teaching in public schools. By this time, school boards throughout the country were busy purging teachers with left-wing politics.

The Zeal for Democracy program attempted to balance anti-Communist ideology and democratic idealism with enough leeway to allow local school boards to emphasize one or the other. Given the climate of repression, the anti-Communist component was much safer, therefore more favored; in some sections of the country, democracy and related ideals such as collective bargaining, civil rights, and civil liberties were, themselves, considered subversive. Teaching anti-Communism became an important part of the social studies curriculum throughout the 1950s. Some states, using the federal program as a model, designed their own courses. In *Teaching American History*, a handbook for teachers published in 1955 by the New York State Department of Education, one of the units is titled, "How Can We Fight Communism?"[23]

In 1962, a group of social scientists reviewed the way the Cold War was treated in high school history texts dating back to the 1950s. After quoting from the most frequently used texts, the authors concluded that "the individual and cumulative effect of these viewpoints is to produce a sadly distorted interpretation of Soviet diplomacy and of the relations between the two global giants after 1945." "More devastatingly," the writers continued, "the student is generally left with only one possible interpretation of the rise of Communism in the Twentieth Century: that it is a conspiratorial movement, a worldwide, backstairs palace revolution, moving by stealth and bombs to accomplish its nefarious objectives."[24]

At the college level, history, political science, and economics could not be taught except in the context of the anti-Communist phobia. According to the most widely read economics text of the period, Paul Samuelson's *Economics*, "Karl Marx, an exile from Germany, worked away at the British Museum vowing that the bourgeoisie would pay for the suffering his boils caused him as he sat working out his theories of the inevitable downfall of capitalism."[25] Direct exposure to Marx's writings, much like sex education, was taboo. Nor were there opportunities for a student to learn about native radicalism. Thoreau, for instance, was interpreted as an eccentric nature lover, whose theory of civil disobedience represented his own peculiar response to the kinds of injustice that no longer existed. Left-leaning professors were purged from faculties. Paul Baran, one of the few Marxist scholars to have tenure at an American university, was harassed by Stanford's administration until his death, constantly having to defend himself against attacks by wealthy alumni.

Teachers were not the only victims of the anti-Communist crusade. Truman's Loyalty Program encouraged states, communities, and private corporations to set up programs of their own. Since the CP had only 80,000 members at its peak at the end of the war (reduced to 10,000 members in 1957), it was hardly a threat. But millions of Americans during the 1930s and after had supported various liberal causes side by side with the Communists. Now these citizens were clay targets for right-wing repression. A host of groups joined the campaign to destroy "subversion": the American Legion, the U.S. Chamber of Commerce, various leaders of the Catholic church (especially New York's Cardinal Francis Spellman and the television personality, Bishop Fulton J. Sheen), Southern racists, and big and small businessmen who sniffed an opportunity to destroy the power of organized labor.

By 1953, some thirty-nine states had made it a crime to advocate the violent overthrow of government. In Connecticut, it was a crime to print "scurrilous or abusive matter concerning the form of government in the United States." In 1951, Tennessee made advocacy of violent revolution punishable by death, and in 1954, the Democratic Governor of Texas, Allan Shivers, urged the legislature to make membership in the CP a capital crime (cooler heads prevailed and the punishment was set at twenty years and a $20,000 fine).[26] More commonly, state and local agencies demanded that employees take loyalty oaths.

Many communities set up their own subversive review boards. In Detroit, the FBI, the city government, and the auto manufacturers cooperated. The Ford Motor Company, which had a long history of hiring goons to infiltrate the workplace and inform and beat up on union organizers, now put FBI men on its payroll to keep an eye on the assembly lines. The Detroit city government purged leftists from civil service jobs and, in the process, helped destroy the United Public Workers Union. One of the workers fired in Detroit was a black garbageman who had worked for the city since 1925. He was a thirty-second degree Mason and had a son fighting in Korea. But he had also supported Henry Wallace, had attended a Paul Robeson concert, and had gone to meetings of a group, the Civil Rights Congress, which appeared on Attorney General Tom Clark's list of subversive organizations.[27]

The Anti-Communist Crusade in Hollywood

Congress was also on the trail of alleged subversives. Its committees carried out 26 investigations of Communism between 1946 and 1948, and another 109 over the next six years.[28] The House Committee on Un-American Activities was especially busy; its headline-grabbing investigation in October 1947 of "Communist Infiltration of the Motion Picture Industry" helped set the pattern.

Movies, themselves, reinforced the anti-Communist ideology, especially before television, when the newsreel was a part of every movie show, along with the double feature, a film short, a half dozen Bugs Bunny, Tom & Jerry, or Donald Duck cartoons, and a serial or two. Publisher Henry Luce was a pioneer in the newsreel. His newsreel *March of Time* lasted from 1935 to 1951, when newsreel techniques were adapted for television. Immediately after the war, however, every major movie studio had its own newsreel unit. Fox had *Movietone News*, MGM had Hearst's *News of the Day*, Warner had *Pathe News*, Universal had *Newsreel*, and Paramount had *News*. The newsreel was a highly contrived propaganda art. Typically, an authoritative male voice described the news in an emotional and subjective way while martial music blared in the background. The film clips did not necessarily have anything to do with the event being described, but were chosen to evoke a charged response in the audience, as if General MacArthur in Korea were as real as John Wayne hitting the beach at Iwo Jima. In Luce's words, *The March of Time* was "fakery in allegiance to truth," and other studios followed that policy. During the 1930s, Hearst and Luce had used their newsreels to support the fascist side in the Spanish Civil War. While the less ideological studios showed films of the battles, Hearst and Luce specialized in stock shots of desecrated chruches to make it seem that the Communist-backed Republicans were at war against religion.

As the Cold War came into focus, other studios followed Luce and Hearst in slanting their news. The saga of the encroaching red menace became standard movie fare. An article in the *New Republic* gave a description of postwar newsreel technique: "When Cardinal Spellman and President Truman spoke on St. Patrick's Day, it was the anti-Communist portions of their address that were singled out for screening. Extensive shots of army maneuvers, diving planes, smoking rockets, and General MacArthur reviewing his troops in Japan are screened while sound tracks blare do-or-die college marching songs...."[29] No matter what the newsmakers really said or did, the message received by the moviegoing audience was clearly urgent. A simple speech became transformed on screen into a Paul Revere-like call to arms. Week after week the nation was shown in a state of crisis. As young people went to the movies virtually every Saturday afternoon, these newsreels undermined the objectivity of even the most skeptical members of the audience. Without any available opposing viewpoint, reality became not what was happening in Europe, Washington, or Asia, but what was dramatized on Hearst's *News of the Day* or Luce's *March of Time.*

In October 1947, HUAC began its first investigation of the film industry. Since Hollywood movies were usually non-political or, like the newsreels, right-wing, the movie community seemed an odd area to hunt subversives. Certainly, Hollywood had its radicals and even a few CP members. But more than subversives, HUAC was in quest of publicity; the appearance of Hollywood movie stars was guaranteed to win the committee front-page attention. Many of these celebrities were not eager to play cameo roles in a HUAC production.[30] Hoping to stop the investigation and to rally public opinion against HUAC's tactics, William Wyler, John Huston, and Philip Dunne organized a star-studded Committee for the First Amendment. Among the dozens of entertainers who gave support were Gregory Peck, Lucille Ball, Burt Lancaster, Frank Sinatra, Edward G. Robinson, Robert Young, Henry Fonda, Katherine Hepburn, Leonard Bernstein, Eddie Cantor, Kirk Douglas, Ava Gardner, Benny Goodman, Moss Hart, William Holden, William Huston, Orson Welles, Billy Wilder, and Groucho Marx.* On a radio show, titled "Hollywood Fights Back," Lucille Ball read excerpts from the Bill of Rights. And a planeload of celebrities flew from Los Angeles to Washington, with publicity stops along the way, to deliver a petition protesting the hearings.

Naively, perhaps, the Committee for the First Amendment believed its celebrity status would intimidate HUAC; but the protest backfired. The very presence of so many movie stars brought more attention to the investigation. "MENJOU TESTIFIES COMMUNISTS TAINT THE FILM INDUSTRY," headlined the *New York Times*, reporting actor Adolph Menjou's charge that Hollywood was a "world center of Communism" and that a red invasion might be imminent, aided by a number of Hollywood stars. ("If the Russians come here, I'd move to Texas," Menjou explained, "because I think the Texans would

---

*HUAC's ranking Democrat, John Rankin of Mississippi, had a repsonse. "I want to read you some of the names," Rankin said during the hearings. "One of the names is June Hovick. Another one is Danny Kaye, and we found out that his name was David Kaminsky. Another one here is John Beal, whose real name is J. Arthur Blieding. Another is Cy Bartlett, whose real name is Edward Iskowitz. There is one who calls himself Edward Robinson. His real name is Emanuel Goldenberg. There is another one here who calls himself Melvyn Douglas, whose real name is Melvyn Hesselberg. There are others too numerous to mention. They are attacking the Committee for doing its duty to protect this country and save the American people from the horrible fate the Communists have meted out to the unfortunate Christian people of Europe."

There was no censure of Rankin from his colleagues. Two years after the victory over fascism, fascist-like anti-semetic ideas had become acceptable in Congress, and their proponents were being given the responsibility of defining Americanism. (*Journal of the Plague Years* by Stephan Kanfer, Atheneum, 1973, p. 73).

kill them all on sight.") And, screamed the *New York Post*, "BOBBY SOXERS AND MOTHERS: WOMEN CHEER RO-BERT TAYLOR AS HE URGES BAN ON REDS."[31] The hearings turned from light comedy to serious drama when ten witnesses, all of them leftists, some of them Communists, refused to answer questions about their political affiliation on grounds that such questions from a governmental body violated the First Amendment. These ten witnesses, who came to be known as the Hollywood Ten, were eventually jailed for contempt of Congress.* The response of the movie industry's moguls, meeting in New York at the same time that the House of Representatives was approving the contempt citations by 346 to 17, was quick. The Hollywood executives (who included Henry Cohn, Walter Wagner, Albert Warner, and others) issued a statement abandoning the Hollywood Ten to their fate, and promising that nothing controversial or critical of existing American institutions would ever come out of their studios. For help in eradicating Communist influence in the movies the group invited "the Hollywood talent guilds to work with us to eliminate subversives." Leaving no stone unturned, the moguls also drafted plans for a new public relations campaign, "Movies are Better than Ever."[32]

Gossip columnist and TV personality Ed Sullivan reported in his syndiated column that Wall Street financiers have "not less than $60,000,000" invested in Hollywood. "Reason that Hollywood big shots rushed to New York and barred the 10 cited by Congress," he said, was that "Wall Street jiggled the strings, thas all."[33] Indeed, the big movie studios were all interlocked with corporate conglomerates. RKO was associated with United Fruit, Atlas Corporation and National Can; Twentieth Century Fox was connected with General Foods, Pan Am, the New York Trust, and National Distillers; Warner Brothers was beholden to

---

*The Hollywood Ten were screenwriters Dalton Trumbo, John Howard Lawson, Albert Maltz, Alvah Bessie, Lester Cole, Ring Lardner, Jr., Herbert Biberman, and Samuel Ornitz, producer Adrian Scott, and director Edward Dmytryk. Of the ten only Trumbo, Maltz, and Lardner were able to resume their careers with any success. In 1957, much to Hollywood's embarrassment, Trumbo won an Oscar for the screenplay of *The Brave One*, written under the pen name of Robert Rich.

J. P. Morgan. The Rockefellers, through their Chase Manhattan Bank, were also involved in underwriting Hollywood movies. No wonder the movies changed their tune. Early in 1948, a studio executive told Lillian Ross of *The New Yorker*, "It's automatic, like shifting gears. I now read scripts through the eyes of the DAR, whereas formerly I read them through the eyes of my boss."[34]

The Anti-Communist Crusade in the Courts

New member Richard Nixon of California made his mark on HUAC in 1948. In that year, Whittaker Chambers told the committee that a prominent former State Department official, Alger Hiss, had been the leader of a secret Communist cell in Washington during the 1930s.* Hiss shared with other foreign service officials Ivy League and upper-class credentials, but he was exceptional in that he also supported liberal New Deal programs. Hiss denied Chambers' charges despite intensive grilling by Nixon and other HUAC members. Indicted for perjury, Hiss underwent two trials, the first ending in a hung jury and the second in a conviction; by the time of the second trial Hiss had become a symbol of what Republicans came to call "twenty years of treason" under the Democrats. He was given the maximum sentence of five years.[35]

Another HUAC victim was government economist William Remington, whom the committee accused of secret Communist activity during the New Deal. It took three federal grand juries to hand down an indictment and two trials to get a conviction, but the Justice Department persisted.** In 1954, Remington was murdered by a fellow prisoner in the federal penitentiary at Lewisburg, Pennsylvania.

---

*A perennial witness on Communist subversion, Chambers by now was in the employ of Henry Luce. As an editor of *Time*, posted in the corporate headquarters in New York, Chambers rewrote news reports from foreign correspondents stationed in China to show that Chaing Kai-shek was a popular leader and that the Communists were headed for defeat.

**The foreman of the third grand jury, it turned out, was under contract to ghost-write the autobiography of Elizabeth Bentley, the government's chief witness against Remington.

HUAC also went after treasury official Harry Dexter White, a protege of Henry Morganthau in the Roosevelt Administration and an architect of the International Monetary Fund for postwar financial reconstruction. White came off of a sick bed to deny HUAC's charge of Communist affiliation, and died shortly thereafter. Because the dead cannot defend themselves, his name was bandied about by Republicans and right-wingers as proof that Communists had infiltrated the federal government. Eisenhower's Attorney General, Herbert Brownell, even accused President Truman of having deliberately ignored White's Communist connections when appointing him to high office. The evidence against White has never been made public. According to Brownell, it was too dangerous to national security ever to be divulged. As with Hiss and Remington, HUAC seemed more interested in destroying public officials who had supported the New Deal than in investigating subversion in the postwar years. Speaking of the White case, but disclosing no concrete information, J. Edgar Hoover told the Senate Internal Security Committee that "this situation has a background of some thirty-five years of infiltration of an alien way of life in what we have been proud to call our constitutional republic. Our American way of life...has been brought into conflict with the godless forces of Communism. These Red-Fascists distort, conceal, misrepresent, and lie to gain their ends. Deceit is their very essence."[36]

As the Hiss and Remington cases made their way through the court system, leaders of the Communist Party were being tried and convicted under the Smith Act by federal juries sitting around the country. Although nothing could equal the courtroom drama of the Hiss-Chambers confrontation, "the most sensational spy case of the century" (as the press called it) concerned allegations that two U.S. Communists, Julius and Ethel Rosenberg, gave the Soviet Union secrets of the American atomic bomb program. The news that Russia had broken the U.S.'s nuclear monopoly and tested its first atomic bomb in September 1949 came as no surprise to U.S. leaders. American nuclear scientists had always warned that Russia was capable of developing the bomb, and 1949 was within their estimate of the time it would take. Still, the American people were stunned by the news. Convinced by incessant propaganda that the Soviet

Union was a backward country, they could not believe that the Russians were capable of such an achievement on their own. Moreover, having used the bomb on Japan, the United States easily assumed that the Russians might use the bomb on them. The emotions of the Cold War, always taut, now took an hysterical turn. Many school districts ordered dog tags, like those used in the armed forces, so that after a nuclear attack rescue workers (it was always assumed *they* would survive) could identify the students' bodies. Children also learned to crawl under their desks as protection against nuclear attack. Never before had the American people faced death so intimately, yet so distantly. Fear of the bomb became a major American preoccupation.

In February 1950, a British atomic scientist named Klaus Fuchs confessed that he had given the Russians information about the bomb while working on its development in Los Alamos, New Mexico. In subsequent months, the FBI arrested a known Communist named Harry Gold and a machinist named David Greenglass who, as a serviceman during the war, had worked at Los Alamos. Greenglass, an unbalanced figure who had been involved in some small-scale blackmarket activities while stationed in New Mexico, turned state's evidence. He testified that his sister and brother-in-law, Ethel and Julius Rosenberg, as well as an old college friend of theirs, Morton Sobell, had conspired to pass atomic secrets to the Russians.

The trial of the Rosenbergs took place in March 1951 during the Korean War. Very few people came to their defense; even the Communist Party stayed aloof for a long time. Emanuel Block, the lawyer who took their case, was a sincere and honest man, but he had little courtroom experience and made important legal mistakes. The evidence used against the Rosenbergs, as with Hiss and Remington, was—and remains—controversial. But it seems clear that none got a fair hearing in the tense Cold War atmosphere of that era.[37] Both Rosenbergs were sentenced to death, Sobell and Gold got thirty years, and Greenglass got fifteen years in return for his testimony.* Despite Justice

---

*There was no evidence linking Sobell to the spying that the Rosenbergs were alleged to have been involved in. At any other time, or with a decent defense attorney and a fair judge, the case against Sobell would have been tossed out of court. In 1969, President Kennedy freed Sobell from prison.

William O. Douglas' last-ditch attempt to stay the execution, President Eisenhower gave final approval and the Rosenbergs were executed in the electric chair at Sing Sing Prison in New York, 19 June 1953.

The Rise of McCarthyism

In a Lincoln Day speech in February 1950, at the height of the furor over domestic subversion, the "loss" of China, and fear of the bomb, Republican Senator Joseph McCarthy of Wisconsin held aloft a sheet of paper and said that it contained the names of 205 current State Department employees who were members of the Communist Party. The allegation, carried by the wire services to newspapers all over the country, electrified the nation. Though McCarthy never substantiated his charge, or even produced the names on the list, the mass media reported his accusation without documentation. This was the beginning of the McCarthy Era.*

Suddenly famous, McCarthy escalated his charges to include other federal agencies and all of his critics. He found Communists everywhere. The Democrats fought him; to Acheson, the senator and his friends were "the primitives." But the Republican leadership cheered him on. "McCarthy should keep talking," the respected Senator Robert Taft advised, "and if one case doesn't work out he should proceed with another."[38]

Though Republican moderates like Eisenhower felt that McCarthy was getting out of hand, they were too afraid of losing their conservative support to come out and directly attack him. Even when McCarthy accused former Secretary of State General George Marshall—who as Army Chief of Staff during World War II had been Eisenhower's commanding officer, and a man whom Eisenhower greatly admired—of being part of a "conspiracy so immense and infamy so black as to dwarf any previous such venture in the hands of man," the future president kept his silence.[39] For almost four years, well into the first Eisenhower

---

*The name exaggerates the actual importance of this previously obscure Republican politician. He was merely the most successful demagogue to exploit a form of politics that had earlier been legitimized by the Truman Democrats.

administration, McCarthy dominated the headlines with tales of subversion in high places.

Early in 1954, McCarthy made the mistake of going after the U.S. Army. The Army, it seemed, had given an honorable discharge to a left wing dentist, Major Irving Peress, and McCarthy demanded to know "Who promoted Peress?" In the course of this investigation, McCarthy attacked the patriotism of the dentist's commanding officer, General R. W. Zwicker, and of Secretary of the Army Robert Stevens. The Army hit back by accusing McCarthy of attempting to get preferential treatment for a young member of his staff, who had recently been drafted. The resultant hearings, carried on network television, proved to be the senator's undoing. The Army's counsel, a crusty New England lawyer named Joseph Welch, stood up to McCarthy with eloquence and wit. McCarthy's manic arrogance became transparent and the public turned away from him in disgust. McCarthy became vulnerable for the first time and members of his party, including President Eisenhower, stopped cowering and began to counterattack. A Senate investigation, triggered by Republican Ralph Flanders of Vermont, resulted in a September 1954 vote to censure him for "conduct...unbecoming a member of the United States Senate." McCarthy's career ended then, for all practical purposes. (He died three years later.)

The tidal wave of anti-Communism that McCarthy had ridden to power also began to ebb. A new Supreme Court, led by Chief Justice Earl Warren, whom Eisenhower appointed in 1953, slowly began to erect procedural barriers in the path of the witch hunters. Justice William O. Douglas and Hugo Black, who had stuck doggedly to the Bill of Rights during the height of the red scare, now became the philosophic leaders of the Supreme Court's majority. In the country's political life, the charge of "Communism" was no longer guaranteed to bring either disgrace to the intended target or publicity to the person making the accusation.

The Blacklist

Still, the effects of the red scare lingered on. Hundreds of entertainers remained blacklisted from movies, radio, and television. TV, because it was coming to replace movies as the most popular entertainment medium, was a particular target for right-wing crusaders. In 1950, after Ed Sullivan had presented dancer Paul Draper and harmonica virtuoso Larry Adler on his popular Sunday night vaudeville show, "Toast of the Town," he was inundated by letters from right-wingers about Draper's and Adler's publicly known leftist affiliations. Three days later, Sullivan was told by Kenyon and Echardt, the sponsoring ad agency for Ford Motors, that "Toast of the Town" should never "be used as a political forum, directly or indirectly" and that, in the future, he should take more care about whom he hired.[40]

In June 1950, *Red Channels: The Report of Communist Influence in Radio and Television* was published, listing the names of 151 "subversive entertainers." The introduction, written by Vincent Harnett, a man who made a career out of identifying "communists," charged that the Communist Party U.S.A. was concentrating "more on radio and TV than on the press and motion pictures as 'belts' to transmit pro-Sovietism to the American public."[41] *Red Channels* was an outgrowth of a weekly newsletter entitled "Facts to Combat Communism, Counterattack," which was distributed to about 4,000 subscribers including the personnel departments of such corporations as General Motors, DuPont, Woolworths, Metropolitan Life, Bendix Aviation and R. J. Reynolds Tobacco.[42] The three ex-FBI agents who produced both publications culled radical literature for the names of so-called subversives. Their files went back to the 1930s, so that having one's name listed as a supporter of, say, the Republican side during the Spanish Civil War in 1938 (a cause favored by Communists, socialists, liberals and radicals of all ideological stripes) was sufficient reason to be identified as a "subversive" in 1950. "Counterattack" and *Red Channels* also publicized the investigation of HUAC and similar witch-hunting groups and, for padding their lists, plagiarized other right-wing hate-sheets like the American Legion's "Summary of Trends and Developments Exposing the Communist Conspiracy," and the Catholic magazine, *Sign*, both of which specialized in listing the names of supposed communists.[43]

Red Channels was sent to radio and television stations and advertising agencies, and the men who produced it became virtual Czars of the entertainment industry, determining who got jobs in television and radio.* Critics of the blacklist were many, but most opposed the way the list was compiled and not its existence. The networks and the advertising agencies, for their part, denied that a blacklist existed, but scores of politically-active entertainers, including such well known actors as Zero Mostel, Jean Muir, and John Garfield, suddenly found it difficult to get work.

When blacklisted actor Jack Gilford and New York Yankee baseball player Yogi Berra were scheduled to appear on the "Colgate Comedy Hour," the Yankees threatened to pull Berra off the show if Gilford were allowed to perform. Though Yankee public relations man Jack Farrell admitted that Yogi didn't know "the difference between Communism and communion," the Yankees issued a statement saying that no Yankee player could make public appearances with persons who had been identified as members of Communist-front organizations. As a result, Berra appeared on the program but Gilford was dropped.[44]

Eli Mintz, who played Uncle David on the popular "Molly Goldberg" TV show, and the papa in the family, Philip Loeb, were also victims of the blacklist, as was Mady Christians, who had the role of Mama in the family comedy "I Remember Mama." Christians was a distinguished actress with a long career on the stage. Because of her work on behalf of Spanish Civil War veterans and exiled German writers, she now became unemployable on TV. She died soon afterwards.

The blacklist did to radio and television what HUAC did to the movies; it imposed a dull intellectual conformity on the medium and made it difficult to air any program containing a controversial subject. In the case of television, this was especially tragic. By 1950 Hollywood had long been grinding out films to a standard formula. But in the early days of television, a new generation of writers and directors were creating interesting shows, especially in the areas of comedy and drama. As long as television remained small and did not represent a large financial investment, quality entertainment was possible. But as TV swept the nation in the early 1950s, corporate investment skyrocketed and television executives became more interested in protecting corporate profits than in producing quality programs.

*The Broadway theatre and the Metropolitan Opera Company, virtually alone, resisted the blacklist without harm to themselves.

The threat of the blacklist intimidated television and curtailed its creative potential. Many blacklisted entertainers remained barred from the home screen until late in the 1960s.

Anti-Communism in the Press

Anti-Communist ideology, like the funnies, had long been a staple of American newspapers; even before anti-communism became a postwar issue, the public had become accustomed to the right-wing reality of the newspaper publishers. The huge capital investment necessary to start a major media venture prohibits control to all but the wealthy. Advertising is necessary to make a profit, and business advertisers are obviously loathe to under-write attacks on their own institutions.

A few eccentric millionaires have, from time to time, operated newspapers and magazines with radical slants, but the economics of ideological conformity—i.e., the inability to get corporate advertising—has limited their journals to, at best, small audiences. The Cold War almost wiped out the radical press. The most serious casualty was the New York daily newspaper *PM*, which began publishing in 1940 with a policy of accepting no advertisements. *PM* was started by an intellectual gadfly, Ralph Ingersoll, with backing from Marshall Field III, who had inherited a sizeable portion of the Montgomery Ward fortune. *PM* reflected Field's idea that objective journalism did not mean "viewing with impartiality both sides of the struggle between strong and weak, the big and the small, the monopolists and the independents."[45] With a daily circulation of 160,000, *PM* struggled gamely in the highly competitive New York news-paper market. In 1946 it opened its pages to advertisements but was unable to land any big accounts. In 1948 the newspaper folded, to reappear briefly with new financing as the New York *Star* and then as the New York *Compass*. A few veterans of *PM* found employment with other daily newspapers. Max Lerner, for example, became a columnist for the New York *Post*, but he no longer advocated radical views. Cartoonist Walt Kelly introduced "Pogo" in the *Star* and then went on to syndicated fame. But whenever the denizens of the Okeefanokee Swamp began to take on the satirical appearances of such political figures as Joe McCarthy, his strip was dropped from many of the subscribing newspapers. Veteran *PM* columnist, I. F. Stone, on the other hand, was virtually blacklisted from major papers and so, in 1951, founded his own independent weekly newsletter. Leftwing journals were routinely harassed by the government during this period. The independent socialist weekly, the *National Guardian*, founded during the Wallace campaign in 1948, opposed the Cold War consensus and led the campaign to free the Rosenbergs. As a result, its editor, Cedric Belfrage, was deported to his native England although he had lived and raised a family in the United States since 1926. The Post Office, cooperating with the FBI, harassed the paper's subscribers and financial backers, and its circulation dropped from 54,000 to 22,000 during the McCarthy period.[46]

Mass circulation magazines found anti-Communism a popular topic. First person reports, written by informers, about life in a "communist cell" were staple fare. So was political fantasy. In August 1948, *Look* ran a story entitled "Could the Reds Seize Detroit?" Staged pictures portrayed a barbarian invasion of the United States. Telephone operators were shown dead on the floor, because, claimed *Look*, seizing the means of communications was a Communist priority. Other pictures showed criminals released from prison running wild through the streets, bridges blown up, radio stations under attack. "A sickle is being sharpened to plunge into the...industrial heartland of America," *Look* said. But, not to worry; "The Reds will find the Detroit police department tough foes," the magazine assured.

Another popular weekly, *Colliers*, fantasized World War III. The October 1951 issue was devoted exclusively to a preview of the next great war. The cover showed a G.I pointing a bayonet at a map of Russia, while the text described the war and the ultimate American victory. The Russian people would be liberated from Communism and begin to reap the benefits of American freedom. There would be Russian editions of popular American publications, a Russian version of the musical comedy "Guys 'n' Dolls," and a fashion show featuring hats by Hattie Carnegie staged in a huge Moscow stadium.

The way the press treated actual events was also on the level of political fantasy. A well-heeled China Lobby placed ample resources behind the Nationalist Chinese on Formosa and the press used its propaganda uncritically. Communist China was

portrayed as a restless, violent country on the brink of starvation
and economic disaster throughout the 1950s and '60s. Only
Communist terror tactics kept rebellion from breaking out,
according to the American press, and the people lived in fear of
their lives. (In 1971 Richard Nixon, one of the politicians most
responsible for a hard-line anti-Communist policy, visited China
and took along the press. Overnight, and with no show of
embarrassment, the media perception of Communist China was
transformed and the poverty-stricken police state at once
became a thriving experiment in collective living that com-
manded the interest, if not the support, of all thinking people.)

The reporting of events from Cuba, with but one exception,
was in the same propagandistic vein. In 1958, an enterprising
editor from the *New York Times*, Herbert Matthews, spent time
with Fidel Castro's guerrilla forces in the mountains of Cuba and
wrote enthusiastic reports of their progress against the Batista
dictatorship. Matthew's dispatches broke a curtain of silence
about opposition forces in Cuba; those Americans with interests
in Cuba had gladly accepted Batista's insistence that Castro was
dead.[47] It was not hard for the American public to sympathize
initially with the Cuban rebels. Cuba was a haven for American
tourists who could not help but see—behind the glitter of the
Mafia-run gambling casinos—the impoverished condition of the
Cuban people. But support for Castro began to wane when he
began to act as if he truly believed that he was the leader of a
sovereign nation, and not a functionary of the U.S. economic
empire. The press, which had ignored Batista's cruelties, now
played up Castro's mass trials and the sometimes harsh punish-
ments meted out to members of Batista's secret police. Virtually
overnight, Castro's image changed, and his regime was described
as unpopular and held in power by police terror. Reports of
Castro's death and his imminent overthrow became commonplace; and the Cuban exile community in Miami, much like the
exiled Chinese in Hong Kong and Formosa, became a source for
anti-Castro atrocity stories. As with the Chinese Revolution, the
press faithfully predicted the expected Cuban collapse. In 1959
and 1960, the American public was treated to these headlines:
CUBA LOOKS DOWN THE ROAD TO CHAOS (*Life*, 13
August 1954)
THE TRAGEDY OF FIDEL CASTRO (*Look*, 15 September
1959)

HOW LONG CAN CASTRO LAST? (*Fortune*, January 1960)
CUBAN REVOLUTION—ON THE SKIDS (*Newsweek*, 10
October 1960)
CASTRO'S DAYS NOW NUMBERED? (*U.S. News & World
Report*, 31 October 1960)
     No wonder, that when CIA-trained forces landed at the Bay
of Pigs in 1961, the U.S. press expected the Cuban people to rise
up against Castro and welcome the invading troops as their
liberators. Reporting only the news that they wanted to hear and
then believing their own distortions as truth, media people—
like government officials—lived in a world of Cold War fantasy
in which ideological orthodoxy was considered an adequate
substitute for actual facts.

The Anti-Communist Crusade and the Intellectuals

     Only a few intellectuals—including Paul Goodman, C.
Wright Mills, Norman Mailer, A. J. Muste—consistently opposed the anti-Communist crusade. For reasons to be explored in
the final chapter, most intellectuals, even those who had been
active in the radical movement during the 1930s, accepted the
basic assumptions of U.S. foreign policy. Those intellectuals who
had flirted with the Communist Party and had been disillusioned
with their contact with Stalinism, and so had given up on the Left
in general, were especially prominent in this regard. Consequently, there was very little dissent when the Truman administration began harassing Communists, even though the harassment quickly spilled over to the independent Left. Indeed, it
became popular for intellectuals to confess their youthful brush
with radicalism as a form of innocent idealism or naivete. Now
grown up, they saw through the Marxist "lie" and had become, in
C. Wright Mills' term, "celebrants" of the American way of life.
     McCarthy, however, split the intellectuals into two camps.
The hardline anti-Communists believed the Communist menace
serious enough to warrant a moratorium on civil liberties. One of
their leading spokesmen, Irving Kristol, even denied that civil
liberties were being infringed upon. Other intellectuals, however, were beginning to think they had been conned and that the
threat of Communism, at least at home, was greatly exaggerated.
The thaw in the Cold War that followed Stalin's death and

Khruschev's speech in 1956 denouncing the Stalinist past destroyed the ideological framework for hardline anti-Communism. Events in the late 1950s gradually destroyed the myth of a monolithic Communist movement emanating from the Kremlin and bent on worldwide subversion. But the damage had been done. The old Left was on its death bed; the few intellectuals who had tried to keep the radical tradition alive had no audience, for the persistence of the anti-Communist ideology had taken its toll of the young. Responding to the crises of the 1960s—civil rights, the war in Vietnam, poverty, and social disaffection—a new generation would rise to create a new radical movement. But this new Left, ignorant of history, was bound to make serious mistakes. In 1968, during the height of the anti-war movement, Paul Goodman wrote:

> We now have the abnormal situation that, in the face of the extraordinary novelties and complexities of modern times, there is no persuasive program for social reconstruction, thought up by many minds, corrected by endless criticism, made practical by much political activity. The failure of the intellectuals during the forties and fifties is a major cause of the present generation gap. The young are honorable and see the problems, but they don't know anything because we have not taught them anything. We few who during that period were not co-opted are now sufficiently honored by the young, but what we say has no weight. Being isolated, we were necessarily eccentric and utopian. Being few, we did not know enough. So the young have only gut issues, not politics.[48]

The impact of the anti-Communist crusade—the silencing of the postwar generation and the temporary but effective suppression of native radicalism—continued to influence American life long after the crusade itself had run its course.

PART TWO:
Life in the United States

*I'll tell you what's wrong. We're lonesome.
We're being kept apart from our neighbors.
Why? Because the rich people can go on
taking our power away. They want us hud-
dled in our houses, with just our wives and
kids, watching television, because they can
manipulate us then. They can make us buy
anything, they can make us vote any way
they want.*

                —Kurt Vonnegut, Jr.

What, me worry?

                —Alfred E. Newman

*What this country needs is a good 10¢
psychiatrist.*

                —Henry Morgan

Prologue:
A Sense of Place

I asked him if each of the two spots had a special name. He said that the good one was called the sitio and the bad one the enemy; he said these two places were the key to a man's well-being, especially for a man who was pursuing knowledge. The sheer act of sitting on one's spot created superior strength; on the other hand, the enemy weakened a man and could even cause him death. He said I had replenished my energy, which I had spent lavishly the night before, by taking a nap on my spot.

He said that while I remained rooted to my "good spot" nothing could cause me bodily harm, because I had the assurance that at that particular spot I was at my very best.
—*Carlos Castaneda,* The Teachings of Don Juan, a Yaqui Way of Knowledge. *(University of California Press, 1968), pp. 18, 34*

The postwar years nailed the coffin shut on the American past. Despite government policies described as conservative or middle-of-the-road, revolutionary changes were taking place in everyday life. Indeed, the disruption of traditional habits and values led many people to accept the rhetoric of the status quo for psychological comfort, as a last familiar connection to the past. It was during this period that long-existent tendencies, accelerated by the war, transformed the economy into a centralized, corporate-controlled juggernaut—carving up urban neighborhoods and isolating small towns, sending the population sprawling indiscriminately across an indistinguishable suburban landscape, and making the superhighway the dominant symbol of a new, streamlined, high-speed America.

Rural America was dying. New highway construction brought death to backroad towns and contributed to random commercial sprawl, boosting standardized corporate enterprise at the expense of neighborhood, family business. The postwar period fossilized the independent tinker and inventor, drove poets to the academy and academicians to the Pentagon (where intellectuals were at long last appreciated), and made life precarious for small entrepreneurs who could not compete against corporate giantism. Mechanization and a cruelly efficient agricultural policy drove family farmers off the land and into the cities which, already overcrowded, were not prepared for the influx. Good intentions, such as urban renewal, destroyed cohesive neighborhoods, and the urban immigration of poor whites, blacks, and Puerto Ricans sparked white flight to the suburbs.

Peter Bogdanovich's movie *The Last Picture Show* illustrates what happened to small-town America in the postwar era. The once-lively Texas town where the movie takes place is almost deserted. Sagebrush whips down its empty main street, now given over to cross-country truck traffic rather than to local enterprise. The social life has moved to the suburbs of a nearby city; the inhabitants grope for the lost opportunities of a happier past. Even the town's lone movie theater is closing down. The last feature is *Red River*—Howard Hawks' classic treatment of the cattle frontier. In this, the last picture show, John Wayne stands tall against the Texas range, envisioning a cattle empire and the coming of the American civilization to the southwestern plains. He and Montgomery Clift put through the first cattle drive to a railhead in Kansas, overcoming storms, a spectacular stampede, and inhospitable terrain. They are heroic figures, mythic Americans, white men with an expansive vision and the will to succeed. But the Texas of their dream has fallen into the mindless ennui of Bogdanovich's characters. The remaining people who still possess a vision of life, like Sam the Lion, are dying off and there are few young people to fill their boots.

In *The Lonely Crowd*, one of the best selling books of 1950 and still a standard text, sociologist David Riesman separated social character into three distinct types: *Tradition-directed* people take their social cues from the web of ritual, custom, and religion that defines a static, primitive society. Time is stationary. The goal of this society is communal harmony rather than progress or individual self-fulfillment. According to Riesman, tribal and peasant cultures exemplify "tradition-directed" peoples. *Inner-directed* character types, in Riesman's words, "acquire early in life an internalized set of goals" based on such values as progress, individual fulfillment, and the will to succeed. John Wayne in *Red River*, as in most of his movie roles, was the archetypal inner-directed American male—strong, confident, persistent no matter what the odds. The Puritan work ethic is the ideological underpinning for this American character type who flourished during the frontier days of the nineteenth century and into the early twentieth century. *Other-directed* people are peer-oriented, "sensitized to the expectations and preferences of others" as Riesman put it. The life-styles of other-directed peoples are defined by their immediate environment, and they strive, above all else, to change with the times so that they will always fit in with the most current style. Other-directed character types willingly choose the comfortable niche; they avoid risks and they seek security rather than adventure or individualized self-achievement. Other-directed people also respect authority and fit readily into hierarchical corporate structures. According to Riesman, other-directedness has come to replace inner-directedness as the predominant character type of postwar life.[1]

If not to their past or themselves, whom could other-directed Americans look to for their values, cultural tastes, and social guidance? In the postwar years, mainstream American culture began to stagnate. Immigration had closed to a trickle after 1924, and the only new additions to the ethnic melting pot were the Puerto Ricans who settled in the cities of the Northeast during the 1950s.[2] Up through World War II, the United States perceived itself as a pluralistic society. But hard times during the Depression caused entire families to take to the road in search of jobs and better living conditions.* The wartime experience further disrupted older living patterns. Still and all, at the end of the war, the mold for a mass-produced, homogeneous image of America had not yet hardened. But the economic demands of corporate growth soon changed this. Ethnic eccentricities, local mannerisms, and regional diversity were all subjugated to the necessities of mass marketing techniques. Advertising—which next to military spending became the most essential prop for the domestic economy—sanctioned the destruction of the old ways and propagated the notion that consumerism was the highest form of patriotism.

World War II was inner-directed America's last stand. The veterans were very much a part of the past they had left behind. Bill Mauldin's bearded, grimy cartoon characters, Willy and Joe, symbolized the American G.I. Although they had no stomach for global intervention or the elitism of the officer corps, they fought the war with a quiet heroism and—despite their grumbling about conditions in the field—earned the country's gratitude and respect. Willy and Joe were not cut out for the corporate mold. They were opinionated, too unkempt, and too damn independent to make any company team.

The military is a good place to examine the growing dominance of the other-directed corporate organization man in the American character during the postwar period. The World War II platoon was a metaphor for the American melting pot. Its members had a sense of place, an understanding of personal tradition, a feeling for roots, and an ability to articulate identity.

*During the westward migrations of frontier times, families moved together as unified clans or with neighbors or other migrant families of the same class, religion, or ethnic background. In the postwar era, when families moved to the suburbs, or from farm to city, they did so in isolation; they were not part of a larger cohesive grouping that could sustain the old customs even under the strain of moving into a new environment.

In novels, movies, comics, and television serials, the platoon became a Noah's ark of ethnic diversity. The standard platoon, with its stereotyped Irishman, Italian, Pole, and Jew became an accepted cliche. In Norman Mailer's World War II novel, *The Naked and the Dead* (1948), the platoon has all the standard ingredients. We find Sergeant Croft, a redneck; Joey Goldstein, the Brooklyn Jew; Gallagher, Boston Irish; Julio Martinez, Mexican-American off the streets of San Antonio; Brown, a businessman; Polack Czienwica, whose name speaks for itself; Minetta, an Italian; Red Valsen, the wandering Scandinavian from the northern plains; Hearn, the Ivy League idealist, representative of the cultured, educated WASP; and General Cummings, whose triumph over Hearn marks, for Mailer, the triumph of the fascist mentality. Though the ethnic differences and confrontations within the novel are not central to the plot, they serve as convenient identifying points, familar to the reading public of the time.

The Korean War was fought in comic books by a platoon featuring an Irish sergeant named Mulvaney and a blond, all-American Joe Palooka-like character called G.I. Joe. Their buddies were predictable: the urban Jew, the Italian from the slums, the Midwestern farmboy, the Southerner, and the Pole whose last name always ended with "ski." (Black, yellow, and brown men were not represented, though President Truman ordered the military integrated in 1948. Sometimes an American Indian was added to the platoon to serve, naturally enough, as a scout.)

The peacetime, post-Korean War army, represented best by television's popular "Phil Silvers (Sgt. Bilko) Show," exploited the same ethnic metaphor and even integrated black men into the company motor pool. The humor in this series was often based on ethnic traditions and there was no effort made to disguise or soften the customs of the past. Though television tried to gloss over conflict and to emphasize tolerance in a low-key way, the novels and the more serious movies about war (especially Herman Wouk's *Caine Mutiny*, James Jones's *From Here to Eternity*, and Stanley Kramer's *Paths of Glory*) made no attempt to show that the melting pot worked. Prejudice and ignorance were honestly exposed and there was little expectation that these tensions would be resolved, except momentarily in the crisis of battle. But it was a situation still in flux that contained the elements of both confrontation and growth. WASPs might hold power, and racism and prejudice might be embedded factors in U.S. life. But there were other dynamics, and the melting pot was still a simmering stew that prevented the democratic process from becoming hardened and stale.

Now consider Vietnam. This was not a war for Willie and Joe. The grunts in the rice paddies (the majority of them white working class or black) alone saw the war at first hand. They wore peace symbols, smoked dope, shot smack, and wanted only to return home to forget, which was hard. In peace, they became forgotten warriors; there were no parades to welcome their return, heroism was neither their style nor their desire. That segment of the population that wanted to have heroes in Vietnam (that thought heroism was possible in such a war) heaped their gratitude on the returning prisoners-of-war, most of whom were Air Force men, careerists, professional volunteers. The Air Force, more than any other service branch, reflected the values and structure of the civilian corporate world.

As Paul Goodman has pointed out, corporations diffuse responsibility. Executives, with narrowly defined powers, are not responsible for the whole. Members of the board of directors cannot be responsible for the activities of the executives down the line whose operations they can hardly know about. And the corporation itself is a legal nonentity. The airmen who bombed Indochina never saw the country they were destroying, except from 30,000 feet. (The generals and the presidential advisors, planning the raids, did so from the Pentagon, thousands of miles away.) Like corporate executives, the airmen commuted to work (in B-52s), dropped their bombs, and returned to the comforts of home base without ever having to personally confront the consequences of their acts. As organization men, they took no moral responsibility for what they did; most considered themselves anonymous members of the Air Force team doing their best to carry out their orders. The POWs were the perfect symbols of modern America: white men without roots, circling the planet in clean, highly automated aircraft, dropping bombs wherever and whenever management ordered.

The process of moral apathy and cultural decay was expressed in a less decisive arena in the differences between the comedy routines of two popular humorists, Fred Allen and Steve Allen. Fred Allen had a popular Sunday night radio show in the 1930s and '40s, a feature of which was the "stroll down Allen's Alley." In this routine, Fred Allen would call on "neighborhood" residents and ask them pertinent and often topical questions. The responses were strictly for laughs, of course; but as with the best of humor, they often told us essential things about ourselves. The characters who lived along Allen's Alley were all regional stereotypes: Senator Beauregard Claghorn, a bellowing unreconstructed Southerner who upheld the merits of the ante-bellum South; Titus Moody, a taciturn, tight-lipped Yankee; Ajax Cassidy, an irascible Irishman; and Mrs. Pansy Nussbaum, the neighborhood gossip, who each week would greet Allen's knock with a line like, "So who were you expecting, King Farouk maybe?"—or "Emperor Shapirohito?" The humor in these encounters was invariably pointed and intelligent. The four foils for Fred Allen each held strong opinions and possessed a keenness and wit rooted in the identities of their characters. They could spot phoniness and hypocrisy in an instant and would never be taken in by the fads and rhetoric of the day. Their images, though carefully shaped, attested to a strong faith in democracy, and radio listeners could identify with them in a positive way.

In the late fifties, Steve Allen brought a similar routine to television. His gimmick was "the man in the street" to whom he also would pose topical questions. The characters who answered these queries included Gordon Hathaway (played by Louis Nye), an ingratiating, somewhat intoxicated, "other-directed" suburban executive who held no opinions and strived earnestly to say only what he thought would please; a nervous, edgey character (Don Knotts) who shook like a jackhammer and whose physical demeanor expressed eloquently the confusion in his mind; and Tom Poston's anonymous man in hopeless quest for identity. When Steve Allen would ask this character his name, he would go into shock. His complexion would whiten, his muscles tense, his eyes pop, and his expression become blank. The mere possibility that others could perceive him as an individual with a name of his own and an opinion to share was more than he could handle.

What happened in the years between the confident, self-possessed, articulate America of Fred Allen's "Allen's Alley" and the anxiety-ridden, panic-stricken TV wasteland of Steve Allen's "man in the street?" What happened between the willing conscripts of World War II like Willie and Joe, and the Air Force professionals raining death on the people of Indochina? What were the forces that so changed the American character during the postwar era?

Chapter Five

The American economic system, judged by its total achievement, is the most successful in the present day world. By the same standard of judgement, it is more successful than any in recorded history.
—*A. A. Berle,* The American Economic Republic, *1963*

Moloch! Solitude! Filth! Ugliness! Ashcans and unobtainable dollars! Children screaming under the stairways! Boys sobbing in armies! Old men weeping in the parks!
—*Allen Ginsberg,* Howl

V-J Day ended fifteen years of economic privation. For the first time since the stock market crash of 1929, Americans had money to spend and the promise of consumer goods to spend it on. The war had created a full-employment economy with plentiful overtime and with job opportunities that even extended to women and minorities. But with industry geared to military production, consumer goods were strictly rationed or unavailable. There were shortages in virtually every consumer category, and durable goods like cars, radios, farm machinery, furniture, and appliances were old, worn out, or out of style. Even more, there was a nationwide craving for luxury items, large and small, that had been cultivated by Hollywood movies even during the hard times of depression and war. Spending money piled up. Accumulated wartime savings totaled $150 billion, a sizable nest-egg for a historically unprecedented spending spree. So, once the war ended, industry raced to convert to peacetime production and to gain a competitive edge in the impatient consumer market.

When consumer goods began to fill the shelves in the months following the Japanese surrender, there was a rush to spend the wartime savings. The demand was irresistible. In Los Angeles, police had to control the enthusiasm of gum-starved customers when bubble-gum appeared on the market for the first time since the war. (During the war, sugar was rationed and the gum was a black market item.) As another indication of the coming prosperity, Columbia Pictures boasted of spending $60,000 for Rita Hayworth's wardrobe in the movie *Gilda*. Included in this array of fashion were a $35,000 chinchilla coat and a $10,000 ermine wrap that she dragged around with her throughout the picture but never wore. After a decade and a half of pinching pennies, watching budgets, limiting purchases to the absolute necessities, and keeping a wary watch for bill collectors and creditors, the consuming public was finally having its day.

The period of affluence that began in 1946 would last more than two decades. Even the demobilization of eleven million servicemen and women brought only a trifling amount of unemployment at the end of the war. To the American people who had lived through the trauma of the 1930s, the ease with which the country achieved reconversion was truly miraculous. The lingering fear of another depression gradually gave way to a sense of overwhelming confidence in the capitalist system and a reinforcement of the feeling of righteousness that had come out of the victory in the war. To many, it seemed like a crossing of an economic divide. For the first time in history, a society had achieved the potential of producing a sufficient quantity of goods to provide every citizen with adequate comfort and economic security.[1] "The year 1946," reported *Life*, "finds the U.S. on the threshold of marvels, ranging from runless stockings and shineless serge suits to jet-propelled airplanes that will flash across the country in just a little less than the speed of sound..."[2]

The Ideology of Affluence

Postwar affluence was predicated on the involvement of the federal government in the national economy. With World War II, Keynesian economics became accepted, in fact if not in principle, as the surest way of leveling the boom-and-bust cycle that had always plagued capitalism. Even the Eisenhower administration, which promised to cut military spending ("more bang for the buck") in order to balance the budget, managed a balanced budget in just one out of eight fiscal years. In 1958, a report commissioned by the Rockefeller Brothers Fund acknowledged the acceptance of Keynesian economics in business circles. "Public expenditures in support of growth are an essential part of the economy," the report said. "Far from being a hindrance to progress, they provide the environment within which our economy moves forward."[3] The three recessionary periods that did beset the economy between 1945 and 1960 showed the importance of government spending as a stimulus.

After the pent-up demand for consumer goods began to exhaust itself at the end of the 1940s, the economy started to wind down. Unemployment was up to 8 percent in 1949 and still over 5 percent the next summer when the Korean War broke out. Then military spending pushed the economy forward. Between 1950 and 1953, the Defense Department budget increased from $14.3 billion to $49.3 billion, while as a percentage of the Gross National Product (GNP) it almost tripled from 5 percent to 13.5 percent. As a result, unemployment in 1953 dropped to a decade-low of 1.8 percent.

After the Korean settlement, cutbacks in military spending

brought about a brief economic slump with unemployment rising to 5.5 percent in 1954. But the economy boomed for the next three years; the period between 1955 and 1957 represented the peak of fifties affluence. With a military budget stabilized at about $40 billion a year (or 10 percent of the GNP), a tremendous demand for durable goods, inspired by the growth of suburbs, pushed the economy to new heights. The nearly 8 million new cars sold in 1955 set a record, and the more than 1.6 million new housing starts that same year still stand as an all-time high. Sales of TV sets and other home appliances climbed dizzily during this period. "Never has a whole people spent so much money on so many expensive things in such an easy way, as Americans are doing today." *Fortune* Magazine observed of this boom. "Their appetite, as Hamlet put it, 'grows by what it feeds on.'"[4]

Flushed with profits, industry expanded rapidly to meet demand. But new, automated machinery limited the number of new jobs created so that, despite the growth in the economy, unemployment remained over 4 percent. Over-expansion and the saturation of the consumer market in 1957 and 1958 brought about the most serious recession of the fifties. Industries like auto, steel, aluminum, and appliances had expanded too fast and were producing more than the market could absorb, causing massive job layoffs. Unemployment rose to almost 7 percent in 1958. Though President Eisenhower urged the public to spend more, it was federal deficit spending that brought about the economic upturn. The U.S. stepped up its space program in response to Russia's first Sputnik satellite in 1957 and increased its military budget. Still, the economy remained sluggish with unemployment remaining over 5 percent into the sixties. Between 1950 and 1960, the GNP had grown by 3.2 percent a year to the total of $506 billion. Yet, in the 1960 presidential campaign, Democrat John F. Kennedy attacked the rate of economic growth under Republican leadership and promised to "get this country moving again."

Production, spurred by government spending, became the orthodox method for achieving economic prosperity. "Whether we need or even wish the goods that are produced," John Kenneth Galbraith noted, "their assured production means assured income for those who produce them."[5] The size of the

Gross National Product, the sum total of all goods and services, became the standard by which the economy was measured. Implicit in this idea was the assumption that the environment could be exploited at will and without any bad effects; that the earth's resources were unlimited; and that the human and natural resources of the planet could be ordered to underwrite American prosperity. In 1953 *Life* boasted that "our highly productive capitalist system" has enabled "6 percent of the world's population to produce about half the world's manufactured goods."[6] In succeeding years, U.S. wealth, in contrast to the rest of the world, accelerated rather than diminished. Despite this record, Americans weren't satisfied. For capitalism—no matter how big its size, no matter how great its wealth—still had to expand. So in 1959, the Americans for Democratic Action, in attacking the Republican record, commented, "We have the resources and machines, the science and skills to expand production and consumption at an accelerated rate, even relative to our growing population. But we are not seizing boldly the historic opportunity."[7]

A statement such as this indicates the narrowness of the dialogue, even after the McCarthy Era. The ADA, despite its anti-Communism, was the voice of liberalism in U.S. politics. But even it did not contest the thrust of the country's economic empire; after all, the resources that the ADA glibly claimed for the U.S. belonged, in many instances, to other countries. Besides crude petroleum and the strategic metals that were noted earlier, a partial list of resources for which the U.S. depended on other nations would include the following: coffee, cocoa, bananas, chicle (for chewing gum), tin, antimony, cadmium, asbestos, mica, quartz, natural rubber, silk, diamonds (for industry as well as jewelry), burlap and cortage fibers, sugar, hides, wool, wood pulp, newsprint, lead, zinc, copper, bauxite, waxes, tanning extracts, and vegetable oils.

Military Spending

America's economic well-being rested, not only on the profits from overseas investment and export, but on the oversize military budget necessary to protect those same profits. As Galbraith noted, military spending was the key to postwar economic policy. "If a public sector of the economy supported by personal and corporate taxation is the fulcrum for the regulation of demand," Galbraith said, referring to the Keynesian model, then "plainly military expenditures are the pivot on which the fulcrum rests."[8] This emphasis on military spending was a perversion of John Maynard Keynes' own ideas. An English economist who tried to make capitalism more cognizant of social needs, Lord Keynes had urged public spending for the public good: welfare, irrigation projects, hydroelectric dams, hospitals, parks, and the like. But American corporations were hostile to any public program that might compete with private invest-ment, and so were the businessmen in the Truman and Eisenhower administrations. Despite a federal budget that grew from $38 billion in 1947 to almost $77 billion in 1960, social programs continuously got shortchanged. In relation to the GNP, federal non-military spending actually declined from 7.4 percent in 1939 to 6 percent in 1960.[9]

Continuing wartime patterns, defense spending favored a few large corporations. Between 1950 and 1960, twenty-one firms got 50 percent of the defense contracts.[10] The lines between the military and its corporate contractors disappeared, just as they had during World War II. Corporate executives once again moved freely between executive suites and Washington, and retired military officers capped their careers by going to work for private industry—sometimes as production consul-tants, more frequently as lobbyists paid to influence their old cronies still in uniform.

The complexity of advanced weapons encouraged this corporate-military relationship. Enlisted men and draftees often lacked the skills to handle sophisticated equipment, so corporate employees—managers, engineers, and technicians—had to be hired to do the job. During the 1950s, as H. L. Nieburg has pointed out, the Air Force, then going through its most expansive period, "fostered a growing band of private com-panies which took over a substantial part of regular military operations, including maintaining aircraft, firing rockets, build-ing and maintaining launching sites, organizing and directing other contractors, and making public decisions."[11] The idea of civilian control over the military now had a new twist.

Military spending, however, had certain disadvantages. In

the long run it promoted inflation by producing wealth without increasing the stock of consumer goods that it could be spent on. In addition, it ate up investment capital. While the U.S. was putting its money into military technology, other countries, especially West Germany and Japan, were upgrading their industrial facilities with the most up-to-date technology. In the 1970s, the industrial plant of basic American industries would become obsolete in comparison with the more modern facilities of the foreign competition.[12]

Private Profit vs. Public Need

Statistically, the U.S. had become wealthy in a way that few but the most visionary science fiction writers a decade earlier could possibly have foreseen. But public spending for vital government services was neglected. The $6.5 billion that industry paid for advertising in 1951, for instance, was $1.5 billion more than the public as a whole invested in schools. Galbraith described how production for private use far outweighed public expenditures even though the two facets of the economy were complementary. Roads, highways, traffic police, highway patrols, parking spaces, and hospitals, for instance, were all connected to the number of private autos produced and consumed. "Although the need for balance here is extraordinarily clear," Galbraith wrote, "our use of privately produced vehicles has, on occasion, got far out of line with the supply of related public service. The result has been hideous road congestion and chronic colitis in the cities."[13]

The businessmen who ran the Eisenhower administration opposed any regulation that restricted corporate freedom. The federal regulatory agencies, originally created to act as watchdogs over the private sector, readily fell in line. The Atomic Energy Commission, for example, was staffed with go-getters who took more interest in promoting the use of atomic energy than in assuring its safety. Likewise, the Food and Drug Administration was headed by men with close connections to the food and drug industries, so that many dubious products, later to be found carcinogenic, were allowed into the marketplace after the most perfunctory testing. No agency seemed to have the authority to deal with the toxic wastes turned out by the rapidly expanding chemical industry. The companies were left to cope with the proliferating wastes however they saw fit, which usually meant dumping them, unprotected, on vacant sites and abandoning the sites when they filled up. In 1952 the Hooker Chemical and Plastic Company abandoned one such dump site near the Love Canal in Niagara Falls, New York, The company knew that the chemicals it left there were toxic, but it did nothing to keep the public out. Not until years later did the resulting birth defects and other serious illnesses in the surrounding residential neighborhood become a public scandal.[14] Thousands of similar dump sites are scattered around the country—many of them dangerous, most of them unguarded.* And the burden of cleaning them up has been left solely to the public.

Hard Sell, Easy Credit

Overseas investment and military spending were necessary to sustain the expanding economy. But inflated consumer spending was another prop in maintaining domestic prosperity. Unlike military spending, which can be regulated to the finite dollar, consumer spending is neither predictable nor inevitable. People are not inherently acquisitive; left to themselves they would probably buy what they need plus a few self-indulgent baubles. The function of advertising is to counter this tendency, to cajole the public into heavy spending. As the trade journal *Advertising Age* acknowledged in 1955, "We are already so rich that consumers are under no pressure of immediate necessity to buy a very large share—perhaps as much as 40 percent—of what is produced, and the pressure will get progressively less in the years ahead." But the alternative, to produce only what is necessary or has social value, was unthinkable. "If consumers exercise their option not to buy a large share of what is produced," the journal warned, "a great depression is not far behind."[15] Thus, the importance of advertising. As economists Paul Baran and Paul Sweezy write, the sales effort in the

---

*The Environmental Protection agency in 1979 estimated the number at between 30,000 and 50,000. From 1,200 to 2,000 of these may be especially hazardous. This estimate was probably low, since the EPA was still discovering new but unreported dump sites.

American economy "has advanced to the status of one of its decisive nerve centers. In its impact on the economy, it is outranked only by militarism. In all other aspects of social existence, its all-persuasive influence is second to none."[16]

The needs of the postwar economy dictated the undermining of the once-hallowed American values of moderation and thrift. Money withheld from the marketplace has no economic use; for prosperity to be maintained, people had to buy whatever industry produced. This was something new in American life. Dating back to colonial times, thrift was considered something of a moral imperative. Frugality, after all, was one of Benjamin Franklin's thirteen enumerated virtues that he claimed were the basis for prosperity, independence, and a good life. (Temperance, silence, order, resolution, industry, sincerity, justice, moderation, cleanliness, tranquility, chastity, and humility were the others.) "If you'd be wealthy," he wrote in *Poor Richard's Almanack*, "think of saving more than getting."* As American society evolved, thrift became a social obligation, a part of the Puritan Ethic. Thrift was a necessary hedge against the inevitability of old age; it was money under the mattress for a rainy day, and the assurance to doting parents that their offspring would have the advantages that they themselves may have lacked. Not until the New Deal did the government provide minimal protection against economic hardship. Social Security lessened the fear of poverty in old age. Unemployment insurance eased the threat of job insecurity. And now a seemingly unending postwar boom was diminishing the fear of a new depression; confidence in the economy inspired increased spending. But thrift was still ingrained. "A penny saved is a penny earned," Benjamin Franklin had said.

The credit industry had its origins back in 1919 when General Motors introduced its first Time Payment Plan.**

---

*Franklin also wrote, "For age and want, save while you may. No morning sun lasts a whole day." Updated by John Maynard Keynes, that advice went, "Thrift may be the handmaiden of Enterprise. But equally she may not...For the engine which drives Enterprise is not Thrift but Profit."

**Installment buying plans had become commonplace in large retail establishments around the turn of the century, but the privilege of buying on credit was then given only to favored customers.

(Henry Ford, being an old-style entrepreneur, retained his commitment to thrift. His idea was to mass-produce cars cheaply, but sell them strictly for cash to those who could afford to pay.) Between 1919 and 1963, GM helped its customers finance the purchase of nearly 50 million cars. This made possible frequent style changes and so kept the market for new cars humming.[17]

During the postwar era, GM-style credit was extended to the general public, and "buy now, pay later" plans caught on widely as a means of stimulating sales. In 1955, a peak year in new car sales, 30 percent of the purchasers had yet to pay off the debt on their previous car.[18] Overall, from 1954 to 1960, installment credit rose from $4 billion to $43 billion. Total outstanding consumer credit rose from an identical $8.3 billion figure in 1940 and 1946 to $21.5 billion in 1950 and $56.1 billion in 1960.

The establishment of the Diner's Club in 1950 led to a further revolutionizing of the credit industry. Initially, a prestigious Diner's Club card enabled its wealthy holders to charge meals (usually business lunches) at a few select restaurants that were part of the plan. By adding a carrying charge to every bill, the Diner's Club made a tidy profit. Drawn to the scent of easy money, competitors began to enter the field. Carte Blanche was organized in 1958, followed by American Express and Bankamericard in 1959. The first three had selected memberships, limited to men with established credit ratings. But with Bankamericard, banks began issuing their cards to all male clients. Competition led to the addition of more businesses in more places, so that it soon became possible to make a credit card purchase anywhere in the world. Credit cards boosted the economy in two ways. By making cash unnecessary, it brought convenience to shopping. And by adding an annual interest as high as 18 percent on unpaid bills, it provided added profits to the banks and lending institutions that issued the cards.

One way to look at this phenomenon is to say that credit was democratized; easy credit was available to rich and poor alike. But, as we shall see, the consumer paid dearly for the privilege. Another way of interpreting the credit boom is to note that easy payment plans, combined with the social pressure and the pervasive influence of the middle-class lifestyles shown on TV, encouraged people to buy goods that they otherwise might have done without. Moreover, low-income people paid higher carrying charges than the rich and were more likely to lose the merchandise through default on their payments. Thus, it was as profitable to extend credit to the poor as it was to lend money to the rich. As *Fortune* summed up in 1956, the credit industry, more than anything else, is "a boon to the banks."[19]

There still remained the problem of luring consumers to the marketplace and persuading them to part with their money. This was the central task of advertising. "Americans had to be 'sold' new habits, new ways of viewing life, new ambitions," wrote William B. Dutton in his book, *Adventures in Big Business*, published 1958. "Unceasing change and improvement in automobiles, kitchen appliances, foods, clothing, and in countless items adding to home comforts had to be matched by increasing change and improvement in people's desires. The homeowner had to be made to aspire to a better home; the two-car family had to become an ordinary occurrence."[20] The emphasis here is unabashedly on the coercive *had to be made.* "The fact that wants can be synthesized by advertising, catalyzed by salesmanship, and shaped by discrete manipulations of the persuaders," suggests Galbraith, "shows that they are never urgent. A man who is hungry need never be told of his need for food."[21]

People also had to be taught to feel good about spending money. "We are now confronted with the problem of permitting the average American to feel moral even when he is spending, even when he is not saving, even when he is taking two vacations a year and buying a second or third car," said Dr. Ernest Dichter, a pioneer in motivational research who brought psychoanalytic techniques to the field of advertising. "One of the basic problems of this prosperity," he observed of the postwar boom, "is to give people the sanction and justification to enjoy it and to demonstrate that the hedonistic approach to life is a moral one, not an immoral one."[22] To hasten this educational process some of the most brilliant people in the U.S. went to work. Sociologists and psychologists joined artists, writers, and account executives in hustling products. Advertising became a sophisticated marketing medium as huge corporate investments made it necessary to take the guesswork out of the commercial jingle. According to

Robert Carney, chairman of the board of the advertising agency Foote, Cone and Belding, "Just before the war, our employees were mostly copywriters, artists and media buyers." But "today," in 1956, "we have as many people in research, merchandizing and marketing."[23] Social scientists found a place in advertising the way research physicists found a home in the Pentagon. Lucrative salaries, far greater than any academician could make, and the feeling of being an important cog in the workings of the affluent society, made this work appealing. In earlier times, social scientists shunned the marketplace and considered businessmen to be crude, uncultured Babbits. Now these social scientists had a place in business; as marketing took on new importance, so did their position in the corporate world.

The collaboration worked on many levels. Advertisers used the social-class studies of sociologists like L. Lloyd Warner and Burleigh Gardner to aim their commercials at the people most able to buy. These theoreticians found themselves in demand, and Gardner even opened his own research business. As more academicians came to do advertising research, their corporate orientation was passed on to their students and became institutionalized in university sociology and psychology departments. As a result, the objectivity of sociology as a social science was compromised. As C. Wright Mills wrote in 1953, "The sociologist in the applied focus no longer addresses 'the public;' more usually he has specific clients with particular interests and perplexities. This shift, from public to client, clearly destroys the idea of objectivity."[24] Paralleling the experience of other academic disciplines, the availability of research grants paid out by industry and business determined the kind of research that was to be done. Just as cancer research lacked funding because scientists were busy solving military problems, social-science research was diverted from urgent social problems to such marketing studies as the sexual implications of smoking, of bathing, the theory that baking a cake was for a woman much like giving birth, and the idea that shaving for men was an act of castration (which meant that shaving commercials had to reinforce the idea of manliness in their message).[25]

The importance of sociology in market research was buttressed by David Riesman's theory in *The Lonely Crowd* that Americans were becoming "other-directed" and that their tastes, habits, and values could be altered by peer group pressure. But there was another school of motivational research that insisted that the consumer was still "inner-directed" and subject to the basic human drives that could be best understood by the psychoanalytic method. Dichter, a Viennese psychologist, was the first to bring Freud to the marketplace.[26] His Motivational Research Institute was established in 1946 to provide advertisers with psychological insights into consumer habits. While psychologists and sociologists argued among themselves about who served advertising more accurately, the American consumer was probed, studied, and eventually tricked into becoming a more responsive consumer. The trickery went so far as subliminal advertising, which was successfully tested in 1957 at a New Jersey movie theater. During the showing of the main feature, messages such as "Eat Popcorn" and "Coca-Cola" were flashed onto the screen at a speed that could not be picked up by the conscious eye. On the nights of the experiment, consumption of popcorn rose by one-half and Coca-Cola by one-sixth.[27] Public outrage stopped subliminal advertising from then being put to public use. Yet the distinction between that sort of conditioning technique and the more subtle use of peer group pressure and sexual symbolism to sell products was indeed fuzzy.

The Importance of Television

Television changed the advertising industry as it transformed the American way of life. Probably no other single force had as much effect in socializing the American people, in shaping their tastes, habits, and opinions, and in smoothing out their regional and ethnic differences as did television—especially after 1952 when television became available to virtually every American home. "The industrial system," wrote Galbraith, "is profoundly dependent on commercial television and could not exist in its present form without it."[28]

Live radio's final decline was signaled in 1948. In that year, CBS raided NBC and signed such network stars as Jack Benny, George Burns and Gracie Allen, Edgar Bergen, and Bing Crosby for future TV appearances. "Howdy Doody," the most popular children's show in video history, had begun broadcasting the previous year. But in 1948 Milton Berle brought his weekly comedy show to the home screen and put television on the map. New York *Daily News* columnist Ed Sullivan started his "Toast of the Town" vaudeville show the same year. By 1950 such entertainers as Groucho Marx, Ken Murray, Sid Caesar and Imogene Coca, Eddie Cantor, Sam Levenson, and Garry Moore had made the transition, with Lucille Ball, Red Skelton, Red Buttons, Jack Benny, Jimmy Durante, Martha Raye, Bob Hope, Jackie Gleason, Phil Silvers, George Gobel, and Danny Thomas soon to come. All the while, "Television Playhouse," "Kraft Theater," and "Studio One" were presenting serious, original dramas by playwrights Paddy Chayefsky, Reginald Rose, Rod Serling, Gore Vidal, Robert Alan Arthur, and Tad Mosel. Because of production limitations, the settings of these shows were always in the characters' homes, but these "kitchen dramas" explored the problems and aspirations of a still struggling America recently home from the war. The number of stations went from 17 in 1947 to more than 2,000 after 1952, and the number of cities with reception jumped from 8 to more than 1,200.

Meanwhile, completion of the first transcontinental micro-wave relay in 1951 enabled more than 9 million people to watch the first live nationwide broadcast, the signing of the Japanese Peace Treaty. That same year, the coaxial cable was completed coast to coast and NBC began to broadcast nationally with a hookup of 61 stations. 1951 also witnessed the live coverage of the Kefauver hearings on organized crime, which showed television's potential as a news medium and held the public transfixed to the television screen as it would not be again until the Army-McCarthy hearings of 1954. By 1956, two out of every three American families had at least one TV, and by 1960 the figure was up to 87 percent.

Television advertising was corporate gold, and by 1949, major corporations had pre-empted prime-time TV. In addition to the "*Texaco* Star Theater," there was the "*Colgate* Comedy Hour," the "*Camel* News Caravan," the "*Ford* Theater," the "*G. E.* Theater" (hosted by Ronald Reagan), the "*Philco* Playhouse," "*Kraft* Theater," "*Bell Telephone* Hour," "*Alcoa* Theater," and the "*Gillette* Cavalcade of Sports," which sponsored Friday night boxing from New York's Madison Square Garden. The ability of the large corporations to foot the bill for television's production costs gave them an advantage over smaller, regional competitors. Because corporations would only spend money on items that appealed to mass homogeneous tastes, it narrowed the range of products being advertised. Thus the trend toward standardization of product was strengthened.

Advertising moved into television on the basis of its radio experience. In the early days of television, production costs were low enough for sponsors to support entire shows and depend, as in radio, on the "gratitude factor" for their reward. The first big network show was Berle's "Texaco Star Theater." Using tried-and-true burlesque format, stale jokes, high energy, and plenty of slapstick, "Uncle Miltie" became a national TV sensation. Every Tuesday at 8 p.m., 75 percent of the TV owners, plus an untold number of friends, relatives, bar patrons, and evening walkers, were tuned in. Berle's impact on the country was so great that shopkeepers who were ordinarily open on Tuesday nights closed because no one was out shopping, though in bars, as *The New Yorker* noted, people stood four deep, "laughing, nudging one another, and neglecting their warm beers."[29] At first, when it was still a rare commodity, televison brought people together. People gathered in bars or were invited to neighbors' houses specifically for an evening of television. But as television gained entrance into every home, bars emptied (except around World Series time, when they became male enclaves) and people stayed home alone.

Because vast sums of money were not yet at stake, advertising remained unobtrusive. On "Toast of the Town," a long-legged woman dressed in an Old Gold package did a tap dance. A midget named Johnny did the advertising for "I Love Lucy" by cupping his hand to his mouth and saying, "Call for Philip Mor-reeees," while a recording of "On the Trail" from the *Grand Canyon Suite* was played in the background. The advertising pitch on Berle's "Texaco Star Theater" was handled by a burlesque comedian named Sid Stone who would set up a portable table of Texaco products at center stage and give a hard-sell spiel about the various Texaco products. His delivery was a deliberate parody of the P. T. Barnum stereotype; he would preface his remarks by rolling up his sleeves and in a glib huckster style say, "tell ya what I'm gonna do," which became a standard tag line emulated by millions of school kids throughout the country. The advertising pitch would end abruptly with the appearance of a keystone cop, waving a nightstick, who would chase Stone off the stage. Sid Stone was an integral part of the Berle show, and the advertisement for Texaco was a part of the entertainment. The fact that a major corporation would allow its products to be sold by a fast-talking, fly-by-night salesman, continually being hounded by the police, indicated how informal the presence of advertising was in the early days of TV. However successful Stone was in selling Texaco products, by no twist of the imagination was he selling the desired image of a respectable, middle-class, corporate man. Later, middle-class style, even more than the advertised goods, became television's more important product.

Television soon fell victim to its own rapid success. The cost of prime time rose from $15,000 an hour, which was the total budget for the first Berle show, to $150,000 on up in the mid-1950s.[30] Rising costs made it impossible for a single sponsor to produce one show. In the mid-1950s, the networks began to produce their own shows and to allow outside producers such as Warner Brothers and Disney to create their own program packages. Under this system, advertisers would buy specific time slots, not specific shows; now they could scatter their messages at different times and on different stations, rather than rely on the popularity of one particular show to sell a product. Having long had a hand in producing entertainment, the ad agencies now had the opportunity to devote their creative talents wholeheartedly to selling products. As the program content became routine and formulaized, the advertisements began to stand out. Oftentimes more money and creative energy were lavished on a 30-second commercial than on the 30-minute program it appeared with.

There are no statistics to accurately measure the impact of television and TV advertising on American life. That television stimulated sales, there can be no doubt. When Walt Disney produced a series of three one-hour shows in 1955 on the life of frontiersman Davy Crockett, he parlayed its success into a $300 million industry, selling Davy Crockett dolls, toys, T-shirts, and fake coonskin caps.[31] Studies by social scientists also attest to television's impact. One study on the effects of advertising found that the public is able "to hold in memory, as we would say of a computer, a very large number of TV campaign themes correctly related to brands." The report concluded, "The economic impact of TV advertising is substantial and documented. Its messages have been learned by the public."[32]

Children especially were targeted as potential customers for advertising appeals. As Clyde Miller told advertisers in his book *The Process of Persuasion*:

> It takes time, yes, but if you expect to be in business for any length of time, think of what it can mean to your firm on profits if you can condition a million or ten million children who will grow into adults trained to buy your products as soldiers are trained to advance when they hear the trigger words "forward march."[33]

The trade publication *Printers Ink* had similar advice for marketing strategists:

> Eager minds can be molded to want your products! In the grade schools throughout America are nearly 23,000,000 young boys and girls. These children eat food, wear out clothes, use soap. They are consumers of today and will be the buyers of tomorrow. Here is a vast market for your products. Sell these children on your brand name and they will insist that their parents buy no other. Many farsighted advertisers are cashing in today...and building for tomorrow...by molding eager minds.[34]

From the early morning cartoons and cowboy movies, through the daytime game shows and the late afternoon kiddie shows, through the evening news and the prime-time network programs, on through the late movie or Jack Parr or Steve Allen's "Tonight," television sold goods, creating among its viewers a bond which Daniel Boorstin called "a community of consumers." "Men who never saw or knew one another," Boorstin wrote, "were held together by their common use of objects so similar that they could not be distinguished even by their owners....Never before had so many men been united by so many things."[35] But, to look at it from another perspective, never had so many men (and women) been so dependent on material goods for their identity. And never before had community been so synthetically derived, divorced from both collective historical tradition and personal experience.

Chapter Six

"...the fulcrum of corporate power is the investment decision. The uses for capital for investment purposes are, in the final analysis, decided by a small handful of managers. They decide how much is to be spent; what products are to be made; where they are to be manufactured; and who is to participate in the processes of production. A single corporation can draw up an investment program calling for the expenditure of several billions of dollars on new plant and product. A decision such as this may well determine the quality of life for a substantial segment of society: men and materials will move across continents; old communities will decay and new ones will prosper; tastes and habits will alter; new skills will be demanded; and the education of a nation will adjust itself accordingly; even government will fall into line, providing public services that corporate developments make necessary.
—Andrew Hacker, in The Corporate Takeover, 1960.

The 1950s were boom years for big business. Corporate profits, after taxes, ranged from a low of $16.8 billion in 1954 to a high of $26 billion in 1955, while corporate assets rose from $441.5 billion in 1945 to $1,206.7 billion in 1960. These profits accentuated the trend toward monopoly, thus placing corporate decisions in fewer and fewer hands.[1] Advertising and marketing techniques hastened this trend. Small businesses, operating on a limited volume, could not afford national advertising, especially on television. Nor could they spend money on the motivational research needed for sophisticated marketing techniques. Large corporations had the further advantage of operating overseas, where profit margins were higher. Beginning in the late 50s, the big corporations also benefited from automated production techniques and a new computer technology.

The postwar period was a period of mergers and expansion. From 1951 to 1961, the largest 100 industrial corporations acquired 884 other firms.[2] Because so little production was concerned with life's necessities, the industrial giants had to diversify their holdings as a hedge against a perfidious market. If one product failed, a corporation needed others to take up the slack. Small business, producing a limited number of products, could not absorb market adversity; the failure of one product could drive the entire business under. As economist A. A. Berle wrote in the early sixties, "The major part of the American economy is controlled by a few hundred (at most) clusters of corporate enterprises, each of whose major decisions are determined by a central giant."[3] The growing corporate conglomerates of the 1950s became the huge multinationals of more recent years, many of them having greater assets than foreign countries.

The Beer Industry

What happened in the beer business was typical of the monopoly tendencies that became dominant with the postwar economy. And beer, a dependable no-risk product with an assured market (some might call it a basic need), was a more stable business than most.

Beer is brewed by fermenting malted cereal grain, usually barley and corn with the addition of hops. Additives are put in during the brewing process to reduce costs and alter flavor. Rice, unmalted barley, tapioca, sugars, and syrups are the ingredients most frequently used. The chemical composition of the water— especially its alkalinity—is another factor that determines taste, so proximity to a quality water source is a prerogative for quality beer. Beer has always been a highly profitable and high-volume business. In 1949 the industry grossed $4.5 billion, two-thirds the gross of the auto industry, the nation's largest. In that year, the American public quaffed 85 million barrels of domestic beer and ale, a figure that worked out to about 200 bottles per man, woman, and child. Schlitz, the number one selling beer that year, earned an estimated $20 million profit after taxes.[4]

In many ways, beer symbolizes the democratic, egalitarian pretensions of American society. In 1961, the *Harvard Business Review*, in a marketing survey for beer, observed that "people drink beer in all social classes and for similar reasons. Beer is considered to mark the absence of authority; it is an invitation to informality."[5] Brewing had long been a family business. Products differed from city to city and region to region and the brewers took pride in the distinctiveness of their product. The recipe for brewing was often a closely guarded family secret, and the taste of the product was keyed closely to the locale where it was brewed. Tradition held that in cold climates a heavy beer with a strong hops flavor and a high alcoholic content would sell. Warmer regions called for a lighter brew. The quality of the local water was important in the brewing process, and brewers often boasted of using pure or natural mountain-fed spring water.

While there have always been a few large, dominant beer producers, competition was relaxed and the big breweries often looked favorably on the smaller locals. Once a year, in prewar days, Gussie Busch of Anhauser-Busch of St. Louis held open house for his competitors, and brewmasters from all over the country would come to the Budweiser brewery to tour the plant and talk shop. In 1945 the brewers spent $1 million on a cooperative ad campaign to present beer as an important part of American life. At this time there were about 460 breweries, a decline from the 700 that were operating after the repeal of prohibition in the early 1930s; the others had succumbed to the Depression. Between 1945 and 1950 the industry stabilized at 450. Then the larger corporations began to go after the national market, undercut the locals, and consolidate their position.

In the 1940s, the big regional breweries began to go nationwide for the first time. In 1945 Pabst of Milwaukee bought out the Hoffman Beverage Co. of Newark and set out to prove that it could produce a beer of uniform quality anywhere in the country. Other big brewers followed suit. By carefully adjusting ingredients and by altering the brewing process, they found it possible to manufacture a standard beer, so that no matter what the quality of the available water, the beer would taste the same. New breweries built in the postwar period were larger and more efficient than the older ones. In 1951, Anhauser-Busch opened a Newark plant that could produce one million barrels a year. By contrast, a typical local brewery, like the Fitzgerald Brewery of Troy, New York, produced only 300,000 barrels a year. However good their product—and many local and regional beers were famous for their unique taste—the small brewers did not have the volume of profit to advertise or to modernize their plants. Unable to keep up with the highly capitalized nationals, they fell rapidly behind.

Television and suburbanization helped determine the market by reducing the number of neighborhood taverns. Neighborhood bars usually featured a local product on draft. This was the only way local breweries could compete with the large national breweries, for it was cheaper to sell beer by the barrel than to bottle it or to market it in cans and six-packs, which meant an investment in expensive packaging equipment. But packaged beer, which had become a grocery item during the Depression, gradually came to dominate the market. By 1954, it represented 75 percent of all beer sales.[6] Big nationals could also afford to advertise on network TV. Thus, in every part of the country, the nationals had the advertising clout to overwhelm the hard-pressed local product. In a sense, the idea of a local beer lost its meaning. The advertisements of the national brand beers appeared everywhere.

The big breweries had another advantage. With a national base, they could move into specific territories, cut their prices, and outsell the local beer. The local brew could not compete, for it had no other territory to compensate for short-run competitive losses. When the drinking public had become accustomed to the national beer, about the time that the local beer had gone out of business, the national beer could raise its price without losing sales. Between 1950 and 1960, the number of brewers declined from 450 to 170. (A decade later the number was down to 70.) In 1946, the seven leading beers controlled just 20 percent of the market. In 1952, their control was up to 34.7 percent. This pattern continued through the next two decades so that by 1970 the ten largest brewers controlled 70 percent of the market and had combined sales totaling $11.1 billion.

New York City once produced more than a dozen different beers: Rupert, Trommers, King, Kip's Bay, Loewers, Ehlings, Fidelio, Horton's Lion, Knickerbocker, Rubsum-Horman, Piels, Rheingold, and Schaefer. In the 1970s, the two surviving breweries moved out of the city. Rheingold, by then, had become a subsididary of Chock Full O Nuts, while Schaefer was owned by Arnold's Bread. New York City no longer produced its own local beer.[7]

The disappearance of hundreds of small breweries and the monopolization of the beer business did not result in better distribution or a better product. What progress there was was measured only in the volume of sales and the growth of profits of a small number of corporations.

The Transportation Industry

The power of a few strategically located corporate decision makers to determine the life of the broader society is well exemplified by events in the transportation industry during the postwar era. In the movie *The Last Picture Show*, Peter Bogdonovitch's remembrance of rural America in the early postwar years, a tractor-trailer roars down a windswept main street of a dying Texas town and kills a dim-witted boy who, in his mindless way, had been sweeping dirt off the usually empty street. The lad is a fixture in town, and in earlier times the townsfolk who gather at the boy's body might have cared for him and felt a loss at his death. But their world has already come to be dominated by the highway and the pathetic youth is not a cause for their concern but a barrier to high-speed traffic. The truck driver climbs down from his cab, apologizing, horrified by the death. But the townspeople tell him not to worry. "He was a dumb kid," they say, "always gettin' in the way. He was bound to get hit one of these days."

During the postwar years, as never before, the automobile became the dominant factor in American life, and highways spread across the landscape like a gigantic concrete blob, isolating rural towns, carving up neighborhoods and destroying street culture, bringing congestion and pollution to all major cities. The private automobile became the personal metaphor from which Americans drew their self-image of potency and strength and by which they showed off their status and affluence. As George T. McCoy, president of the American Association of State Highway Officials, observed in 1956, "Highways and motor vehicles are truly the keystones of the American way of life."[8]

"Excessive economic concentration," writes Bradford Snell in the introduction to his study on *American Ground Transport*, "can restructure society for corporate ends."[9] As early as the mid-1920s, automobiles had begun to saturate the economy on the basis of one car per family, leading the automakers, especially GM, to adopt a new marketing strategy. Continued expansion could only come through planned obsolescence—so a family would have to buy a car every few years—and through encouraging two-car families and by making the automobile necessary for commuting. This latter strategy, especially as applied by GM, meant gaining control of mass-transit companies in order to destroy them.

The destruction of mass transit by monopolistic business practices made sense for GM's corporate policy. Efficient mass transit was a barrier to expanding corporate profits. One bus, for instance, renders 35 private cars unnecessary; a streetcar, subway car, or railroad car can replace 50 private vehicles on the commuting highway; and one train can haul as much freight as 150 tractor-trailers or as many passengers as 1,000 cars.[10] With enough capital for expansion, it was inevitable that GM would move to drive out all competition and increase the market for its private vehicles.*

*In terms of public efficiency, of course, highway travel is wasteful and expensive. A single lane of freeway, with cars carrying an average of 1.6 people (the national average is 1.1) can carry fewer than 5,000 people in

During the 1920s GM began to take over bus transportation, establishing Greyhound in 1926 and setting up holding companies to invest in interurban electric bus and trolley lines throughout the country. Wherever it invested its money, it forced a conversion from pollutant-free electric trolleys and buses to its own diesel-powered buses. In some cities, GM would buy up existing electric street railways, scrap the system or let it deteriorate so it would lose revenue, and then switch over to its own buses to reverse the decline. By 1955, GM had been involved in the replacement of more than 100 electric transit systems with its own buses in 45 cities, including New York, Philadelphia, Baltimore, St. Louis, Oakland, Salt Lake City, and Los Angeles.[11]

The only improvement here was in GM's profit margin. Diesel is economically inefficient. Engineering studies have shown that in comparison to electric transit, diesel buses have 28 percent shorter lives, 40 percent higher operating costs, and 9 percent lower productivity than their electric counterparts.[12] But this worked to GM's benefit. Declining mass transit makes private commuting necessary, and GM makes 10 times as much profit selling automobiles as it does selling buses.*

GM also used its economic prowess to destroy commuter railroads. During the 1930s, GM began manufacturing diesel locomotives. These locomotives had half the life of electric

one hour. By contrast, a railroad track can move 50,000 people in the same hour with less pollution and obviously with less congestion in the city proper. As for freight, for distances over 400 miles, railroads can move twice as many ton-miles of freight as trucks while using half as much fuel. (*Super Highway—Super Hoax* by Helen Leavitt, Doubleday, 1970, p. 3; "Not Working on the Railroad" by Edward T. Chase, *Commonweal*, 29 June 1973).

*The U.S. government has long been aware of GM's responsibility in destroying mass transit. In 1949, a federal jury convicted GM, Firestone Rubber, and Standard Oil of California (three corporations that stood to gain by private vehicle use) of criminally conspiring to replace electric mass transport with GM manufactured diesel buses. Justice was done, however: the court staggered GM with a $5,000 fine and forced H.C. Crossman, the GM executive responsible for carrying out this policy, to pay $1.00. ("Report on American Ground Transport" by Robert Snell, Subcommittee on Anti-trust and Monopoly, Senate Judiciary Committee, 26 Febuary 1974).

locomotives but cost three times as much to make. They also polluted more than electric locomotives, leading many cities to insist that diesel trains stop at their border and change to electric locomotion, a time-consuming and expensive inconvenience. As the nation's largest shipper of freight, GM was in a position to persuade railroads to invest in its locomotives. In 1935, electric locomotives outnumbered diesels by seven to one. By 1970, diesels predominated by 100 to one.[13] In almost every other industrial country, railroads are run on electricity and are prosperous and efficiently run. By contrast, American diesel-powered railroads have been losing money since the war. Passenger and commuter traffic suffered the most, leading to increased dependence on highway commuting and auto profits.

How did this dependence on highway traffic come about? Certainly, as the activities of GM indicate, it was neither inevitable nor a matter of public choice. At the end of World War II the U.S. still had a healthy railroad system and the potential for modernizing its mass transit. Highway transportation was not an important factor during the war. Ninety percent of all military freight and 97 percent of all military personnel travelled by rail, while motor vehicle registration dropped from 30 to 25 million cars between 1940 and 1945 as the auto industry retooled to build tanks, trucks, jeeps, and planes.[14] Inter-urban trains, despite mismanagement by GM subsidiaries, were still in existence, concentrated in the Chicago area, Los Angeles, Iowa, the Southwest, the Carolinas, and greater Pittsburgh. In other cities, the rights-of-way were still available for mass transit purposes if public money had become available to build commuter lines. The inter-urban systems were an obvious model for postwar mass transportation. They were cheap, fast, and efficient. At its peak, the Pacific Electric Railway that served the Los Angeles area operated 760 miles of service at a capital investment of $100 million. Before it was taken over and liquidated by GM and Standard Oil of California, it was the largest inter-urban in the country, scheduling more than a thousand trains a day from the center of Los Angeles to such outlying stations as Redlands, Corona, Santa Monica, Redondo Beach, and Balboa, carrying light freight as well as passengers.[15] Its last line, to Long Beach, was abandoned in 1961, leaving Los Angeles completely at the mercy of the private automobile. Congestion and air pollution were the result, and in 1973 the federal government would propose an 80 percent reduction in the city's auto traffic in a last-ditch effort to combat smog.[16]*

Commuter railroads suffered the same way. By 1960, only one-fifth of all work trips in urban areas were by mass transit, and most of the rail lines were concentrated in a few big cities. The experience of the New Haven & Hartford Railroad, connecting Boston with New York and serving the suburban areas of Westchester and Fairfield counties, was typical. In 1956 the railroad began converting from electricity to diesel. This was the beginning of its road to bankruptcy. As the Interstate Commerce Commission (ICC) noted in a 1960 report, during 50 years of electrified operation, the New Haven had always shown a profit. In 1955, the year before conversion, it netted $5.7 million carrying 45 million passengers and 814,000 carloads of freight. By 1957, a year after, it was losing $9.2 million with 35 million passengers and fewer than 700,000 carloads of freight. In 1961, it was declared bankrupt and an ICC report censured GM for contributing to its ruin.[17]

The Long Island Railroad suffered a similar fate. Unable to compete with government-subsidized highway traffic, the LIRR was allowed to deteriorate. Though it remained one of the busiest commuter lines in the country, in 1973 it still had seventy cars built in 1927 in operation and accidents and breakdowns were commonplace. Other commuter lines were also using passenger cars of prewar vintage over roadbeds too old for high-speed use.[18] The deterioration of these railroads fed the congested highways and made the private auto seem even more essential. It was a closed cycle that only a change in public policy could break. But by the end of the war, the federal government

---

*Air pollution scientists found that 88 percent by weight of all the contaminants found in Los Angeles' air could be traced to internal combustion engines in trucks and private cars. The economic costs were also considerable, with two-thirds of the downtown area becoming devoted to garages, parking lots, and roadway. Billions of dollars in revenue had been lost because land utilized for highways cannot be taxed and in Los Angeles one cloverleaf might take up as many as 80 acres of land. By 1960, Los Angeles had spent $900 million on 310 miles of freeway, yet congestion had grown worse. (*Interpretations and Forecasts*, Harcourt, Brace, Jovanovich, 1973, p. 370).

was wholly committed to auto use and was ready to subsidize the auto industry the way that it had subsidized the railroads a century before.

In 1944, Congress passed the Defense Highway Act, with construction costs to be split 50-50 by the federal government and the States. The need for a new highway system was supposedly national security. But in 1944, the war was almost over and, as we have seen, most military traffic was moving by rail. The real impetus for the program came from intense lobbying by the auto industry and its allies in oil, rubber, and steel.

Building upon the 1944 precedent, the auto and highway lobby won passage twelve years later of a law authorizing the 41,000-mile interstate highway system. This system of four-lane superhighways has been 90 percent federally funded, the money coming from a Highway Trust Fund created by a tax on gasoline. The Highway Trust Fund was to the automobile industry what the land giveaways of the nineteenth century were to the railroads. Under the 1956 law, the money in the trust fund could be used only for highway construction, nothing else, for sixteen years. The system was self-perpetuating. More cars consumed more gas and fed more money into the trust fund to finance more highways which, again, encouraged the use of more cars.

It would be simplistic to overemphasize the economic aspect of the highway-auto glut, for the private car seemed also to fulfill the psychological needs of the American people—needs which Detroit learned how to manipulate and exploit. The lure (and myth) of the American frontier, with its emphasis on rugged individualism, has always encouraged privatism and isolation. Individuals gained succor not from belonging to a secure community but from their own material possessions and sense of status. Detroit, with its interest in motivational research studies, exploited this tradition with a vengeance. Emphasis was placed on style rather than on mechanical efficiency or safety. As Lewis Mumford wrote, "The present motor car has been the result of a secret collaboration between the beautician and the mortician; and according to sales and accident statistics both have reason to be satisified." Auto technology stagnated; automakers stressed superficial changes at the expense of engineering design. In 1964, an executive at Ford acknowledged that "the automatic transmission," introduced in 1939, "was the last major improvement in the American auto industry."[19] Cars were made bigger, heavier, flashier, and more powerful, but not safer or more economical to run.

The availability of cheap imported oil encouraged waste. Big, high-compression engines used up more gas than smaller six-cylinder engines, and after World War II Detroit began emphasizing V-8's while cutting production on the more economical sixes. In 1945, the small Nash 600 was getting up to 30 miles to the gallon. By 1974, despite the challenge from gas-saving foreign imports, the best an American car could do was 24.6 miles per gallon, and of the thirteen most fuel-efficient cars in the world, only the eighth was made in the U.S.[20] The Cadillac, as a high-priced, big, deluxe car, was getting 20 MPG in 1949; in 1973 the equivalent model was down to 13.5.[21] These gas-guzzling, high-compression, high-horsepower engines had no practical utility, except to consume gas and boost ego. Cars were built with speedometers registering up to 120 miles an hour, although, even in the wide-open spaces of the Great Plains, speed limits were 75 mph at the maximum and in most areas of the country, before the high-speed interstates were completed, it was unlawful to go over 55.

Despite urban congestion and the problem of parking space, the size of American cars was increased throughout the period. Automobile manufacturers resisted bringing out small, compact cars because big cars meant bigger profits and because their motivational research departments reported that consumers craved bigness as a psychological need. But was the craving natural? Or was it conditioned by advertising and by the postwar emphasis on material goods as the measure of a person's worth? Advertisements continually stressed size over convenience, style over performance. In 1956 a Pontiac commercial described "Your Big Pontiac" and showed a group of people, supposedly representing the "smart consumer," chanting, "We're everybody...We want a big car, and style too." Mercury was described as the "Big M," and Lincoln advertised "Never before a Lincoln...so long and so longed for." The Chevrolet grew two feet in length during the period, becoming bigger than the Oldsmobile of ten years earlier.[22]

The transition from a people on rails to a people on wheels

reflected changes in American culture. There was a romance to train travel that was lacking with the private automobile. Despite the awesome size of the big iron locomotives and the cold, rythmic clacking or iron and steel, the railroads maintained a human dimension and reflected warm personal values. To mobile Americans, the rumbling of a distant freight or the haunting sound of a railroad whistle at night often brought with it a remembrance of some special moment, a recognition of a forgotten childhood memory, a yearning for the road, or a mystical feeling for home. Yet riding the railroad was practical; trains took people places and brought them home. "219 done took my baby away," sang New Orleans jazzman Jelly Roll Morton about the number 219 train from New Orleans to Chicago. Ever hopeful, he added, "217 goin' to bring her back someday." Glenn Miller captured this same spirit in his song, "Chattanooga Choo-Choo," with its closing line, "Why don't you carry me home?"

The men who worked the rails, like John Henry and Casey Jones, became the legends of American folklore. Traditional songs like "I've Been Working on the Railroad" were passed down from generation to generation and still are sung today. The image of a railroad engineer has always been a friendly one. Railroad engineers wave to children in a powerful, age-old custom. But that is not how people usually view the drivers of cross-country tractor-trailer rigs, high above the road, isolated in their lonely cabs, proud of their machismo image and their reputation for hard driving.

There are few musical celebrations of the interstate highway. When, in the 1940s Nat "King" Cole sang about getting "kicks on Route 66," he was singing about a funky two-lane hardtop that wove its way through city and rural town from St. Louis to Los Angeles. Gradually, during the postwar era, Route 66 became absorbed by Interstate 40. There are no honkytonks and greasy-spoons spread out along its length—only franchised restaurants and gas stations, all corporate-owned, all selling similar pre-packaged standardized products—nothing to sing about. During the 1950s, songs about cars emphasized drag racing (as with "Maybelline") and death (as with "Teen Angel"). In *The Wild One,* a movie that, along with *Rebel Without a Cause,* provided teenagers with identity (about which, see

Chapter Nine), motorcycles were a metaphor for violence. And in *Rebel*, a "chicken" contest—in which two cars were driven off a cliff—gave the competing teenagers a yardstick for bravery. In the 1946 MGM musical *Harvey Girls*, the railroad song, "On the Acheson, Topeka and the Santa Fe" evoked the excitement and optimism of an innocent America. But the music of the postwar era, when it dealt with the automobile, celebrated alienation, isolation, violence and death.

The Nuclear Option

Cheap energy, especially oil, made car culture possible and contributed to the affluence of the times. American foreign policy supported the oil conglomerates in their quest for foreign domination while favorable tax policies made it possible for the oil companies to amass huge profits at the well-head while maintaining low prices on the domestic market.

Even when they were forced to share their profits with their host governments (as Exxon did in Venezuela and Aramco in Saudi Arabia), the companies were able, throughout the 1950s, to keep control of production. In some cases, as in Iran under the Shah, the ruling circles were corrupt and easily bought off. Other countries, like Saudi Arabia and Kuwait had just emerged from feudalism and lacked an educated civil service to challenge Aramco's control. In Venezuela, which supplied most of America's imported oil during the war and immediately thereafter (the Middle East oil fields then came on line to augment the supply), the corrupt right-wing government of Colonel Marcos Perez Jimenez allowed U.S. oil companies a free hand. It was after Jimenez's overthrow in 1958, at the hands of the social democrat Romulo Betancourt, that the idea of concerted action by the oil-producing countries first emerged. The new Venezuelan government charged that the oil companies were depleting the country's oil reserves and—by pushing production throughout the Third World—were artificially keeping the price of oil down. In effect, the oil-producing Third World was underwriting the success of the American oil-based economy and getting very little in return. By joining together, the oil producers could limit production to protect their own reserves, force up prices, and gain control of their natural resources. In 1960, the Organization of Petroleum-Exporting Countries (OPEC) was founded with Venezuela, Saudi Arabia, Iran, Iraq, and Kuwait as charter members. But it would not be until the 1970s that these countries would have the expertise and political independence to band together to control the international oil market.

Meanwhile, since profits came out of production and not out of marketing, the oil companies had to find outlets for their self-created oil glut. The more oil they could produce, the more they would profit—hence, gas guzzling automobiles and the growth of the petrochemical industry. The Marshall or European Recovery Plan (ERP) was also used to create a demand for oil. European countries, even those with ample coal reserves, were forced to convert to oil use, much to the advantage of the American oil giants who used the ERP to penetrate the European energy market.*

In the U.S., energy consumption almost doubled between 1939 and 1960 from 23.07 quadrillion BTUs to 45.35 quadrillion BTUs. The hunger for cheap energy could not be met by petroleum alone. Oil was best used for transportation and as the basis for petrochemicals. With the advent of television, stereos, freezers, air conditioners, all-electric homes, and other new uses for electricity, additional sources of energy had to be found to run electric generating plants. Small hydro dams existed in many parts of the country, but they were not profitable for private utilities to operate. In the postwar years many were abandoned, some dismantled.

Simple solar collectors to heat hot water had been used in places like Florida and Southern California early in the century. But as the private utilities gained control of the electric grid, the promise of solar technology was forgotten. Energy conservation

---

*When the European nations submitted their requirements for ERP assistance they assumed continued reliance on their own domestic coal resources and the rehabilitation of their railroads. The initial European request for aid listed 47,000 freight cars and no trucks. But the Marshall Plan provided just 20,000 freight cars and 65,000 trucks. By mid-1950, 11 percent of the value of all Marshall Plan aid was in oil, supplied for the most part by American oil corporations active in the Middle East.(*Middle East Oil and the Energy Crisis* by Joe Stork, Monthly Review Press, 1975, p. 61).

was not even considered as a possible option. A return to coal to run electric generating plants was far more likely. The resources and the labor force were available. The railroads would have to be improved, but the tracks and the right-of-ways were in place. Safety and environmental protection were problems, but scrubber technology to reduce pollution would soon be available. Mine safety standards would have to be upgraded; European coal mines had much better safety records than their U.S. counterparts. But the oil companies were making windfall profits and capital was available to modernize the coal industry.

For a number of reasons, the country chose to generate electricity by nuclear fission instead of with the more traditional coal-fired furnaces. By the war's end, billions of dollars had been invested in the Manhattan Project. The research necessary for nuclear energy was advanced, and a huge industrial infrastructure in place. To let the technology go idle, now that the war was over, would have meant writing off this fabulous investment. Moreover, many of the scientists who had worked on the bomb were eager to put their work to peacetime use. As a general who witnessed the Alamogordo bomb test from a shelter near the blast zone put it, "There was a feeling in that shelter that those concerned with its nativity should dedicate their lives to the mission that it would always be used for good and never for evil."[23]

More practically, nuclear scientists knew that the basic theory of nuclear fission was known to scientists all over the world, and that America's monopoly of the bomb would quickly end. As nearly as May 1945 there was agreement among the leaders of the bomb project that the country ought to expand its industrial plant for nuclear energy, stockpile nuclear weapons, and encourage industrial development and application.[24] These steps would assure American nuclear superiority when other countries, for instance, the Soviet Union, perfected their own nuclear technology.

With the beginning of the Cold War, the United States, through the new Atomic Energy Commission, stepped up its bomb testing program and, after the Soviets exploded their first nuclear bomb in 1949, began development of the hydrogen bomb, which was successfully tested in 1952. Despite evidence from the Japanese bombings that the effects of nuclear radiation lasted many years, the government showed little interest in health hazards posed by radioactive fallout. Though nuclear scientists working at Los Alamos had warned as early as 1946 that "the most worldwide destruction could come from radioactive poisons," the government pursued its program to build bigger and dirtier bombs in the name of national security.[25] And, in 1950, when the U.S. began to use Nevada as its primary test site, President Truman pooh-poohed the dangers. "Let us keep our sense of proportion in the matter of radioactive fallout," Truman said. "Of course we want to keep the fallout in our tests to an absolute minimum, and we are learning to do just that."[26] In point of fact, throughout the 1950s, fallout from nuclear bomb tests scoured vast areas of the country: after one blast, radioactive residues were found around Troy, New York, two thousand miles from the test site. In Nevada itself, in order to train the military in nuclear combat, soldiers were sent on maneuvers in proximity of ground zero. Years later, a huge proportion of them would contract cancer, leukemia, and various other radiation-linked diseases.[27]

The AEC, with President Eisenhower's approval, adopted a deliberate policy to downplay the hazards of radiation. Officials toured communities near the bomb zone assuring people that they faced little danger. The AEC and the military provided films to schools and civic clubs with the same message: the government was taking all necessary precautions and there was no danger from fallout. In the mid-fifties, however, scientists began to question these assurances. Strontium 90 carried by air currents to all parts of the country, was recognized as a particular hazard, especially to pregnant women and nursing mothers. The AEC and government officials dismissed these dangers: given the repressive climate it was easy to portray the scientists who spoke about these dangers as unpatriotic. The bomb tests continued.

At the same time, the AEC promised all kinds of benefits from nuclear power. Operation Plowshare would change the topography of the earth: canals would be dug, harbors would be deepened, mountains would be moved—all by clean, safe nuclear explosions. A nuclear reactor program for the generation of electricity was even more promising. Once developed, nuclear reactors would replace oil as the chief thermal source of electricity, reserving oil for use in the chemical industry (plastics especially), agriculture, and of course transportation. Coal would be ignored; the industry promised that nuclear reactors would produce electricity too cheap to meter.

To private industry, nuclear energy was attractive for a number of reasons. First of all, the technology was developed through public funding. Second, nuclear generation promised increasing profits. In the United States, private utilities are regulated monopolies. Individual states regulate private utilities and assure them a rate of return, i.e., profit, based on the size of the capital investment. The greater the investment (called the rate base), the greater the revenues and the higher the profits. Though the expense of plant construction is included in the rate base, fuel costs are not—they are passed on to the consumer, but with no profit added. The ideal form of energy from this point of view is one in which construction costs are high and fuel costs relatively low. As it happens, coal plants are cheaper to build than nuclear plants, but their fuel costs are much higher. So nuclear power promised much greater profits than did coal. Encouraged by government subsidies and a favorable regulatory climate, the utility industry moved into the nuclear field.

The first plan was to build a breeder reactor in order to guarantee a continuous supply of nuclear fuel. The first reactor, in Idaho Falls, was successfully tested in 1951, but an accident in 1956 destroyed the reactor core and killed three workers. Likewise, the Fermi Breeder Reactor near Detroit had to be shut down after a few months of operation when a partial fuel meltdown almost went critical. In the meantime, however, uranium deposits were discovered in South Africa, the Belgian Congo (now Zaire), Australia, Canada, and within the United States, assuring the nuclear program a supply of fuel. In 1956, construction permits were issued for the first generation of nuclear reactors in Rowe, Massachusetts, Indian Point, New York, and Dresden, Illinois. Despite accidents, rising construction costs, and growing apprehensions on the part of environmentalists and some labor leaders, health workers, and nuclear scientists, plans for more and bigger reactors were put forward in the 1960s.[28]

Nuclear power was supposed to encourage economic growth. Under the trickle down theory, economic growth creates prosperity which trickles down to the poorest Americans, enabling them to improve their standard of living. But consumption of energy in the United States was not at all equal. Indeed, the distribution of energy was skewered on the basis of class. And the great corporations, rolling in prestige and profits, were the most self-indulgent wasters of electricity.

Monuments To Affluence Are Made Of Glass

Beginning in the early 1950s, major corportations, rolling in profits, began building fabulous new headquarters for themselves in the downtown areas of the larger cities and, in a few instances, on large tracts of former farmland in suburbia. These new skyscrapers changed the skyline of the great cities and offered the public, through the aesthetics of architecture, the image that corporate America had of itself. These new modern buildings described the spirit of the times. In contrast to the way the government skimped on public housing projects, the corporations spared little in building monuments to themselves.

The two most influential architects of the postwar period were Frank Lloyd Wright and Mies Van der Rohe. Wright was a humanist who strived for an architecture that would celebrate democratic values and the natural surroundings. His designs, he insisted, were keyed to the landscape and to the activities of the people who would live and work within. Mies, on the other hand, was a technocrat who dreamed of idealized buildings. "We are not trying to please people," he once said. "We are driving to the essence of things."[29] Mies's philosophy of aesthetics articulated the corporate values of mass society. "The individual is losing significance," he stated: "his destiny is no longer what interests us. The decisive achievements in all fields are impersonal; and their authors for the most part are obscure. They are part of the trend of our time toward anonymity."[30] Author Cranston Jones has given a good description of the polarity between these two influential architects. "For Wright, architecture was a symphony embodying man's hopes and dreams, the machine was a tool for poets. For Mies, architecture was an expression of the essence of the twentieth century, in terms of technology, science and economics."[31]

Wright and his followers were virtually ignored by the corporations commissioning new buildings. It was Mies who set the aesthetic standard and whose disciples received most of the contracts. Skidmore, Owings and Merrill, which was known in the world of architecture as "the firm for big businesses," (their first major project was designing the Oak Ridge Atomic Energy plant in Tennessee during the war) was the primary beneficiary. Their Lever House, completed in 1952, was the first New York skyscraper to embody Mies's principles, and it set the style for office buildings during the next two decades. The Lever House was a 21-story building with glass and aluminum siding encasing a steel framework. As the corporation headquarters for a leading manufacturer of soap products, the building was functionally designed. As Cranston Jones noted, "The cost of keeping such a huge mirror bright and sparkling was considered negligible compared to the advertising value of seeing the immense panes of glass being sudsed down in good Lever Brothers soap by window washers suspended in a special gondola."[32] But glass-faced buildings did not all house the offices of detergent manufacturers. The function of glass as an advertising medium was limited, to say the least.

Corporations spent billions of dollars on new office buildings, often tearing down perfectly serviceable structures in the process. The older buildings were often quite beautiful with their intricate brickwork and stonecut filigree; but the corporations were interested only in what was new, so down came the brick and stone. The older buildings had also been more energy efficient due to their thermal mass. In the new buildings, as Lewis Mumford and other critics noted at the time, the glass siding intensified heat in the summer and let in cold in the winter. Huge central heating and air conditioning units were needed in order to create a totally artificial climate at great energy cost. Moreover, the buildings were plopped down without regard for the seasonal path of the sun, and in many cases were shaded the year round, thus negating one purpose of the glass and adding to the winter chill.[33]Between 1947 and 1960, total consumption of energy rose from 33 quadrillion BTUs to 44.6 quadrillion BTUs, and during the next decade rose another 22.8 quadrillion BTUs causing electric outages and cutbacks in service—especially during the hottest days of summer, when their air conditioning units were operating at full blast.

During the postwar era, the corporate world had the financial resources and the authority over investment decisions to reshape the world; their choice, in virtually every sector of the economy, was to cushion themselves at public expense. In transportation, energy, construction and other basic industries and in the more mundane consumer sectors such as beer, the corporations proved unwilling to allocate resources in a democratic way or to plan rationally for the long term. Behind their decisions was a conviction that the U.S. could continuously waste its own resources, control more than its share of Third World wealth, and finesse actual problems with new technological development, like nuclear power, regardless of the effect on health, safety, and the environment. This same monopolization of capital and resources took place in agriculture as we shall see in the next chapter, with similarly awesome results.

Chapter Seven

"Before I left the United States in the early fifties there existed among our leaders deep concern about the future of the family farm. It was the big issue of the day. How to maintain the position of family farming in American agriculture was constantly debated and discussed. There was a concern back in those days. There was interest. When I returned in 1961, however, this atmosphere had changed. Gone was the widespread concern over family farming in this country....

"...Where in former days, farm professionals would hotly argue the best approaches of getting more resources for small farmers, establishing families on better land, organizing marketing co-ops; now they seem more concerned with techniques of production on only the biggest farms—the automated devices, input-output records, advanced engineering designs—that kind of thing."
—Howard Bertsch, administrator of the Farmers Home Administration, 1964.

"How can he find himself on a farm? Is that a life? A farmhand?"
—Willy Loman in Arthur Miller's play, Death of a Salesman, 1949.

Between World War II and 1970, rural America had an out-immigration of 25 million people. This, according to a federal task force on rural development was "one of the largest migrations of people in recorded history," far outranking in numbers of people on the move the European emigration to the United States and the settling of the western frontier.[1] Farmers had been abandoning land since before the Depression, but not until after the war did it become admitted policy to drive small, independent family farmers off the land. Between 1933 and 1941, even despite the hard times, farm population dropped from 32 to 30 million. At the end of the war it was down to 24,420,000, or 17.5 percent of the national population. Returning veterans and slackening defense work caused it to spurt briefly upward, to 25,829,000 in 1947. But 1947 was a drought year and the beginning of the final decline. The 1950 farm population was 23,048,000, or 15.3 percent of the population; ten years later it was down to 15,635,000 or 8.7 percent. In seven out of thirteen years between 1948 and 1960, the farm population dropped by more than one million, an average of about 3,000 people a day. More than one million owner-operated family farms went out of business during those years. But a large proportion of the dispossessed were poor, black Southern sharecroppers and tenant farmers. Between 1940 and 1960, 90 percent of the agricultural population of the Mississippi Delta left the region because of mechanization, racism, and lack of job opportunities in other fields.[2] By 1960, there were more people crowded into urban slums than there were living on farms.[3]

Family Farms in Crisis

In 1941, sociologist Walter Goldschmidt studied two small farming communities in California's San Joaquin Valley—one based on corporate agriculture, the other on family farms. Arvin, where the corporations dominated, had 48,000 tillable acres in alfalfa, fruits, and field crops with a yield of $2.46 million. The town supported few retail stores. Because migrant labor was essential to the economy, auto and auto supplies made up 36 percent of the retail trade. There was a grade school but no high school, and no civil or community organizations. Dinurba, where family farms dominated, had only 28,000 tillable acres but its crops (the same as Arvin's, with dairying and market gardening added) were worth $2.54 million. In addition, Dinurba supported over a hundred stores, two banks, and two newspapers. The houses were well kept-up and the standard of living was higher than in Arvin: people in Dinurba spent five times as much money on clothing, sporting goods, and jewelry. The town had a high school, a community swimming pool, and many civic organizations. The message of the Goldschmidt study was clear. Where family farms existed, small towns prospered. Shut down the small farms, bring in corporate agribusiness, and rural America dies.*4

The veteran returning from the war found rural America much as he left it. The word "agribusiness" had not yet been coined, and most farms were still diversified and family-operated. Farmers planted a variety of grains, used alfalfa and clover to add nitrogen to their soil, pastured their livestock, kept chickens and a milk cow or two, used manure to fertilize the cropland, and kept a vegetable garden for home use. The farmer was an independent entrepreneur skilled at a variety of crafts. If hog prices dropped, the farmer would sell his pigs and expand his cattle operation. He'd use a portion of his grain to feed his stock and sell the rest off as a cash crop, offering corn, soybeans, wheat, oats, and hay—whichever grain would fetch the best price.

Good weather during the war years and increased demand led to record yields and high prices, allowing farmers for the first time since World War I to make a decent profit. Total farm income advanced 165 percent during the war, and when peace came farmers had $14 billion in bank deposits (up from a prewar total of $3.9 billion) and $61.8 billion in real estate. Even more important, the total mortgage debt had declined 23 percent during the war and the threat of bank foreclosures on agricultural land was less than ever before. With heavy farm equipment

*Goldschmidt's conclusions, because they were critical of the agribusiness trend, were suppressed by the USDA which had commissioned the study. In 1947, he included them in a book, *As You Sow*, which was vilified by spokesmen for the agribusiness giants who challenged his methodology, conclusions, and politics. More than a decade later, as we shall see, Rachel Carson, author of the book, *Silent Spring*, was abused by the same interests for her scientific challenge to agribusiness orthodoxy.

soon to appear on the market for the first time since the war, the farmer had enough capital to invest in modern machinery and thereby increase productivity.

Yet the boom statistics tell only part of the story. Overproduction has always been the biggest problem of American agriculture, keeping prices down and impoverishing marginal farmers. World War II accelerated this process. At war's end, the two million largest farming operations were marketing 79 percent of the crop and receiving a major share of the farm subsidies.

"The war has strengthened the small farmer's competitor immeasurably," wrote Lee Fryer in *The American Farmer,* a book published in 1947 that argued the case for the family farm. The war years, explained Fryer, "expanded the big farm, and increased its production efficiency by 40 percent. While the family farmer's financial position has improved, the big farmer's economic strength has grown like a giant, so that with all of his savings bonds and reduced debt the small man's position is not better. It may be worse."[5]

"Family farmers are being crowded relentlessly onto a smaller area of land," Fryer warned. "Three-fifths of all farms are now too small to support a family satisfactorily..... A million farmers may face dispossession, when commodity prices decline again to the 1939 level, because their farms are too small to be solvent." The well-established family farmer who believes "he is secure and in a position to compete successfully...may not have considered where he will be when the cost of production is set by a corporate farming industry that is using and exploiting a teeming migratory labor supply and reducing the family farmer's labor to a low competitive value."[5]

Growth of Agribusiness

The large land holdings, which were the basis for corporate farming, were often put together by financial manipulations (little of it legal) on the part of businessmen, crooked politicians, and real estate speculators—and not by the toil of ambitious, hard-working farmers.[6] Typical is the history of the Kern County Land Company, whose vast holdings included some of the most fertile farmland in California's Central Valley. The company was put together illegally by two robber barons, James Ben Ali Haggin and Lloyd Trevis, following passage of the Desert Land Act in 1877 which granted plots of 640 acres of land to settlers who would put in irrigation. By hiring scores of vagabonds to apply for these grants, and by bribing land office agents and the local courts, the two hustlers put together their empire. Bonafide settlers who had broken the land and were cultivating wheat were dispossessed by corrupt judges for having "illegal titles." By 1960, Kern County Land controlled about 2,800 square miles of land, was raising cattle and crops, and had discovered oil.*[7]

One reason that agriculture was so attractive an investment to banks and corporations was the availability of migrant labor. As small farmers were dispossessed, so were their hired hands. Farming villages like Dinurba disappeared as migrant labor, moving with the harvest, replaced owner-operators and their helpers, and family farms became consolidated into plantation-size assembly-line units. Mexican-Americans, Filipinos, blacks, and other minority people worked in the fields with no protection from the law. Migrant workers were underpaid, ill-housed, given no health protection (despite their often harmful work with toxic biocides), and were at the mercy of the large growers. Attempts by the labor movement to organize farm-workers, especially during the 1930s, were suppressed violently. Often, federal agencies worked hand-in-glove with the growers to allow laborers from Mexico to illegally enter the country, providing cheap labor. Migrants who protested these brutal conditions or who were active in organizing labor unions were blacklisted and deported. The attitude of the country as a whole reflected that of the growers. A picture in an issue of *Life*

*During the 1960s, Kern County Land Company sold out to Tenneco, a large conglomerate that pioneered in vertical integration; it controls every facet of its food production from seedbed to market. It also has subsidiaries that produce farm machinery, agricultural chemicals, and packaging materials. Typical of many corporate growers, Tenneco has little interest in long-term management of its land. Says Simon Askin, Tenneco's Vice-President for Agriculture and Land Development: "We consider land as an inventory, but we are growing things on it while we wait for price appreciation or development. Agriculture pays taxes, plus a little."("The Vanishing Small Farmers" by Peter Barnes, *New Republic*, June 12, 1971) magazine in 1954 showed a migrant performing stoop labor in the fields of California. Its caption was: "At work picking carrots for Joe Maggio Company in Imperial Valley is a *bracero*. Mexicans do not mind bending and the sun does not bother them."[8]

For big-city employers, the mass displacement of small farmers was an event to be welcomed. In 1945, the U.S. Chamber of Commerce called for a program to depopulate rural areas in order to make more people available for industrial jobs. Implicit in its thinking was that a labor surplus, by creating competition for jobs, would weaken the growing union movement.[9] The U.S. Department of Agriculture, reversing the course it had taken in the 1930s, also threw its weight behind agricultural concentration.

During the Depression and under the New Deal the USDA, taking a holistic view of agricultural life, had experimented with ways of keeping people on the land by improving their living conditions and teaching them improved farming methods. In the South, a small number of sharecroppers and tenant farmers who might otherwise have moved to northern slums were relocated on federal land and organized into agricultural cooperatives. The Farm Security Administration (FSA) worked to improve rural health facilities and other social services. The Rural Electrification Administration (REA) brought cheap electricity to even the most back-country farms. But reform projects, with the exception of REA, never got past the pilot stage; with the coming of the crisis and the abandoning of the New Deal, they were allowed to die.

Crop subsidies had been another New Deal measure to keep small farmers on the land, where they could at least be self-sufficient. But the perversion of this policy began almost immediately when the corporate-dominated American Farm Bureau Federation was given a hand in administering the subsidies.* After World War II, the program was used to enrich

---

*The American Farm Bureau Federation was founded in 1919 with money provided by the corporations that made up the grain trust, including the railroads, the Rockefeller interests, and the Chicago Board of Trade (which contributed $1,000 to the first 100 farm bureaus organized). From the beginning, the Farm Bureau worked hand-in-glove with the USDA, in order, as President Wilson's Secretary of Agriculture expressed it, to ward

the largest farms, many of them corporate-owned. In the South, white farmers froze blacks out of the subsidies; throughout the country, small farmers were victimized as agribusiness gained control of the subsidy programs. In 1947, the farmers in the top third of the industry were harvesting 80 percent of the subsidy, and the top one percent reaped 15 percent.[10] The situation grew worse as the USDA became more and more interconnected with the big farmers. By 1959, according to Senator John J. Williams of Delaware, the three largest growers in the country collected more price support money than all of the farmers in Delaware, Maryland, New Jersey, and Pennsylvania combined.[11] The expanded subsidy program coincided with the revolution in farm technology; thus, in effect, the government financed the mechanization of the large growers.

Agriculture, to the makers of national policy, was an economic problem to be solved without regard for human, social, or environmental effects. Overcrowded cities, unemployment, social ennui, crime, traffic congestion, juvenile delinquency, pollution, the difficulties faced by the rural poor in adjusting to city life—these problems didn't interest the USDA. Industrial efficiency and maximum profit were the sole criteria for shaping policy. Statistics like yield per acre and production per worker, both of which rose impressively during this period, spurred their policies on.* Transfixed by their statistical balance sheets and

off agrarian "bolshevism." Financed by corporate interests, and offering such services as cheap insurance programs to bolster farm membership, the AFBF became the most influential agricultural agency in the country. The politics of the Farm Bureau have long coincided with that of big business. During the New Deal, it attempted to kill Rural Electrification and succeeded in destroying the FSA. It initially fought the cooperative movement and has consistently opposed attempts to organize farm labor. In 1949, Allen B. Kline, a farmer with a seat on the Federal Reserve Bank in Chicago, who in 1953 would become president of the Farm Bureau, told a television audience "that it's a good thing to emphasize the complete interest of all the rest of the economy in having relatively few people produce the necessary food. We have done an extraordinary job in America in getting that done. We want to continue to do it." (*The Decline of Agrarian Democracy*, Atheneum, 1969).

*In 1900, according to USDA statistics, one farmer could supply enough food for seven people. In 1935 one farmer produced enough food for ten humbled before the great god of technology, they were unable to take note of the human fallout of their agricultural policy.

Adapt or Perish

During the Eisenhower administration, USDA policy hardened and agribusiness became the dominant force in rural America. Corporate interests began saying that the country needed two million fewer farmers, and Secretary of Agriculture Ezra Taft Benson was keen to the idea.[12] (Consider, for a moment, the uproar if farmers got together and said that the country needed two million fewer corporate executives.) What the farmer needs, said Benson, "is an opportunity for full employment. Under-sized, under-capitalized, and under-equipped farms cannot furnish such employment, nor can those who operate them possibly earn an adequate income without part-time work or other occupations." What Benson was calling for was a return to the nineteenth-century doctrine of Social Darwinism, or survival of the fittest. "What right have we in our generation to refuse to others an opportunity to earn what we proudly call an American standard of living?"[13] he asked. Refuse opportunity? Benson had the dispossessed farmer coming and going. Not only did the government have no evidence of people wanting to leave the farm, but it supplied no jobs or retraining programs for those who *had* to.

Benson proposed to scrap the whole subsidy program, while maintaining the USDA's extension services which had already come under agribusiness control. But Democrats opposed him and Congress voted to continue crop subsidy programs, even to expand them from corn, cotton, wheat, tobacco, rice, and peanuts to soybeans, sorghum, and dairy products. While this slowed the process of liquidation, it did not reverse the trend. As the major share of the crop subsidies went

people, but in 1957, the average was twenty-three people. (In 1970 it was over forty.) Corn yield per acre remained constant at about twenty-nine bushels from 1870 to 1940, then rose to thirty-eight bushels in 1950 and fifty-five in 1960. None of these statistics take into account the quality of the food produced. Nor do they include the investment and labor for the support industries that make industrial farming possible.

to the richer farmers, they continued to expand at the expense of the others. Manipulating the agricultural economy to support agribusiness remained government policy. The Soil Bank Program, introduced by Benson in 1956 in an effort to reduce the crop surplus and raise prices, further compounded the inequality. The idea of the Soil Bank was to create a long-range conservation reserve. Farmers were paid money to take land out of cultivation—were paid, in effect, for not farming. Small farmers had little excess land to put into the Soil Bank. The large landholders, on the contrary, could afford to put whole sections of their least productive land into the reserve and reap a financial reward. In 1960, nearly 30 million acres were out of production.[14] In the words of Benson's outspoken assistant, Earl Butz, the order of the day was "adapt or perish."*

With farming in decline, rural areas tried to right themselves by luring industry away from the large cities. Towns competed with one another to attract industry, and offered corporations tax breaks to relocate in their communities. What this represented, in effect, was working people subsidizing industry in exchange for the jobs that industry might provide. But it was a buyer's market. Industry could shop around for the best tax breaks, the most lucrative real estate deals, and the lowest wage scale. But, unlike industry, farms got no tax subsidies; indeed, the system of property taxation assessed farmland at its market value, i.e., its speculative worth as a potential real estate development. An equitable tax system based on land use would have saved many family farms. Instead, rural communities, in keeping with the times, helped destroy their own native industry in order to attract corporate investment from the outside.

Because of the Jeffersonian tradition, the family farm has

---

*Butz was Assistant Secretary of Agriculture from 1954 to 1957, and later Secretary of Agriculture under Nixon and Ford until he was forced to resign for telling a racist joke. In between, he was dean of agriculture at Purdue University. He has also been a corporate director of J.I. Case (a subsidiary of Tenneco), of Ralston Purina, International Minerals and Chemical Corporation, and Stokely Van Camp. Before entering graduate school in agricultural economics, Butz worked on his father's farm, but as a government official his advice to the family farmer was consistent: adapt or perish.

always been a staple of political rhetoric, hailed even by those politicians supporting policies that drive it out of existence. But the media in the postwar years were less tactful than the politicians. They either ignored the small, independent farmers entirely or made them an object of ridicule. The cowboy, war hero, and pioneer remained heroic American archetypes, but not the farmer or the rancher. Postwar drama was concerned with suburban life, family squabbles ("kitchen drama"), or the problems of organization men on the rise. Movies about agriculture were on the level of Ma and Pa Kettle on the Farm, presenting farmers as poor, uneducated rubes, comedy fodder for sophisticated city-slickers. No wonder Willy Loman in Arthur Miller's play, *Death of a Salesman,* is shocked when his favorite son, Biff, announces that he wants to be a farmer.

Technological Change

The policy of rural depopulation is usually presented as an inevitable result of technological progress. When a farmer goes out of business and auctions land, livestock, and machinery at a price well below what they are worth, neighbors mutter about "hard times" or about his or her "run of bad luck," as though nothing can be done to redirect the hands of fortune and fate. But though progress may be inevitable, the path it takes is a matter of human choice. The question always has to be asked: Who is progressing at the expense of whom? And who gets to decide the particular form that progress will take?

Technology is neutral. The wonders of technological advancement that in America have led to giganticism, centralization, and unequal distribution of power and wealth could just as easily have led to the development of intermediate technology and the creation of decentralized, small-scale enterprise. In agriculture, as in other areas of life, the corporations that controlled the new technology opted for bigness and capital-intensive production.

The drift of agricultural technology was exemplified by a *Fortune* magazine article entitled "Power Farming," depicting some of the new machinery that was coming onto the market in the mid-fifties. Included in the layout were an 80-horsepower tractor pulling a 5-bottom plow; a 24-foot disc harrow pulled by a

117-horsepower diesel crawler (valued at $16,000); 4-row grain drills that deposited chemical fertilizer alongside the seeds; a 125-bushel manure spreader; an insecticide spreader capable of treating 100 acres in eight hours; a 2-row self-propelled cotton picker worth $15,400, that could do the work of seventy cotton pickers; a celery harvester worth $9,500 that could be converted for lettuce, and (with a crew of thirty-two) would dig, trim, wash, and pack the crop; and a 14-foot grain combine that could handle 150 bushels per hour and would cost $5,800.[15]

By emphasizing bigness, and by creating machinery that only the wealthy could afford, agribusiness placed farmers at the mercy of the banks and forced them also to follow the economies of scale. The tractor, cutterbar, rake, and baler that are needed to make hay cost the same whatever the size of of the hayfield. But only when the acreage reaches the maximum of what one machine can "properly" handle does the investment begin to pay off.[16] A $9,500 celery harvester, for example, is useless in a ten-acre celery patch that one market-gardener might carefully cultivate him/herself. But on a thousand acre spread, with celery plants filling the horizon, such a machine becomes a necessity. Agribusiness used technology to aid the grower with the thousand acres. But it did nothing to improve the life of the family farmer, still working the ten acres with rototiller, hoe, and hand.

The USDA promoted capital-intensive technology through its research and extension services connected with public land grant colleges. These schools were authorized by the Morrill Act in 1862 to provide practical education for people living in rural areas. They also do research. Fueled by USDA grants, their research has increasingly been carried out for the benefit of the big corporations involved in agriculture. According to Jim Hightower, former director of the Agribusiness Accountability Project, a public interest research group,

> The basis of land grant teaching, research, and extension work has been that "efficiency" is the greatest need in agriculture. Consequently, this agricultural complex has devoted the overwhelming share of its resources to mechanize all aspects of agricultural production and make it a capital-intensive industry....It generally has aimed at trans-

forming agriculture from a way of life to a business and a science, transferring effective control from the farmer to the business executive and the systems analyst.[17]

Land grant colleges serve as "think tanks" for agribusiness. They also educate future farmers and agribusiness executives and carry the latest research findings to the field. Through the National Association of State Universities and Land Grant Colleges (NASULGC), they maintain a politically powerful united front that cooperates with industrial organizations and farm groups like the Farm Bureau to direct research funding for the benefit of their constituents. Agricultural research is a big part of the USDA's budget: though the number of farms declined in the years between 1945 and 1960, the budget for research grew almost 300 percent, from $38 million to $126 million a year.[18]

Corporations often give research grants for projects that seem potentially useful to them, but the public helps pay for these grants too, since they are tax-deductible. The grants save agribusiness corporations from having to build their own research facilities; they can utilize graduate students rather than their own employees to carry out experimental projects. If the research is successful, the company that financed it is usually awarded the license to make the new product, often under exclusive agreement.

The case of Stilbestrol, also called DES, illustrates the nature of agricultural research. DES is a chemical additive mixed with cattle feed to "increase the efficiency rate at which cattle convert into pounds." This means that cattle consume less feed and are ready for market in a shorter time. DES was developed at Iowa State University in 1956 and was patented by the Iowa State Research Foundation, a public body. Without competitive bidding, the Eli Lilly Company was authorized to manufacture and distribute DES. The licensing agreement gave the university a 5 percent royalty on net sales, with Lilly keeping the rest. From 1956 to 1972, when DES was banned in the United States as a suspected source of cancer, Iowa State University earned $3 million from royalties and Lilly earned about $60 million.

DES revolutionized the cattle industry. At one point, three-fourths of all the cattle slaughtered annually were being fed the drug. According to its proponents, "a thimbleful of stilbestrol in a ton of feed makes cattle gain weight 15 percent faster at a 10 percent saving in feed per pound of grain, which adds $90 million annually to the profits of cattlemen."[19] DES was especially useful to specialized feedlot operators, who began to flourish during this period. Traditionally, cattlemen kept their stock on pasture or on winter feed that they grew themselves, using the manure from the cattle barn as part of their fertilizer. DES now allowed them to remove cattle from pasture at an earlier age and ship them off to centrally located feedlots. There they were force-fed grains laced with chemical additives to combat the contagious diseases that the overcrowded feedlots gave rise to. These feedlots were usually highly mechanized, too expensive for the average farmer. Moreover, as the livestock industry became more specialized, the feedlot operators stopped growing feed and, instead, purchased it in bulk from specialized dealers who bought the grain from farmers and packaged it with chemical additives. The feedlot operators had cows, but no fields. The manure accumulated in the cattle pens, leached into the water table, and polluted wells, lakes, and rivers. Great piles of rich natural fertilizer were now going to waste, to become somebody else's environmental problem. But that was all right, because the agribusiness corporations were busy selling costly chemical fertilizers to the farmers to replace the manure.

With DES, agribusiness was quite aware that it was involved in a shady practice. In 1955 the influential magazine *Farm Journal* advised cattlemen, "If you feed stilbestrol to your cattle, better not say anything about it when you send them to market. You might end up getting less money." The reason was not difficult to fathom. Though DES did accelerate the fattening process, weight increase came from watery fat, not from additional protein. The *Farm Journal* article quoted one meat packer as saying, "Stilbestrol cattle just don't cut out a carcass that's as good as they look on the hoof." But, added the *Journal*, "It's not only stilbestrol that's responsible—it's the shortcut, cheaper, fattening methods promoted by every agricultural college around. The beef we're seeing today doesn't measure up to the old corn-fed beef. It looks plump and good on the outside, but when you cut it open the quality isn't there." The *Journal's* advice to cattlemen concluded, "So while it is hard to nail down anything concrete at these markets, one fact stands out; if you feed stilbestrol, better keep mum about it."*[20]

Chemical Farming

This same pattern of government and agribusiness collaboration was evident in the development of biocides, those chemical poisons used by farmers to kill insect pests (pesticides) or unwanted weeds and grasses (herbicides). Chemical biocides are one of the most profitable aspects of agribusiness. Before World War II they were used sparingly. Herbicides had not yet been developed and neither had the most potent insect killers. Farms were then small enough for a farmer to cultivate mechanically, with a horse or tractor-drawn cultivator, turning over the soil between the crop rows, burying the weed, and improving soil tilth as s/he went. Technology should have made the task of mechanical cultivation easier, as tractors became more dependable, cultivators improved in design. A farmer today can sit in an air-conditioned tractor listening to a stereo tape deck while cultivating the crop. But except for a few stubborn traditionalists, most farmers have stopped mechanical cultivation in favor of chemical spraying; not because it is cheaper or more efficient or better for the crops or the soil, but because farm publications dependent on chemical advertising urge its use and the USDA's extension service willingly goes along.

Controlling insect pests is a graver problem than controlling weeds. Without some system of pest control, a farmer is certain to lose a portion of the crop. Time and again in human history, insect plagues have caused famine. But with or without pesticides, surplus and not the threat of famine has been the rule for American agriculture. Even without the use of biocides, scientific agriculture can minimize damage. Good soil management, crop rotation, plant genetics, use of pest-eating insects

---

*In the late 60s, evidence that DES was a carcinogenic drug became irrefutable. Twenty-one countries banned its use and Sweden and West Germany prohibited the importation of U.S. beef for fear of harmful residues. In the United States, the USDA attempted to regulate the use of DES but resisted an outright ban. The cattle industry had become so geared to the use of drugs and chemical additives to speed up growth that a return to the natural way of raising cattle would, spokesmen insisted, lead to economic disaster. In 1972, when DES was finally banned from the market, there were sixteen other USDA-approved suspected cancer-producing drugs available to take its place.

such as ladybugs and praying mantises, rotenone and pyrethrum compounds, and insect sterilization programs, all contribute safely to effective pest control. Pesticides in use before 1945 included such natural materials as pyrethrum and rotenone, some inorganic compounds like sodium arsenite, and a variety of metallic salts. While these agents were not without their problems, they all broke down quickly without leaving toxic residue either on the plant or in the soil.

But the postwar technological revolution violated many of the basic precepts of scientific agriculture. Monoculture became favored over crop rotation in many areas because it was easier and more "efficient" for a farmer to specialize in just one crop. Good soil management was thwarted by the excessive use of chemical fertilizers and the idea, promoted by the USDA, that soil was necessary only to absorb water and chemicals and hold the plants upright. Although plant genetics improved rapidly through USDA research, emphasis was on aiding mechanized harvesting, which meant that plants were developed primarily for the toughness of their skins rather than for nutritional quality, taste, or their resistance to disease and pests.

The repudiation of scientific agriculture brought an escalating reliance on hard pesticides whose development had been hastened by World War II. Organophosphates like Malathion and Parathion, for example, were derived from German nerve gas. DDT, a chlorinated hydrocarbon, was developed to prevent malaria among American soldiers in the South Pacific. Other chlorinated hydrocarbons followed: Aldrin, Dieldrin, Endrin, etc. A shared characteristic of these hard pesticides is that they do not decompose efficiently into the soil; their residues remain toxic for long periods and are stored in the fatty tissues of animals that eat contaminated food. The poison is subsequently passed along the food chain in increasingly higher dosages: for instance, from field corn to cows and then, by milk, into human beings. Mothers who eat contaminated foodstuffs store the poison in *their* fatty tissues and pass it along to nursing offspring. Pesticides are spread far and wide by the wind and by birds and other mobile animals. They have been discovered in fish and in non-agricultural areas. Even penguins in the Antarctic have been found to contain residues of hard pesticides in their fatty tissue.

Though heavy pesticide use became prevalent after World War II, it has had little effect on the insect problem. In 1904, the crop loss due to insects was estimated at 9.8 percent, without any use of dangerous chemical poisons. Between 1942 and 1951, when hard pesticides were coming into common use, the figure dropped to 7.1 percent in the average year. Between 1951 and 1960, despite increased use, crop loss rose to 12.9 percent, higher than it was before the invention of these chemicals.[21] By this time, the soil had become saturated with toxic chemicals; as successive generations of insects developed immunity, stronger and stronger doses had to be administered. Pesticides with DDT as a major ingredient tripled in application from 1947 to 1954, from 53,000 tons to 164,000 tons. Their use leveled off at this figure, but organic phosphates and other chlorinated hydrocarbons became popular. The quantity of the latter doubled between 1954 and 1963, to 149,000, and use of the former jumped from 2,000 tons in 1954 to 102,000 in 1963. Herbicidal use also rose tremendously, from $4 million worth in 1947 to almost $26 million in 1963.

As with DES, biocide research focused narrowly on agricultural use rather than on human or environmental side effects. Nevertheless, the USDA was long aware of the dangers involved. In 1948, E.G. Moore of the Agricultural Research Administration admitted that DDT and similar chlorinated hydrocarbons were "highly toxic to man."[22] But no effort was made to pinpoint their effect or regulate their use. It was not until after 1962, with the publication of Rachel Carson's *Silent Spring*, that the USDA was forced to acknowledge publicly the dangers to human health of indiscriminate use of biocides.*[23]

---

*Though Rachel Carson did not advocate an outright ban on pesticides, only that they be used with caution, the USDA and the agribusiness research establishment waged a bitter campaign against her. Typical of this attack was a review in *Conservation News* by F.A. Soraci, director of the New Jersey Department of Agriculture. "In any large-scale pest control program," Soraci wrote, "we are immediately confronted with the objection of a vociferous, misinformed group of nature-balancing, organic gardening, bird-loving, unreasonable citizenry that has not been convinced of the important place of agricultural chemicals in our economy."

In response to *Silent Spring*, the National Agricultural Chemicals Association doubled its public relations budget. An industry spokesman said, "If man were to faithfully follow the teachings of Mrs. Carson, we

Chemical fertilizer became another major cost in farm operations during the postwar years. Previously, farmers used barnyard manure (diversified farms had plenty) supplemented by small amounts of chemical fertilizer and such organic substances as rock phosphate, granite dust, wood ash, bonemeal, cottonseed meal, treated sewage, and sludge. Between 1945 and 1955, the number of acres for crops declined, yet chemical fertilizer use rose from 14 million tons in 1945 (up from 8 1/2 million tons in 1940) to 24 million tons in 1960. In more recent years the use of chemical fertilizer has skyrocketed even more, contributing directly to the energy crisis because—as with biocides—so much electricity, oil, gas, and coal go into manufacturing it.

would return to the Dark Ages." When "CBS Reports" presented a balanced program on the controversy, three out of five sponsors, including Standards Brands (a food processor), the manufacturer of Lysol Soap, and Ralston Purina, an agribusiness giant, withdrew sponsorship. The American Medical Association joined the outcry, urging doctors to write for industry publications to counter the growing concern of patients with biocide poisoning.The Nutrition Foundation (created in 1941 by Campbell Soup, Coca-Cola, General Foods, General Mills, H.J. Heinz, Libby McNeil & Libby, Safeway, United Fruit, and other corporate giants to publicize the food industry's "concern" for good health and nutritional food) charged that Carson's conclusions were "distorted" and that "food faddists, health quacks, and special interest groups are promoting her book as if it were scientifically irreproachable and written by a scientist."

The popular press, including the Luce publishing empire, the *Saturday Evening Post* and *Readers Digest* also made personal attacks on Carson without challenging her evidence. "Many scientists sympathize with Miss Carson's love of wildlife," a *Time* reviewer allowed, "and even with her mystical attachment to the balance of nature. But they fear that her emotional and inaccurate outburst in *Silent Spring* may do harm by alarming the non-technical public, while doing no good for the things she loves."

The USDA, in response to Carson's challenge, revised its figures on crop damage due to pests. In the early 1950s, before the biocide controversy began, the USDA had estimated that 10 percent of any given crop was destroyed by insect pests. The new post-Carson figure was put at 25 percent, supposedly to prove that pesticides were necessary to avoid famine. This was a strange argument. If pest damage had risen 15 percent during a period of intensive pesticide use, then the USDA's position contradicted itself and pesticides were a self-evident failure. (*Since Silent Spring* by Frank Graham, Houghton-Mifflin, 1970).

Changes in the American Diet

Throughout the fifties and accelerating into the sixties, large corporations consolidated their hold on agriculture and transformed the food industry. Suburban development drove market gardeners out of business making it difficult for city people to enjoy freshly harvested native vegetables in season. Instead, they paid the transportation costs of produce shipped in from a few growing areas, primarily in California.* Supermarket chains, which came to dominate the grocery business after World War II (during the 1930s they accounted for less than 5 percent of the retail food volume), also aided the corporate farmers, some of whom sat on interlocking boards of directors.[24] Supermarkets demanded a standardized product and emphasized the way it looked on the shelf, rather than its nutritional quality. This meant that the extra care a small truck farmer could give his produce meant nothing, because it brought the same price as a tough-skinned, overripe vegetable that looked good coated in wax and wrapped in plastic. Moreover, the chains often did centralized buying and paid on a fixed schedule to suit the convenience of their own accounting offices and this hurt the cash flow of the small grower.

Just as artificial chemicals were injected into the soil as a substitute for natural mineral elements, artificial additives, many of them dangerous to human health, were put into food. And despite advances in agricultural technology, the American people ate less fresh food. According to the USDA, household consumption of milk and milk products and of fruits and vegetables declined about 10 percent between 1955 and 1965. At the same time, the USDA claimed a growing popularity of snacks. "As a people we are eating a surprising amount of food and drink between meals," the USDA said. Among those "foods" growing in popularity the USDA listed soft drinks, potato chips, cookies, crackers, doughnuts, and candy. As the report expressed it, Americans were "eating more of our calories in sweets than ever before."[25]

---

*In the 1960s, U.S. agribusiness began expanding into the Third World, where land and labor are cheap and the regimes place no limits on chemical farming. Fruit and produce imported from Mexico, the Philippines, and Latin America are produced by U.S.-owned corporations.

New technology often meant a decline in the nutritional value of food. The introduction of hybrid feed corn, for instance, raised crop yields in the early 1940s but lowered the percentage of protein in the crop. In 1911, the mean protein concentration of feed corn was 10.3 percent. By 1950 the top grade among five hybrids contained only 8.8 percent.[26] The protein value of wheat also diminished with modern agricultural methods: the best wheat crops had up to 17 percent protein in 1940, only 14 percent in 1949.[27] When farmers began to complain about the low quality of their livestock feed, fishmeal was added to boost protein content. The U.S. imported enough fish protein, mostly from Peru, to wipe out half the protein deficit in Latin America; that it was diverted to make up for the deficiencies of modern hybrid corn is a sufficient commentary on the rationality of American agriculture.[28]

Presweetened breakfast cereals were introduced in 1949, coincidental with the coming of television. Advertising for these new cereals was aimed primarily at children. Breakfast manufacturers like Kellogg's, General Mills, and Post competed with each other by introducing new and gimmicky brands designed to appeal to children with a sweet tooth. Old standby cereals like Wheaties, Corn Flakes, and Rice Krispies were de-emphasized in promotional budgets. In 1959, a USDA publication observed that "sugar-coated cereals that are ready to eat cost more, per ounce, than many unsweetened ones. Buying sugar-coated cereals can be an uneconomical use of food money." But in 1962, a release noted that these presweetened products—"cereals shaped like stars, doughnuts, and snowflakes...cereals with cutouts and games on the back; and sugar-coated cereals" are "good for between-meal snacks" and are "available at your local food store in almost endless display."[29]

Along with the other dietary changes came an ever-growing reliance on meat. Between 1900 and 1950, consumption of beef in the United States averaged around 60 pounds per person each year. With the help of DES, imported fishmeal, and other advances in the livestock industry, meat became the staple of the American diet. Between 1950 and 1960, the level of consumption rose to 100 pounds per person.[30]

Challenge to the USDA

Despite evidence of declining nutritional value in food, the USDA consistently maintained that there was no relationship between soil health and food quality. The orthodox view was that the nitrogen-phosphorous-potash (NKP) chemical fertilizer formula alone was sufficient to grow food and that the nutritional content of a crop had nothing at all to do with the richness of the soil. The correct USDA line, as expressed in the 1959 Yearbook of Agriculture, stated:

> Composition is controlled by hereditary factors of genes which also control other characteristics of the plant such as size and shape. Thus we find that the seemingly plausible preaching that depleted soils produce foods of poor nutritional quality and that this is the basis for extensive supplementation of minerals and vitamins has no basis in scientific fact.[31]

The USDA might just as well have been arguing that the world was flat, a doctrine that during its time also had the sanction of official orthodoxy. As Dick Simmons and Lee Fryer state in their book, *Earth Foods*, "The fact is that neither plants nor men, nor even a grain of salt, can violate a basic law of thermodynamics, which says: 'The sum of matter and energy in a closed system is constant.' "[32] Soil lacking in plant nutrients cannot support crops high in nutritional value. Photosynthesis helps plants grow, but vitamins and minerals do not all fall magically from the sky; and one has only to observe the difference between a healthy-looking plant grown in rich soil and a sickly-looking plant grown from the same packet of seeds but in poor soil to understand this argument. Yet the USDA considered this self-evident scientific fact to be heresy and attempted to suppress or debunk all conflicting evidence.[33]

There was almost no popular resistance to the USDA policies during this postwar period. The fate of J. I. Rodale and Louis Bromfield is indicative. In May 1942, Rodale began publishing *Organic Farming and Gardening* magazine, advertising it as "a new kind of agricultural magazine designed to help you build soil fertility in a natural way, and to get the crops that are fit for human as well as animal consumption." In trying to spread his ideas to the agricultural community, Rodale ran up against the agricultural establishment that was bent on establishing chemical farming techniques throughout the land. Because of his advocacy of health foods and other "faddist" phenomena, Rodale was vulnerable to a counter attack by his critics, who had the weight of government authority and corporate money behind them. Rodale never succeeded in making an inroad into American agriculture and so changed his emphasis from organic farming to organic gardening, creating in the process a small publishing empire, catering almost exclusively to affluent health enthusiasts and home gardeners. The drift of modern agriculture, at least during this period, completely passed him by.

Another proponent of small-scale scientific family agriculture was novelist Louis Bromfield. During World War II, he returned from self-imposed exile in France to a farm in his native Ohio. Malabar Farm was a self-conscious experiment in the modern scientifically advanced agricultural techniques. Organized on a collective basis, Malabar became a model of its type, visited by thousands of farmers and friends of agriculture during the late 1940s and early 1950s. Bromfield was influential in the New Agriculturists or Friends of the Land Movement which, like the Rodale publication, attempted to counter the USDA-backed chemical revolution. Innately conservative and seeing himself as a traditional Jeffersonian, part of the American mainstream, Bromfield shunned the more declaratory promises of Rodale's organic movement for a slower trial-and-error experimental technique. Bromfield preferred the chisel plow (which churned up and mixed the soil) to the mouldboard plow (which merely turned it over like a sandwich), advocated crop rotation, diversified farming, trash mulching rather than clean cultivation, use of manure and green cover crops as the basic fertilizing ingredients (with some chemicals where absolutely needed), and grassland farming to prevent erosion on hilly land. In the Malabar garden, organic methods proved their worth and Bromfield accepted Rodale's argument, denied by the USDA, that a balanced soil made fertile by organic methods results in pest-free crops that taste better and have greater nutritional value than their chemically-grown equivalents. In a series of books, *Malabar Farm, Pleasant Valley,* and *From My Experience,* Bromfield argued for a new agriculture that would utilize technological advances to build upon what was best and most scientific in the older, natural way of farming. But like Rodale, he was frustrated by the growing authority of the agribusiness interests; though his books were popular, his influence was marginal.

Throughout the postwar era, agricultural reform, like all other reform movements, proved an impossible undertaking, and those who advocated it were consigned to the outermost fringes of respectable society. Rachel Carson's *Silent Spring* proved the first break in the agricultural consensus. But it was not until the counter-cultural movement of the late 1960s that the hegemony of the USDA and the agribusiness corporations came under popular challenge. The resulting ecology movement popularized the idea of organic farming. A natural foods industry developed to meet the demands of the growing number of people concerned with the health and nutritional factors of the American diet. Young people began to buy up rural farms and homestead in the Jeffersonian tradition. In the Midwest, many commercial farmers, concerned with the rising cost of oil and the degradation of their crops and soils from an overdose of chemical fertilizers and biocides, made a successful transition to organic methods. Even then, control of farming and the food industry remained in corporate hands. The alternative agricultural movement, lacking financial capital and political power, remained on the economic fringe.

Chapter Eight

Whatever people made of their cities in the past, they expressed a visible unity that bound together, in ever more complex form, the cumulative life of the community. Today a rigid mechanical order takes the place of social diversity, and endless assembly-line urban units automatically expand the physical structure of the city while destroying the contents and meaning of city life. The paradox of this period of rapid "urbanization" is that the city itself is being effaced.

—Lewis Mumford in
The Urban Prospect, 1962.

The myth of suburbia fosters an image of a homogeneous and classless America without a trace of ethnicity but fully equipped for happiness by the marvelous productivity of American industry: the ranch house with the occupied two-car garage, the refrigerator and freezer, the washer and dryer, the garbage disposal and the built-in range and dishwasher, the color TV and the hi-fi stereo. Suburbia: its lawns trim, its driveways clean, its children happy on its curving streets and in its pastel schools. Suburbia, California-style, is America.

—Bennett M. Berger in
Working Class Suburb: A Study of Auto Workers in Suburbia, 1960.

The most pressing problem facing postwar America—after reconversion—was housing. Few houses were built during the Depression and the war, and the housing industry was ill-equipped to meet the newly burgeoning demand. Houses still had to be built one at a time with a different subcontractor performing each task: plumbing, carpentry, roofing, masonry, foundation-laying, and so on.

According to the National Housing Agency (NHA), at least 3,500,000 new houses were needed in 1946 just to provide veterans with decent housing, but there was only enough material and labor to build 460,000.[1] In 1947, 40 percent of the veterans were still living "doubled-up" with families and friends. House building, commented *Fortune* magazine in 1947, is "the industry that capitalism forgot":

> Home construction is in the doldrums. In the first five months of the year, in spite of the worst housing shortage since the James River landing, the industry showed no appreciable gain over 1946 except in the price of the product, which advanced enormously.... Any reasonable schedule for filling the nation's housing needs would call for at least twice as many houses as are now being built, at prices a whole lot lower than now.[2]

The postwar era was a seller's market with the law of supply and demand favoring the real estate agent, the builder, the developer, the landlord. The buyer was at their mercy, so desperate was the shortage. Bob Hope told of walking up to a phone booth and seeing a man depositing a hatful of nickels into the coin box. "I said to him, 'Brother, you must be calling China.' He said, 'No, I'm just paying my rent.' "[3]

The housing problem was especially severe for families with incomes of less than $4,000—about two-thirds of the population in 1946. With the coming of affluence, the middle third of the population would begin earning enough money to afford suburban housing, but millions of poor families stayed behind. The 1950 census showed 14.8 million Americans living in substandard housing, with another 6.6 million in overcrowded quarters. Ten years later, after a massive federal effort costing billions of dollars, 8.5 million people still had substandard housing and 6.1 million lived in overcrowded buildings.[4]

The postwar period began the mass exodus of the white middle class from the cities to the suburbs, which until then had been largely rural. Fast on the heels of these white professionals and corporate executives came the white working class. Light industry followed. New highways and the growth of the trucking industry made it possible for industry to move out of centralized industrial areas; automation and new assembly-line techniques made it necessary. Multi-story loft buildings were now obsolete in industry, and the one-story factory sprawling across acres of real estate became commonplace.

As the white middle and then the working classes fled the city, the poor moved in to fill the vacuum, to compete with one another for the remaining jobs and slum housing. White families from the depressed coal-producing areas of Appalachia, black sharecroppers from the South, Mexican-American farm laborers from the Southwest, Puerto Ricans from their native island—all of these different peoples, many of them unfamiliar with urban life, flooded the inner cities and pressed outward into declining white neighborhoods. Black novelist Ralph Ellison, speaking of the shock that traumatized so many black people new to the urban ghetto, described the newcomers as "shot up from the South into the busy city like wild jacks-in-the-box broken loose from our springs—so sudden that our gait becomes like that of deep sea divers suffering from the bends."[5]

Most every city in the country—large and small, north and south—faced this population shift. In Washington, D.C., between 1950 and 1960, the non-white population rose from 35 percent to 55 percent; in Chicago, 14 percent to 24 percent, and in Boston, from 5 percent to 10 percent. Chicago and Cleveland also felt an influx of poor whites from Appalachia, while the majority of Puerto Rican immigrants settled in New York.[6] As early as 1950, inner-city population growth was increasing at twice the rate for non-whites as for whites. Though the white middle-class was moving away, many still commuted to the cities to work. Thus, while the cities were losing their residential tax base, they still had to provide services for the weekday commuters: water, police, fire protection, sanitation, mass transit, etc. The urban newcomers also needed special services, thus adding to the cities' growing financial burden. The rural-dominated Congress and state legislatures were unwilling to provide the cities with much help.

The white exodus to the suburbs was influenced, for the most part, by the cherished American dream of private land ownership and the desire to own one's own house. But the exodus was also hastened by such standard business practices as block-busting and rent gouging on the part of real estate agents and landlords. The 1960 census data for Newark, NJ, for example, showed that blacks paid one-sixth more than whites for equivalent housing. In Chicago, blacks paid one-third more.[7] Blacks and other minority poor were exploited in many other ways. Landlords often subdivided two and three family homes to hold four, five, and six families in inadequate living spaces. Supermarkets often charged higher prices in the ghettos than they did in the suburbs or in middle-class locations. Tenement landlords who had decent relations with their white tenants exploited the newcomers, cut down on services, and were slow with repairs. Thus victimized, and having no legal protection, inner-city dwellers began to seethe with anger and resentment, some of which, having no outlet, was turned on themselves. What were once nice, middle-class neighborhoods began to take on the appearance of demoralized slums, breeding grounds for the riots and rebellions of the 1960s.

Public Housing Policy

Passed over right-wing opposition because it included construction of 810,000 low-cost dwelling units at public expense, the National Housing Act of 1949 declared as public policy "the goal of a decent home and a suitable living environment for every American family."[8] Those aspects of the bill that encouraged private investment and suburban living were, for the most part, fulfilled. By guaranteeing mortgage loans to suburban homeowners, the government encouraged the growth of the suburbs and the construction of single dwellings that led to suburban sprawl. In particular, home mortgages guaranteed by the Veterans Administration made it easy for veterans to buy suburban homes.[9] Public housing for the urban poor, however, lagged far behind. By 1964, only 550,000 low-income public housing units had been built.[10]

The primary forms of urban redevelopment were middle-
and upper-income housing and the construction of corporate
office buildings in downtown business areas. Public officials
would select a site, usually a slum or a blighted commercial area.
The land would then be appropriated by eminent domain, (the
occupants forced to move) and sold to a private developer for a
fraction of the initial cost.[11] Corruption was almost a routine part
of the program with housing administrators, real estate promoters, and leaders in the building trades sharing the lucre. Most of
the developers were real estate speculators or large corporations.
As with defense spending and agriculture, when there was
federal money to be doled out, the corporations were there to
suck the government teat.

Federal funds gave city planners an opportunity to show
their stuff. Utopians at heart, planners believed that a good
environment would improve the lives of individual citizens.
Good schools, good housing, fresh air, etc., were seen as a cure-all
for society's ills. Unfortunately, many of these planners, with
their intellectual abstractions and their idealized conceptions of
the good life, were ignorant of the commonplace needs that
made cities tick, that made neighborhoods liveable. And as
reformers, they believed that good will alone was enough to
provide people with decent homes and that corporations would
willingly subsidize decent living conditions on a non-profit basis.
Their elitism could not be suppressed by a democratic veneer;
they believed with disarming sincerity that they alone knew
what was best for people. Many of them, reacting to the
prevalence of urban slums, were hostile even to the idea of a city.
One of the more influential New Deal planners, Rexford G.
Tugwell, who headed the project that created the Green Belt
demonstration suburbs, had wanted to build "just outside centers
of population, pick up cheap land, build a whole community and
entice people into it. Then go back into the cities and tear down
whole slums and make parks of them."[12] The planners, also,
were almost exclusively men. This meant they thought big, on
the grand scale, without concern for the day-to-day amenities
that make living enjoyable. Moreover, women, much more than
men, work at home; yet men who spend most of their time away
from home in an office, had the power to plan home and
neighborhood life, subjects they were totally ignorant about.[13]

The planners craved order and aesthetic simplicity. A good neighborhood is, of course, an orderly neighborhood. But it's not an order geared to law and outside regulation. It is an order shaped by the rhythms of the people and their culture, their habits and their way of life. A street in a ghetto neighborhood with stoops filled with men drinking beer and playing dominoes, women talking, and kids hanging out on a corner or playing stickball in the street may seem disorderly to a planner; it may seem threatening to a suburban dweller used to quiet streets and to residents who keep to themselves behind closed doors and picket-fenced yards; it may also seem lawless to a cop who lives in the suburbs and who holds these same privatistic values. But despite the noise and apparent chaos, there may well be an order to such a street, an order that in its familiarity is comforting to the inhabitants.

With the best of intentions and a can-do spirit, city planners set out to clear the slums and build housing projects that would improve the quality of life for the poor who would move in. But the planners were doomed to fail. Design is no substitute for political struggle and social change. Many of the more humane housing plans were savaged by right-wing legislators unwilling to use taxpayers' money to buy "frills" for the poor, so usually public projects were built as cheaply as possible. As Lewis Mumford commented, "There is nothing wrong with these buildings, except that, humanely speaking, they stink."[14] The failure of the city planners to get adequate funding for their job should have been a lesson in the limits of technocratic planning. A decent social environment cannot be created without a transfer of political and economic power. The urban planners were trying to create utopia without providing the public access to financial capital or decision-making power.

Destruction of Urban Neighborhoods

Lewis Mumford has written that the function of a city is "to permit, indeed to encourage and incite, the greatest potential number of meetings, encounters, challenges, between all persons, classes and groups, providing, as it were, a stage upon which the drama of social life may be enacted, and with the actors taking their turns as spectators and the spectators as actors."[15] Paul Goodman adds that "history teaches that cities have made people smart because of their mixed peoples, mixed manners and mixed learning."[16] But the city planners and the administrators of housing and urban renewal projects cared little for that kind of diversity. In limiting the freedom of choice that makes city living vibrant, they helped create an environment that bred fear and crime. Diversity flourishes in chaotic, free-spirited, democratic situations that do not lend themselves to bureaucratic control. Knowing little about neighborhood culture and street life, and appreciating it less, planners saw no reason to make its preservation a priority.

In the view of the planners, slums and overcrowding were the root cause of crime. The new high-rise red brick housing projects were seen as antidotes to crime, and this became their most spectacular failure. Instead of diminishing criminal activity, the projects provided an environment where crime could most easily flourish. As Jane Jacobs has pointed out, "A well-used city street is apt to be a safe street," providing, of course, the neighborhood is cohesive and residents feel that this is where they want to be. A street lined with apartment houses and small shops gets maximum use, especially if there are small commercial businesses in the area to provide added patronage for local stores. These stores provide services that cannot be measured by economic standards. Small businesses, as Jacobs shows, are the "eyes" of a street. In a good neighborhood, shopkeepers know the residents and are cognizant of the goings-on in the street. As long as the stores are open and there is coming and going, the opportunity for crime is minimized. Board up the stores, do away with the stoops and public areas where people congregate, destroy the feeling of neighborhood community, create an environment where people shut themselves in their apartments and watch television, and criminal acts become more possible.[17]

That is what happened in the housing projects. With the forced removal of local businesses (in favor of large corporate shopping chains all clustered in one location), and the destruction of side streets that served as public areas, the planners created a combat zone for street crime. Because no social activity took place in the streets or in the ill-defined area between the separate high rises, people shunned responsibility for events out of doors. The biggest gang problems during the postwar years were in the housing projects. There the concept of private "turf" was strongest, for there were no public areas for teenagers to congregate and no streets, alleys, or windowless brick walls (for ball playing) to inspire them with things to do. A Pittsburgh study on the relation of slum housing to delinquency embarrassed its researchers by finding that delinquency rates were higher in the new housing projects than in the uncleared slums.[18]

Federal regulations aimed at separating commerce from housing. The government did not provide funds to improve neighborhoods of mixed commercial and residential use. Good living, according to the planning experts, required residential areas with clearly marked-off areas for shopping centers. Locally owned businesses and stores interspersed throughout the apartment buildings were not wanted, and public policy actively discouraged their remaining in renewal areas. A study of small businesses that were forced to relocate under the public housing laws found that through 1961 only 59 percent of 21,439 evicted firms got payment for their relocation and that in some places 40 percent of them shut down for good.[19]

How this destroys a neighborhood is described by Jane Jacobs writing about East Harlem, a mixed Puerto Rican-Italian neighborhood in New York. In the late 1940s, East Harlem was in the process of self-rejuvenation. Then came "slum clearance": 1,300 small businesses and 500 non-commercial storefront organizations, many of them social clubs that expressed the vitality of the neighborhood, were forced out of the area. The shopkeepers could not afford to rent stores in the new projects. In their place came a few chainstores and supermarkets. Instead of a hodge-podge of small stores catering to the particular tastes of the community, the people had to adapt to the standard brands of corporate enterprise. Moreover, the population, after it had dispersed for slum clearance (and the process of clearance and rebuilding took up to twelve years to complete) could not in many cases return, because income regulations prohibited the more affluent from occupying public quarters.[20]

Where could these families go? The Italians had little trouble relocating to the suburbs or other white areas. But the Puerto Ricans had no freedom of choice. Federal housing policy encouraged the segregated status quo. FHA policy was to refuse mortgage insurance for Puerto Ricans and blacks who wanted to buy homes in white areas, no matter what their collateral. Banks followed the same pattern and, in addition, preferred to invest money in the suburbs (a policy called "greenlining"), making it difficult for city dwellers, white or black, to get loans for home improvement. The former Puerto Rican residents of East Harlem, like minority group members everywhere, could only relocate in other overcrowded slum areas.[21] Nationwide between 1949 and 1960, two-thirds of the more than 600,000 people forcibly removed from their homes because of urban renewal were members of discriminated-against minority groups.[22] (Hundreds of thousands more were forced out of their homes because of the national highway program.) East Harlem, meanwhile, once a neighborhood of diverse ethnic groups and income levels, became a ghetto for poor people of color. This pattern was repeated throughout the country.

Low-cost public housing did not have to be built in high-rise fashion. But it was more economical that way. In 1946, Robert Moses, New York City's most powerful planner, said, "People just have got to move out of the way to make way for buildings that will house more families than the area has been housing." At that time, perhaps 20 percent of the area of greater New York, was privately-owned vacant land; other cities were not very different.[23] But housing administrators were reluctant to build public housing on taxable private property. True, public housing reduced the local tax base. But huge swaths of taxable property were enthusiastically taken off the tax rolls to allow for highway construction. Clearly the commuting needs of the suburban middle class had precedence over the housing needs of the urban poor.

The housing projects failed to provide a decent way of life for other reasons as well. Harrison Salisbury, reporting on the rise of juvenile delinquency in housing projects in New York City during the 1950s, described how "admission to low rent housing projects basically is controlled by income levels.... Segregation is imposed not by religion or color but by the sharp knife of income or lack of income. What this does to the social fabric of the community must be witnessed to be appreciated. The able, rising families are constantly driven out.... At the intake end the economic and social levels tend to drop lower and lower.... A human catch-pool is formed that breeds social ills and requires endless outside assistance."[24] This description of urban housing applies to the problem of rural slums as well. In Appalachia, for instance, the most able and therefore the most mobile young people left in search for jobs in the city. Remaining were the aged, the least competent, and the most impoverished—the people who lacked the will, wherewithal, or capabilities for upward mobility. The result, like the low-income highrise, was an economic and social backwater, a rural slum, a problem area.

Housing officials marked off slum areas by using statistical criteria rather than by walking the neighborhood and talking to the people. Population density and the age of the buildings usually determined what constituted a slum. And when a neighborhood was designated a slum, bureaucratic wheels were set in motion to make it almost inevitable that it would become one. Jane Jacobs tells how, after the war, city planners in Boston designated the densely populated North End as such an uninhabitable area. As a result, legitimate financial institutions like banks and insurance companies blacklisted the area and it became impossible for residents to get loans or credit for home improvements. Banks will not invest money in designated slum areas, a policy called "redlining" that is still going on.

(While poor neighborhoods were blacklisted, a national mortgage market was available for suburban homeowners and builders who could get credit for the asking. For example, in 1959 a savings bank in Brooklyn advertised that 70 percent of its loans were made close to home. Investigation proved, however, that "close to home" meant nearby suburban Nassau County. Due to "greenlining," money deposited in that bank was not available to residents of the neighborhood who banked there. But people in the suburbs found it a ready source of credit.[25] In a sense, urban savings subsidized suburban expansion and thus contributed to the city's own impoverishment. Greenlining, thus, inevitably leads to redlining.)

A boycott by lending institutions is usually the turning point, after which a neighborhood fulfills the expectation of the planners and degenerates into a slum. But in Boston, residents fought back. The North End was a wholesome mixture of small commercial and residential buildings with hundreds of small, interesting, locally-owned shops; the residents were mainly Italian but with a smattering of many other ethnic groups and a diversity of income levels from middle class to welfare poor. It also had a sense of itself as a defined neighborhood, a community. Because the people liked the area and wanted to remain there, they began using their savings to make home improvements. Performing most of the labor themselves, exchanging tools and skills by mutual aid, the North Enders upgraded their neighborhood. No federal money entered the area, and often a primitive bartering system was substituted for financial transactions. By the standards of the city planners, the North End continued to be a slum, yet in 1960 it had the lowest rates of juvenile delinquency, disease, and infant mortality in all of Boston. It also had the lowest rents.[26]

New York's Greenwich Village was another neighborhood community that resisted the planners. In 1958, Villagers won a battle to save their beloved Washington Square Park from becoming part of a major traffic artery. At other times, Greenwich Villagers stopped expressways and urban renewal projects that threatened to remove the old tenement and brownstone buildings that gave the neighborhood its distinction. In 1958, a Village resident named Charles Abrams wrote:

> What is happening in Greenwich Village echoes the rumbling of a new social revolution in America. It is a revolt of the urban people against the destruction of their values; of the pedestrian against the automobile; the community against the project; the home against the soulless multiple dwelling; the neighborhood against the wrecking crew; of human diversity against substandard standardization.

> What is happening in Greenwich Village is a reaction against national homogenesis and against...the sacrifice of the playspace to the parking lot.... It is, in short, the first concentrated stand against the heedless destruction that has been the theme of the slide-rule era, 1935-1958.[27]

Alas, except in special self-conscious communities like Greenwich Village and Boston's North End, this revolution never had a chance. Most Americans, when forcibly uprooted from their homes or neighborhoods, believed themselves to be hapless victims of "progress," something that would benefit them in the long run, if not now. But it was the large corporations making the decisions about where and how to invest capital that caused the destruction of the urban community. And "progress," such as it existed, was a standard that *they* used to measure their own growth and profit. Thus, by willful self-prophecy, the country allowed salvageable neighborhoods to degenerate into slums or into poorly planned, shabbily built housing projects often with more devastating social problems than the old tenement neighborhoods they were supposed to replace.

Spread of the Suburbs

At the end of the war, the suburbs were still largely rural. When you reached the city limits you often came upon a landscape of pastureland, cornfields, gardens, and forests. Market gardeners, many of them with roadside stands to sell fresh vegetables in season, working dairy farms with Holsteins grazing in sight of the city skyline, and well-kept estates of gentlemen farmers and corporate tycoons lined the trafficless, meandering blacktops. Where there was a populated area, it was along the fringe of the city proper and connected to the downtown by interurban transportation systems that included trolley cars and electric buses. But beyond these immediate settlements, deer grazed peacefully and rural life still existed, albeit in its last throes. In Armonk, New York, now the corporate headquarters of IBM and American Can, a general store and blacksmith operated at least until 1950. Stands of feed corn grew where tracts of houses are today, and the county airport, which now services corporate and regularly scheduled jet traffic, offered rides in a single-engine piper cub over the surrounding woodland. John Gunther, surveying the country in 1945, noted that Westchester County "was still the sticks. Suspicion of New York, City, the wicked Babylon," he noted, "can be as acute thirty miles away in Westchester as in the most remote villages of the Adirondaks."[28]

The growth of Long Island's Nassau County, bordering Brooklyn and Queens, was not untypical of what was happening in suburban areas surrounding all major American cities. From 1940 to 1950, Nassau grew from 406,748 to 672,765. Ten years later the population had almost doubled to 1,300,171, and Suffolk County, further east on the island, was also feeling the effects of the suburban sprawl; its famed potato farms were rapidly being replaced by row upon row of tract houses. Meanwhile, the population of New York City declined, despite the World War II baby boom and an influx of Puerto Ricans and poor black families fleeing the segregated South.

The same trend held true in other areas. Orange County, outside Los Angeles, almost doubled in population between 1940 and 1950 from 130,760 to 216,224, and in the next decade more than tripled to 703,925. San Mateo County, south of San Francisco, grew from 111,782 in 1940 to 444,387 twenty years later. In the nation's capitol area, Prince George's County, Maryland, grew from 89,460 in 1940 to 357,395 in 1960, reflecting in part the growth of the federal bureaucracy that was a by-product of the war. Oakland County, near Detroit, more than doubled between 1940 and 1960 from 254,068 to 590,259, and Lake County, in greater Cleveland, went from 50,020 to 148,700 in the same twenty years.

Suburban growth, encouraged by federally guaranteed mortgages and the greenlining policies of banks were also aided by the development of mass production techniques in the building industry. Prefabricated housing had been available before the war. Buckminster Fuller developed his Dymaxion House in 1927, and the TVA built prefabricated communities on a small-scale during the Depression. During the war, prefab housing was thrown up to house workers near defense plants like Ford's Willow Run aircraft plant in Detroit and the Kaiser shipyard in Oregon. The quonset hut was most popular, offering 500 square feet, radiant heating, plumbing, refrigeration and hot water for about $2,500. But their primitive curved design and galvanized steel siding were unattractive and they were never considered a permanent solution to the housing shortage. The American people wanted something more solid than what the prefabricated builders could then offer, and Bob Hope expressed a common attitude when he joked, "The prefabricated houses are really cute. They come in several styles. Some even look like houses. They can be put up in anywhere from two to ten hours by three strong men and brought down in anywhere from five to ten seconds by one strong wind."[29]

Of course, the housing shortage had little effect on the well-to-do who could afford custom-home construction and did not need to wait on the techniques of mass production. The upper middle class pioneered the exodus to suburbia. Many bought old homes in long-established rural communities; others bought plots of land, hired an architect and a contractor, and built from scratch. For them, *Life*, in 1946, conjured up a "Dream House" estimated to cost $75,000.[30] This was at a time when a hamburger, a milk-shake or Saturday afternoon at the movies each cost a quarter, while a bottle of soda pop cost as little as 7 cents.

The solution to the housing shortage developed out of wartime experience. Given a wartime contract to build low cost houses for the U.S. naval base in Norfolk, Virginia, New York builder William J. Levitt experimented with mass production techniques, completing 750 bungalows and 1,600 row houses in eighteen months on a tight budget. This success led the firm to plan for large-scale development once the war ended. To Levitt, land could be turned into a giant factory to produce low cost homes in assembly-line fashion. Basic parts were pre-cut, numbered and assembled in a package and trucked to the building site. One crew of men did nothing but go from site to site laying foundations; another laid the joists and were followed by a crew that put in the subfloor and floor; another crew raised the studs, another fitted the windows, and so forth. The basic structure, a 4½ room house of Cape Cod design, sold for $8,000 in 1949. Originally intended as rental units for white veterans eligible for G.I. loans, the builders began to put the houses up for sale when they realized that people wanted to buy, not rent. And after 1949, when the Federal Housing Act eased mortgage restrictions for non-veterans, Levittown was thrown open to all buyers, as long as they were white.*

---

*Suburban homes, until the early 1960s, were restricted almost exclusively to whites. (Likewise, in many upper middle class suburban developments, restrictive covenants barred Jewish families). The first Levittown home-owners had to sign a contract with a restrictive clause that read, "No dwelling shall be used or occupied by members of other than the Caucasian Race, but the employment and maintenance of other than Caucasian domestic servants shall be permitted..." This restriction was ultimately scrapped—in Levittown, at least. But most developments were closed to

Levitt's first community venture began in what was then a small farm settlement in Nassau County, called Island Trees. Beginning with 300 acres of potato fields, the project upon completion four years later, covered more than seven square miles and had about 68,000 people living in 17,500 Levittown homes. Levitt's success revolutionized the housing industry. Now, contractors would buy up large plots of rural land, bring in bulldozers to clear and flatten the landscape, and throw up look-alike houses one after another. Housing developments began to cover the countryside, sprawling outward from the city limits, bringing with them shopping centers and other suburban conveniences dependent totally on the automobile. The Levitts, meanwhile, after the success of the Long Island Levittown, moved their operation to Bucks County, PA and built another 17,311 houses. It was the first entirely planned community since the construction of Washington, D.C. In 1958, another planned Levittown community went up in Whitesboro, NJ, also within commuting distance to Philadelphia, on land obtained from market gardeners who had been growing peaches, plums, and tomatoes for the Philadelphia market.

The Levittowns were unique for their semblance of community planning. Land was left open for schools, and the projects came complete with community centers and swimming pools. But few developments were built with such awareness. Many lacked school sites, police and fire protection, even adequate sewer systems; houses were simply thrown up wherever there was open land. Suburbia was also developed without regard for the pressing need for new housing. Instead of building multi-unit dwellings which would have further eased the housing shortage, the industry emphasized single-dwelling homes. In the period between 1925 and 1930—before the

blacks until the civil rights movement in the 1960s made "open housing" an issue. Levitt, himself, later promoted open housing. In his Bucks County development, open housing was the official policy. But the first black families that moved in were harassed by some of their white neighbors. This, too, was typical of the white suburbs. Black families who integrated all-white neighborhoods often faced verbal and physical violence. Integrated housing was as explosive an issue as integrated schools. ("Levittown: A Suburban Community" by Harold L. Wattel, in William M. Dobriner, *The Suburban Community*, Putnam, 1958, p. 308).

Depression put an end to new housing starts—20 to 30 percent of new housing was for three or more families; the single family home represented just 60 percent of the market. After the war, private homes represented about 80 percent of the housing starts while high-rise apartment buildings, a new innovation, replaced the neighborly three- to six-story apartment buildings that were so common in pre-Depression urban neighborhoods.[31]

From Los Angeles to Long Island, suburbs all came to look alike, with the standard Cape Cod saltbox, the standard ranch, the standard split-level—little else. Instead of building in economically and ecologically efficient clusters—a group of houses surrounding a common space—private homes were built in strip rows, requiring each home to have its own support system (plumbing, septic and sewage, hot water and space heat). The single-story ranch house or split-level was especially wasteful, given the fact that heat rises easier than it spreads over a large surface. Whether on the plains or in the mountains, suburban land was all level, because a flat terrain was easier to build upon. Even flora varied little from place to place; the nursery-bought Colorado spruce was as ornamental in the suburbs near Boston as it was outside Mobile, Seattle, Detroit, and Denver. Row upon row of "ticky-tacky" houses with trim lawns and sterilized shrubbery inspired a comedy cliche. The man of the house commutes home from work, opens the door and kisses the wife who is waiting for him, martini in hand. But it's the wrong house and the wrong wife. In 1956, the Rays, a black rock'n'roll group, had a hit record along this theme. In "Silhouette," a rejected lover watches his girl friend kissing a rival behind drawn shades. Raging with jealousy, he barges through the front door only to discover it's neither his girl nor her house. She lives in a look-alike house down the block.

The suburban housing boom alleviated the immediate problem of housing for the white working and middle class. But because of the quality of construction, deterioration was rapid. By the 1970s, the building-supply industry would experience an unexpected boom, attributable, according to the *Wall Street Journal*, to the spread of suburbia during the 1950s. The paper quoted a building-supply executive as saying, "Some five million single family homes built in the private housing boom of the early 1950s have reached the age when roofing replacement is required." And, added the *Journal*, "many homes built a generation ago now need major remodeling. Some building supply firms expect their market to increase two or three times as fast as the gross national product over the next few years."[32] As with most other American products, planned obsolescence was a factor in the initial design. "Progress" in home construction techniques did not mean that the new houses would be built to last. Even in 1955, at the height of the suburban boom, Borg-Warner, a large corporation that manufactured, among other products, insulation and air conditioning, advertised, "Will your home be obsolete...even before you move in?"[33].

The Suburban Myth

Suburbia evolved to meet the specific needs of the nuclear family: husband, wife, their children, alone together in a one family house. In the past, members of extended families often lived near one another; grandparents, aunts, uncles, cousins lived in the same neighborhood or on the same city block. As in long-established rural towns, frequent and informal visiting was commonplace; children had a variety of adult role models and the whole family had a wide network of support. In the working class suburbs, this way of life was kept intact, distances permitting. Blue collar workers, with their limited job opportunities, settled in one suburb, as in one job, and tried to maintain old ties. It was customary on week-ends, for instance, for city kin to visit their suburban cousins, "going to the country" to barbecue steak or hot dogs in the backyard.[34]

But when young couples of the upwardly mobile executive and professional classes moved to the suburbs, they usually left their roots behind. Families moved from suburb to suburb following the trajectory of the husband's career. Cut loose from the past, they increasingly drifted away from the culture—familial, ethnic, and religious—in which they had been raised. The husbands became "organization men," in William H. Whyte's famous phrase: "The ones of our middle class who have left home spiritually as well as physically, to take the vows of organization life." [35] Instead of drawing strength from their heritage, this new breed of American looked to the corporate world for values. The corporation and the way of life it represented became the substitute for the traditional web of custom and ritual, the inheritance of our past.

Whyte's "organization man," like David Riesman's "other-directed" character type, became a catch phrase to describe the white collar administrator who inhabited suburbia and supposedly set the style for the rest of the country. The suburbs, to Whyte, were "packaged villages" for the new trend-setters, "the dormitory of the new generation of organization men."[36] Their influence was supposedly ubiquitous. "The organization man furnishes the model for the life style and even in the suburbs where he is a minority, he is influential out of all proportion to his numbers," Whyte wrote. "As the newcomers to the middle class enter suburbia, they must disregard old values, and their sensitivity to those of the organization man is almost systematically demonstrable."[37]

Despite the fact that over half of suburban residents, after the middle fifties at least, were working-class, the idea of the suburbs as the exclusive domain of the upwardly mobile white middle class became widely accepted. The suburban working class, like its urban counterpart (not to mention the poor), became almost invisible in the public consciousness, ignored by the media, known only to the millions of men and women who were part of it. Instead, what Americans perceived was what Bennett M. Berger in 1960 first called the "suburban myth"; an attempt to falsify experience, to render the suburbs as a contented, classless, homogenous, affluent society, "a new melting pot"—a place, as sociologist William M. Dobriner put it, where "social and personal differences are submerged beneath a great wet blanket of conformity" as if "all suburbs are pretty much the same."[38]

Nowhere was this suburban myth demonstrated more clearly than in the situation comedies that were popular on television during the 1950s. In the earliest days of television, during the late 1940s and early '50s, programs were lifted directly from radio and therefore described earlier prewar styles and values. The most popular situation comedy on radio at that time was a program about a Jewish working class family living in an old tenement building in the Bronx. Next to "Amos and Andy," "The Goldbergs" was the longest running serial on radio. When transferred to television in 1948, it met with equal success.

The Goldberg family, living in a small walk-up apartment consisted of Jake, the father; Uncle David, a retired watchmaker; two teenaged children named Sammy and Rosalie; and the feature character, their mother, Molly Goldberg. Gertrude Berg who played Molly also wrote many of the scripts and directed the program. Each episode began with Molly leaning out of the window "schmoosing" with the neighbors. Invariably her gossip was about the adventures and misadventures of her family, neighbors, and relatives. The Goldbergs were part of a dynamic urban Jewish culture and their interests extended well beyond their tiny Bronx apartment. As cultural and ethnic diversity was encouraged by radio and early television, the Goldbergs were conscious of their Judaism and celebrated the various Jewish holidays on the home screen. The three adults in the family all spoke with a trace of an Old World accent and Yiddish phrases were a part of their dialogue. But the accents were there for realism, not comedy. One laughed at the wit of the dialogue and the human problems that were inherent in the plot. The characters also had dignity. The fact of their religion was important to the show, but it was the universality of their mishaps and triumphs that gave "The Goldbergs" its appeal. The sex roles were balanced. Though Molly was the principal character and was a strong, sharp witted woman with opinions about everything, her strength did not come at the expense of either husband Jake or Uncle David. Jake was gentle, David had the tolerance and sympathy for the young that often comes with the mellowing of age. From their poor but comfortable tenement dwelling, the Goldbergs spoke to what was best about human-kind.

The Goldbergs covered the Jewish segment of what was still perceived by the media as a turbulent melting pot. Almost every large ethnic group had a situational series with which it could identify, though the popularity of the shows crossed all ethnic and religious lines. "Life with Luigi," starring J. Carroll Nash, described the life of an Italian-American family. William Bendix starred in "Life of Riley," an Irish-American comedy, and Peggy Wood was the matriarch of a large family of Swedish-Americans in "I Remember Mama." "Amos and Andy," originated on radio by two white vaudevillans in black face, came to television with an all black cast. Though the program was produced by whites and the blacks lived in a falsely comfortable world untainted by racism, the characters did have the same kind of dignity that one saw in the Goldbergs; if they were not shown to be militant activists, at least they were not the Stepin Fetchit caricatures of an earlier day. Even senior citizens had a place on early television. Most situation comedy or drama had a resident wizened sage. And one of the most popular shows of this period, "Life Begins at Eighty," featured a panel of spirited octegenarians who dispensed wisdom with wit and verve in the manner of old people through the ages.

The impact of these early television and radio serials was to bolster the idea of a pluralistic America. A family could rise in the world without negating its past. The melting pot was still a tasty stew and Americans were proud of their differences. But in the early 1950s, these programs disappeared from television. Between Molly Goldberg and Archie Bunker of "All in the Family," there is a void filled only tangentially by Jackie Gleason and his "Honeymooners" series.* Gleason was a product of vaudeville and his comedy belonged to an earlier, class-conscious era. Reginald Van Gleason III, one of his characters, came from depression days when rich boors in top hat and tails were objects of working class laughter and scorn. Finnegan, the barkeep, came out of a time when the neighborhood bar was a community gathering place and bartenders knew everyone's business. "The Honeymooners" described two working class families. The husbands drove a bus and worked in the sewers. Their wives were portrayed as equals and often got the good comedy lines. With the exception of the "Honeymooners" and "I Love Lucy"— the zaniness of Lucille Ball defied place and time—family situation comedies throughout the 1950s described the lives of suburban middle-class nuclear families that were, without

---

*The "Honeymooners" evolved from a skit to series of its own. Gleason played Ralph Kramden, a fat, loud, insecure, bumbling, but not unlikeable, bus driver. His wife, played by Audrey Meadows was tough and took no guff. The Kramdens' lived in a tenement building; their upstairs neighbors were Ed Norton, played by Art Carney, who worked for the Department of Sewers, and his wife Trixie, played by Joyce Randolph.

exception, white, Anglo-Saxon, and Protestent. This became the one family model presented by television.

Father Knows Best

The archetypal family of the 1950s was the Anderson family of "Father Knows Best." Robert Young played the father, Robert Anderson; Jane Wyatt was Margaret, his wife; and three children, Betty, Bud, and Kathy, filled out the family and the cast. "Father Knows Best" was introduced to the television audience in 1953. It was a favorite of the TV critics and had an unusually faithful following. When supposed low ratings caused one network to cancel the series, public outcry encouraged another network to pick it up, a rare occurrence in television. TV critic J. P. Shanley called "Father Knows Best" "the most appealing and believable situation comedy" on TV, noting that its "chief appeal" was "its close relationship to events that occur regularly among families all over the country."[39] But families all over America were not all affluent white Anglo-Saxon Protestants living comfortably in a modern suburban dwelling as was the Anderson family. There was nothing realistic about the Andersons' lives. What was typical was the expectations that their roles described. The Andersons were a model for other American families to aspire to, to copy. The old working class family with its ethnicity intact, though it still existed, became—as a social archetype—invisible. Robert Young wouldn't dream of going off to work carrying a lunchpail with two bologna sandwiches and a mug of coffee, as William Bendix always did on "Life of Riley." Jane Wyatt would no more cook cabbage soup in her modern kitchen than she would serve a dinner of ribs and collard greens. Molly Goldberg's chicken soup, like the audience reaction to "Father Knows Best," by now had become canned. TV had a new message and was selling a more up-to-date lifestyle.

The qualitites expressed by "Father Knows Best" tell us much about the expectations of the suburban middle class during this period; expectations that supposedly had broad appeal. The program was concerned exclusively with the nuclear family. The interests of the Anderson family were totally internalized. When the plot did go outside the family, it usually concerned one of the three kids, who, in contrast to their parents, were adventure-some, almost like ambassadors to the world at large. Betty, the teenage daughter, is shown trying to attract the attention of a shy boy in class and her parents give her support. Bud (younger than Betty) becomes a door-to-door salesman to earn pocket money and needs help in dealing with his customers from Dad. The family is mutually supportive but is structured as a patriarchy, i.e., father knows best. The parents live in virtual isolation except for their children; no other adult threatens their cloistered monogamy. Shanley described the father as a "human being who goofs sometimes but never becomes a low comedy dimwit." His life is centered around the home. He goes to and from work carrying an executive's briefcase, but we do not know what he does. Margaret, Shanley continues, "conducts herself with appropriate dignity. She knows how to keep a budget and attend to other household duties without fluttering. She does not forget to turn off the oven when the cake is baked."[40]

In actuality, Margaret was a handsome and intelligent woman whose impact on the screen was like a domesticated version of Kathryn Hepburn. But the plot of "Father Knows Best" missed few opportunities to make her seem utterly dependent on know-it-all Dad. An episode in which Robert Anderson tries to teach her to drive is an excuse to drag out every patronizing cliche about women drivers. "She can't drive a car, it's too complex," says Bud. Explains father: "Your mother, she's a woman, her attitude toward a car is different than yours or mine." When Margaret does finally sit behind the wheel, she first primps herself in the rearview mirror. Then, grinding the gears and neglecting to look behind, she backs out of the driveway too fast, narrowly misses a passing car, and has the poor, usually unflappable Dad terrified. When she does at last navigate past the driveway, she stops in the middle of the street to gossip with another woman, as cars line up behind, their horns blaring. "Scatterbrained," says Anderson of Margaret; "a female public address system" is what he calls her friend.

Through it all, Robert Anderson has tried to keep his calm. This, too, reflects a white middle-class value encouraged by programs such as this. "Why don't you ever fight, bicker and quarrel?" asks Bud at the breakfast table one morning. Robert and Margaret merely smile at one another sweetly; fighting is

not their style. Then comes the driving lesson and the provocation becomes too much. They glower at one another and have
words. But not in front of the children. Bud comes downstairs
and catches them having a spat. He is shocked and they are
embarrassed. The suburban myth did not sanction openly expressed anger. Bud might just as well have found them screwing
on the living room floor, such is his surprise. The parents, caught
in the act, quickly recover their cool. They were only acting, they
lie to their son. "It gave me kind of a sick feeling to see you and
Mom fighting," Bud says to his Dad with evident relief, Mom
being an appendage that he does not address directly. The
episode ends with the conflict over driving still unresolved but
the parents smiling. Episode after episode, Robert and Margaret
are always smiling. Problems occur, are solved, or are left hanging. But the Anderson family is always smiling.

The formula represented by "Father Knows Best" monopolized the media from the middle 1950s until the early 1970s
when "All in the Family," an updated version of "Life With
Riley," appeared on the screen. The dominant character in this
TV series was Archie Bunker, an old-fashioned blue-collar
family man whom postwar affluence had passed by and recent
history had sought to deny. Like Riley, he is a lovable fool and the
producers of the series, sympathetic to his situation, have cast
him more as a victim of society rather than as simply a bumbling
incompetent. Archie's attitudes are frozen in the 1950s—as they
should be, given his enforced retirement from media life—but it
is the invisible fifties of the white working class unexpectedly
brought back to life. Now he is defensive, bitter, and uncompre-
hending of the forces that have passed him by. The tragedy of
Archie Bunker is not his old-fashioned prejudices and his
appalling ignorance. We can forgive him those; given his place
in postwar life, he could hardly be otherwise. Archie Bunker's
tragedy is that he is the forgotten man of American life. Robert
Young, television's archetypal white middle-class surburban
male, had no politics, no opinions, and no connection with the
world about him. He was the very model of the 1950s
organization man, never angry, trying to keep the lid on by
denying the existence of a crumbling world about him. Archie
Bunker, like the independent American of old, retains his sense

of self and wants to take a public stand. But all through the Dark Ages, when bland, other-directed Bob Anderson was holding forth, Archie was being force-fed political pablum and criminal lies. Patronized, exploited, abandoned, and ignored, Archie Bunker is a remnant of America's past whose creativity and independence have been stifled and whose ignorance and narrow-minded bigotry have now come back to haunt us all. Archie Bunker has a right to be bitter.

Chapter Nine

The idea of a really wide distribution of economic ownership is a cultivated illusion; at the very most, 0.2 percent or 0.3 percent of the adult population own the bulk of the pay-off shares of the corporate world.
—C. Wright Mills in The Power Elite, *1956*

Life for the working classes is not wholly dismal. They are offered a broad fare of engaging distracting involvements: the mass media (Ed Sullivan, football and base-ball games, space shots..., and so on); fish-ing, hunting and camping; unlimited home improvements by the do-it-yourself meth-od; and Catholic religiosity, Protestant self-satisfaction, beer and compulsiveness as outlets that allow them to make their compromise with life in an increasingly middle-class world to which they feel they do not belong.
—Joseph Bensman and Arthur J. Vidich in The New American Revolution, *1971*

Despite the postwar prosperity, income distribution was fairly static. In 1947, writes economic historian Harold Vatter, 36 percent of the population had incomes that were "very low in terms of capacity to support properly a system geared to high mass consumption... The relative portion of the lower strata changed not at all during the 1950s."[1] Another economist, Robert Lekachman, describing the 1950s, observed that "most Americans have never had it so good; possibly 15 percent to 20 percent have had it as bad as ever."[2] And Michael Harrington estimated that at the end of the fifties, 40 million to 50 million Americans were still wallowing in depression-like poverty, but had become neglected and unseen against the backdrop of everyone else's affluence. The poor had become, in Harrington's words, "socially invisible" as the rest of society became preoccupied with its material good fortune.[3] During the thirties, when poverty was a general condition of society, the poor had political power; hence, their situation was a public issue. But the experience of upward mobility that touched so many Americans during the postwar era left the poor ghettoized and easily ignored. Indeed, the whole ideology of affluence, the insistence that the U.S. had passed an historic economic divide, was based on ignoring the millions of poor, denying their existence, writing them out of the national experience. This was easy to do. The media, providing the image by which the American people perceived themselves, focused entirely on the white middle and upper-middle class. And the suburban commuter, driving alone on a new high-speed highway that sliced its way nonstop through a demoralized ghetto, was insulated from that particular reality.

As the chart below (taken from U.S. census statistics) shows, income distribution changed little over the period 1946-1960. In this fifteen-year period, the 20 percent of the families with the lowest income earned, in the mean average, just $580 more in 1960 than they did in 1946. Those in the second one-fifth of the population increased their mean income by $1553, and so forth. The wealthiest 5 percent made the greatest gain, almost $10,000. Using a different method of computation, Richard Parker, in the book *Myth of the Middle Class*, estimated that in 1959, just as in 1945, the wealthiest 10 percent of the population earned approximately 29 percent of the national

Family Personal Income Received by Each Fifth and Top 5 Percent of Families and Unattached Individuals: 1946 to 1960

Percent distribution of aggregate family personal income

Year	Lowest fifth	Second fifth	Third fifth	Fourth fifth	Highest fifth	Top 5%
1946	5.0	11.1	16.0	21.8	46.1	21.3
1950	4.8	10.9	16.1	22.1	46.1	21.4
1955	4.8	11.3	16.4	22.3	45.2	20.3
1960	4.6	10.9	16.4	22.7	45.4	19.6

Average (mean) family personal income in current dollars

Year	Lowest fifth	Second fifth	Third fifth	Fourth fifth	Highest fifth	Top 5%
1946	982	2,178	3,156	4,290	9,091	16,796
1950	1,056	2,418	3,579	4,911	10,254	19,066
1955	1,355	3,200	4,634	6,290	12,722	22,893
1960	1,562	3,731	5,577	7,731	15,493	26,721

income, the poorest 10 percent divided up about one percent of the income, and the income distribution of the middle 80 percent remained basically unchanged.[4] Whatever the method of computation, the evidence is clear that though everyone except the hardcore poor gained during this period, the rich tended to get richer, the middle class tended to stay in its place, and the poor, relative to everyone else, were left further and further behind.

To appreciate how well the rich did during this period it is important to remember that people can consume only so much, that even beyond the point of owning a country estate, private airplanes and a pleasure yacht, there is money left over for investment. Because the rich have surplus capital, that is, money to invest, affluence for them translates into economic ownership and control. In 1958, Richard Parker calculates, 1.5 percent of the people owned 30.2 percent of all privately held wealth and 75.9 percent of all privately owned stock.*[5] This corporate elite continuously rewarded itself. Most working people, for example, were paid hourly wages or straight salaries. But in 1955, thirty-six corporate executives were awarded bonuses of over $250,000 each for the year—this, on top of annual salaries that often topped $100,000. General Motors gave bonuses totalling $94 million to its managerial employees.[6] Such executives, along with doctors, lawyers and the professional people who rose with them, were the ones who benefitted most by the affluence of the postwar years and were the people the commentators wrote about when they ballyhooed the times.

Workers on the Defensive

The key to the new affluence was, as we have noted, mass consumption and its Siamese twin, full production. Less than full

---

*As C. Wright Mills observed in 1956, "...at the very most, 0.2 percent or 0.3 percent of the adult population own the bulk, the pay-off shares of the corporate world." (C. Wright Mills, *The Power Elite*, Oxford University Press, 1956, p.21). In an adult population of 150 million, this represented 300,000 or 400,000 people. But this included only the genuine upper class. On their heels were the up-and-coming corporate managers and white collar professionals who, through stock option plans, tax loopholes and other economic advantages, were carving themselves a sizable, though not controlling, slice of the economic pie.

production would mean higher unemployment and a decline in consumer spending which would lessen demand and cause cutbacks in production in an ever-downspiraling cycle. As such, the role of the working class became two-edged; workers not only had to produce the wealth of the nation, they had to help consume it as well. With automation, the role of consumer began to outweigh that of producer. Production workers could be replaced by machines; consumers could not. Moreover, consumership began to take on added social significance as a worker's sense of him/herself declined in the wake of automation. As automated assembly lines diminished the value of skilled craftsmanship, the working person could no longer take pride in or even identify with the products s/he produced. Increasingly, work became meaningless, the worker alienated from the job. The sense of achievement so essential to psychological well-being no longer came from one's work; instead, it came from the pleasures and status one gained in the consumer role.

In 1946, Congress passed the Full Employment Act, pledging government's responsibility for "promoting maximum production" and "assuring opportunities for those able, willing and seeking to work." The idea of a federal minimum wage also became certified in the postwar era. In response to inflation and liberal pressure, it rose from 75¢ an hour in 1949 to $1.00 in 1955 and $1.15 in 1961. Unemployment compensation, social security benefits, and various other welfare programs were also expanded to provide minimum incomes to the elderly, the unemployed, and the poor. The welfare legislation was especially controversial. The right had always approved welfare for the sick, aged, and disabled, as a form of charity, but had opposed payments to those whom they deemed able to work. This put the unemployed in a Catch-22 situation. Right-wing opposition prevented government from promoting full employment through public works that competed with private enterprise. At the same time, even with the permanent war economy, unemployment remained at over 4 percent throughout the 1950s, except during the Korean War. So the unemployed were accused of being lazy, welfare cheats, and so forth, by the very same people who supported economic policies that limited the number of jobs. Caught in the middle, the unemployed survived on the welfare crumbs that liberal legislators were able to exact from Congress.

The union movement was the one force that enabled working people to share in the affluence of the postwar years. Where unions were strong, working people did relatively well. But the union movement was on the defensive throughout most of the period. As we have seen, the strike wave of 1945-46 was an indication that labor was ready to renew its prewar offensive. But even then, it was facing internal problems. The wartime maintenence of membership clauses that unions won in exchange for the no-strike pledge, meant that new workers in organized industries were automatically entered on to the union rolls. As a result, the unions didn't have to actively win their support, and the new workers missed the experience of having to struggle for union rights. Moreover, many of the cadre who led the organizing efforts before the war left their factory jobs to fight in the war. New factories encouraged a transient labor force. The result was a breakdown in union cohesion.

During the war, women, blacks, and members of other minority groups got high-paying jobs in manufacturing plants for the first time. During the organizing struggles of the 1930s, the CIO had an admirable record of fighting for the rights of black union members. And during the war, under pressure from black labor leaders like A. Philip Randolph, FDR signed an executive order guaranteeing black workers equal opportunities for jobs. Where this law was enforced, in unionized defense plants in the North, blacks were upgraded into jobs previously held by whites. But under the Selective Service Act, servicemen had the right to return to their old jobs with seniority intact. At the end of the war, these jobs, in many cases, were held by blacks who did not want to give them up. The CIO was in a no-win position: blacks and whites were competing for a limited number of good jobs, a situation in which racism was a predictable result. To protect their interests, blacks began to organize their own union caucuses. One of the first was organized in 1949 at Ford's River Rouge plant, where one-fourth of the 60,000 workers were black.[7] Red-baiting destroyed a number of these groupings but the idea of such caucuses survived, especially in the auto industry.

The union movement didn't even perceive the question of women workers as a problem. During the war, women "manned" the assembly lines of heavy and light industry: more than

300,000 women worked in the vital aircraft industry alone, and others worked in machine shops, steel mills, oil refineries, railroad roundhouses, lumber mills, shipyards, the weapons industry, and other kinds of defense plants.[8] Married women constituted half of this workforce and they had the equivalent of two full-time jobs: factory work and housework. Nothing was done to ease the burden. Women with children had an especially hard time, though the Lanham Act financed day-care centers in a few scattered communities. At its peak about 100,000 children were involved, but financing was cut off when the war ended. Given the demands on their time, women could not have taken an active role in the unions, even if their participation had been encouraged—which it was not. Women automatically became union members in unionized shops and the labor leadership, not needing to win their support, simply took them for granted.

Nevertheless, the traditional stereotype of women as the weaker sex was in abeyance during the war years. "Rosie the Riveter," dressed in coveralls and with goggles pressed against her brow, carrying her lunchpail to work, was the heroine of the day. As the Office of War Information acknowledged, war production work "disproved the old bugaboo that women have no mechanical ability and that they are a distracting influence in industry."[9] Annie Oakley, the sharpshooting cowgirl of Irving Berlin's 1946 Broadway musical, "Annie Get Your Gun," expressed this confidence best, "Anything you can do," she sang, "I can do better."

The concern of economic planners in the immediate postwar years focused upon integrating the eleven million returning veterans into the labor force without, as we have noted, causing widespread unemployment. If women were forced out of industry, that was not considered to be "unemployment." Women, therefore, along with blacks, were the first fired. A few unions, especially the more progressive ones in the CIO, fought for the rights of blacks; but nothing was done for women, despite the fact that a survey taken by the Women's Bureau found that 75 percent of the women who held jobs in industry during the war wanted to remain at work. As one woman put it, "War jobs have uncovered unsuspected abilities in American women. Why lose all these abilities because of a belief that 'a woman's place is in her home?' For some it is, for others not."[10]*

Despite the admirable record of women during the war, there was a din of male voices urging women to return to the home. A rise in juvenile delinquency was attributed solely to working mothers—as we shall see, a familiar theme—and not, for instance, to the lack of day-care facilities. Typical was the opinion expressed by Frederick Crawford, head of the National Association of Manufacturers, who said that "from a humanitarian point of view, too many women should not stay in the labor force. The home is the basic American institution."[11]

Women left the labor force reluctantly. Many filed union grievances, insisting that they had compiled seniority, but these were generally ignored. In Detroit, where the number of women working in manufacturing plants fell from 124,000 at V-E day to 63,000 in 1946, women picketed the Ford plant over discriminatory practices.[12] The purge of female and black members, though numerically counterbalanced by the return of servicemen from the war, was a severe (however unrecognized) blow to labor's position. Had the unions fought for the rights of all their members, and demanded job opportunities for women, blacks, *and* returning G.I.s, the labor movement would have been representative of the working class as a whole. With women in the workplace, unions would also have had to grapple with day care issues and with traditional patterns of male behavior. Automation and the diminishing demand for skilled labor had a demoralizing effect on the work force. Workers who no longer had any reason to take pride in their work suffered accordingly. For men, macho behavior was a way of retaining some form of

---

*Many of the displaced women workers had been employed before the war —in traditional low-paying, non-union "female" jobs, such as in laundries, department stores, restaurants, and hotels. Such jobs paid an average of $24.50 a week, compared to $40.35 for the wartime manufacturing jobs. "The nature of postwar employment problems is influenced not only by the number of wartime workers who expect to remain in the labor force," the Women's Bureau commented, "but also by their expressed desire to work in particular industries and occupations. Postwar openings as cafeteria bus girls, for example, are not apt to prove attractive to women who are seeking work as screw-machine operators." ("Separated and Unequal: Discrimination Against Women After World War II" by the Woman's Work Project, New England Free Press, 1972, p. 2, 12. *America's Working Women*, by Rosalyn Baxendall, Linda Gordon and Susan Reverby, Vintage, 1976, p. 311).

ego-gratification; racism was another. White males who experienced their workaday world crumbling and who no longer felt vital to the production process, could at least lord it over women and blacks—an anti-social and self-destructive form of psychological compensation.

Labor Defeated

The labor unrest in 1945 and 1946, great as it was, revolved primarily around basic bread-and-butter issues. Labor wanted to keep the salary gains made during the war without having to work overtime. At the same time, with demand outrunning supply, rising prices were cutting into the value of wages in terms of actual buying power. (It was not until 1954 that real wages, the measure of how much workers could buy with their money, caught up to the wartime level.)[13] Corporate profits, meanwhile, continued to rise even though war production had ended. In October 1945, the Office of War Mobilization and Reconversion estimated that industry could increase wages by 24 percent without raising prices and still maintain prewar profit margins.[14] Of all the labor leaders, only Walter Reuther of the UAW challenged the right of management to arbitrarily raise prices. Using government statistics augmented by the UAW's own research, Reuther insisted that General Motors could raise wages without a price increase; to press his point, he challenged management to open up its books for union inspection. This demand, which would have given labor entrance into the corporation's decision-making process, was turned down flatly, and 200,000 GM workers went out on strike in November 1945. Within months they were followed by 700,000 steelworkers, 200,000 maritime workers, 400,000 coal miners, 300,000 railroad workers, and 200,000 electrical workers. In response, President Truman threatened to use the military to keep the merchant fleet and the railroads moving and to take temporary control of the mines to maintain soft coal production.

In February 1946, after a 30-day walkout, Philip Murray of the steelworkers accepted an 18½¢ per hour wage increase that was suggested by the Truman Administration, and this became the basis for settlements in all the other industries, including auto. Although they had won a wage increase, the auto workers failed to gain access to GM's books and to extract a promise from GM not to raise prices. This proved to be a strategic defeat for organized labor. For, as part of the steel settlement, Benjamin Fairless of U.S. Steel raised prices by $5 a ton—an increase that netted the industry 435 million dollars, more than double what it paid out in wage increases. Other corporations, including GM, also raised prices to absorb both the wage hikes and the increased price of steel. By the end of the year, the cost of living had risen by 18 percent, totally wiping out the gains made by the strikes and leading John L. Lewis to call the miners out on a second strike. Thus began the so-called wage-price spiral that Reuther had hoped to avoid. This pattern of collective bargaining would remain fixed throughout the period. Industry would meet labor's demands by raising prices (higher than necessary to meet the costs of the wage hike), thus passing the cost on to the consumer. Industry would then use its ownership and control of the media to blame labor's greed for the rising cost of living. But this "wage-price spiral" was a misnomer. Higher wages did not cause higher prices; in most cases the reverse was true and union members were in the position of continually playing catch-up.

A congressional investigation, conducted by Senator Estes Kefauver in 1958, explored how large corporations set prices in order to absorb rising labor costs and, at the same time, increase profits. Kefauver found that in industries like auto and steel, where a few large manufacturers determined the market, the corporations set prices without regard to supply or demand. By computing their expected costs and then establishing prices to guarantee profits on the basis of low sales, the big corporations could assure themselves of hefty earnings. In 1956, for example, GM expected to break even with sales at 48.8 percent of total output. Translated into production, this meant that GM could expect a 20 percent return after taxes if it sold all the cars it produced in 36 weeks. Consequently, as economist Daniel Bell explained, "GM could 'take' a four month strike and still come out at its predetermined margin by operating for the rest of the year at full capacity."[15]

The Kefauver Committee also studied the 1957 negotiations between the United Steelworkers of America and U.S. Steel and found that the steel company could run its blast furnaces for just two days a week and still manufacture enough steel to come out in the black. But "the nub of the (Kefauver Committee's) analysis," Daniel Bell wrote, "as applied specifically to the wage-price situation in 1957...is that when wages went up, prices—and profits—went up *even higher*.... In brief, it was quite clear that the steel companies had used their negotiations as an excuse for boosting prices, in order to jack up their profit margins."[16]

In additon, as Kefauver discovered, U.S. Steel used the negotiations with the union as a screen to raise the salaries of its white-collar executives 37 percent higher than what the union members won in their new contract. While negotiations with the union were reported in the press, this salary hike was not made public. In effect, the union was blamed for forcing the cost of labor up when most of the benefits went to the non-union executive staff. This too, was a typical pattern. Between 1950 and 1960, the median wage for union and non-unionized workers rose 39 percent while salaries for executives rose 68 percent.[17] Yet it was the worker whose wage demands were negotiated in public who got blamed for the rise in prices.

Workers with strong union representation managed to keep up with rising prices. In 1948, the UAW introduced the idea of a cost-of-living escalator clause as a hedge against inflation, and by 1950 this idea was included in a number of industrial contracts. The steelworkers won an employer-financed pension plan in 1949, and by 1954 about 12 million unionized workers were covered by health and pension plans. Though these union members were protected, members of weaker unions were not, and the great body of unorganized workers fell further behind, often earning the federal minimum wage.

Labor Accepts the Status Quo

An attempt by the CIO and the AFL to organize the Southern textile industry in the late 1940s was the high point of labor's effort to recruit in non-union industries. The brief, unsuccessful textile campaign was motivated by the South's historic position as a non-union haven for northern manufac-turers seeking lower production costs. White racism, as well as rural distrust of unions in general, made it difficult to unite white and black workers in a common cause. White organizers could not openly meet with black workers, and blacks organized in the

South at the risk of their lives. A tradition of violence—tacitly accepted (and at times encouraged) by Southern lawmen and FBI agents—prevented black/white cooperation. The rivalry between the CIO and the AFL did not make the organizing task any easier. The CIO had split from the AFL in 1937 because of the latter's refusal to organize unions on a trade or industry-wide basis. The craft-oriented AFL was also more interested in bread and butter union issues than in reform. After the war, the AFL decided to compete with the CIO for new members, and organizers from both federations headed for the mill towns of the South. Almost at once, the AFL began to red-bait the CIO in order to curry favor with corporate leaders. "Let me give Southern industry this warning," AFL president William Greene said in 1946, "grow and cooperate with us or fight for your life against Communist forces." But anti-Communism, then, was not an issue, not even in the South. As one AFL organizer commented in 1946, "Hell, these folks down here don't even know what rheumatism is, much less Communism."[18] The AFL also used the CIO's progressive civil rights record to appeal to Southern racism. The rivalry made a difficult task impossible. The AFL abandoned its organizing effort by 1947; the CIO persisted until 1952 despite the virulence of southern racism but with few results. The failure to organize the South weakened the bargaining position of workers in the North, due to the constant threat of runaway shops.

As we have seen, after 1947 Communism did become an issue in the labor movement as it did everywhere else. The Republican victory in the 1946 congressional elections and the growing mood of Cold War reaction, forced the CIO to move closer to the mainstream of the Democratic Party, even though CIO leaders were not enamored of Harry Truman. (The CIO, in fact, had been Henry Wallace's main bulwark of support for the Vice Presidential nomination in 1944.) Left-wingers in the labor movement who supported Wallace's presidential campaign were now isolated from the majority in the CIO. The Progressive Party fiasco seemed to confirm the wisdom of the CIO's support of Truman. The New Deal was dead and the Communists, who had done so much to organize the CIO, were shown to be politically ineffectual.

The Taft-Hartley Act of 1947, passed by a conservative

Congress over President Truman' veto, was proof that the era of militant labor was over. Taft-Hartly seriously compromised labor's right to strike. It first provided for a 60-day cooling off period at the end of a contract during which time strikes were prohibited. This period could be extended another 80 days if, in the opinion of the President, a strike threatened "national security." (Between 1947 and 1959, Truman and Eisenhower invoked Taft-Hartly seventeen times, despite the fact that there was never a declaration of war to fulfill the requirements of national security.) The law also prohibited the use of mass-picketing to keep company-hired scabs out of a factory; outlawed secondary boycotts, a vital weapon in pressuring employers to settle a strike; outlawed the closed shop; and authorized state legislatures to adopt "right to work" laws banning even the union shop. Finally, Communists were prohibited from holding union office—an obvious violation of union democracy not to mention the Bill of Rights. To add insult to injury, all labor leaders had to file affidavits that they were not Communists.

In 1949 and 1950, the CIO expelled ten of its member unions, including the West Coast Longshoremen and the Mine, Mill, and Smelter Workers (featured in the movie *Salt of the Earth*). Other CIO unions were encouraged to raid the membership of the expelled unions. An eleventh union, with Communist leadership, the United Electrical Radio and Machine Workers (UE), quit the CIO when a rival union, the International Brotherhood of Electrical Workers (IUE), was set up to compete with it. UE, though it dwindled in size, persevered and earned a reputation as one of the more democratic unions in the country.*

As a result of the CIO's purge of its "Communists" many of its most active cadre, who at one time or another had been close to or members of the Communist Party, were lost. Beyond this,

---

*The UE was fiercely red-baited by both the government and industry. But UE was able to stay alive, in part, because some corporations saw the benefits of a divided union movement. Thus in 1955 when UE and IUE were contesting to represent the workers of the San-o-tone Corporation of White Plains, New York, executives were instructed "that in the present weakened condition of the UE, it is advantageous for the Company to deal with them... We urge our supervisors NOT TO DISCOURAGE any employee voting for the UE in the next election." (*The Great Fear* by David Caute, Simon and Schuster, 1978, pp. 280-282).

many independent radicals also suffered in the general purges. Those who weren't blacklisted from the labor movement had to stick to bread-and-butter issues lest they provoke suspicion. In some unions, especially the National Maritime Union (NMU), with its once strong Communist caucus, the purging of its left-wing led to a takeover by criminal elements. Other unions became involved in Cold War politics, assisting the CIA in working to tame the labor movements of France, Italy, and Latin America.

If Communism was considered the bane of the CIO, corruption was the plague of the more business-minded AFL. Unions like the International Longshoreman's Association (ILA), the Teamsters, and the Operating Engineers were riddled with gangsters and racketeers who pocketed members' money. Sometimes corruption and anti-Communism went hand-in-hand. From 1947 until he was exposed in 1953, ILA President Joseph P. Ryan regularly dunned shipping companies for a secret fund to keep Communist labor organizers off the docks. During this period, Ryan reportedly spent $48,725.18 to fight Communism. This sum included $2,331.60 for golf club fees, $10,794.85 for insurance premiums, $942.30 to repair his Cadillac, and $546.15 for a luncheon at the Stork Club, a posh New York restaurant whose owner, Sherman Billingsley, was notorious for hiring scab labor and opposing unionism.[19] The longshoremen were expelled from the AFL in 1953 after public hearings and the movie *On The Waterfront* made them a public scandal. In 1956, the Teamsters and two smaller unions received the boot. The next year a Senate committee headed by Senator John McClellan, with Robert Kennedy as chief counsel, began investigating corruption in unions like the Teamsters. Their leaders were shown to be exercising dictatorial rule, embezzling union funds, taking bribes from industry to stay out of certain plants, and—a Teamster specialty—signing "sweetheart" contracts that profited both the employers and the union officials at the expense of the workers.

The CIO's political purge and the AFL's initiation of steps to limit corrupt practices helped clear away the obstacles to a merger of the two organizations. The united AFL-CIO formed in 1957, gave the House of Labor more centralized leadership and political influence. But the virtues of the CIO's independence—

its social reformism and its support of black workers—were compromised by the AFL's conservative bread-and-butter unionism. Especially in the skilled crafts, which were the backbone of the federation, the AFL remained an alliance of closed guilds that prevented outsiders from entering high-paying fields. Since they no longer competed with each other for members and influence, there was no incentive for the CIO to challenge the AFL to become more democratic, or for either to go out and organize the unorganized and unemployed.

Automation and the Triumph of Management

Wartime research, especially in the new glamour field of electronics, further threatened job security. The theory and use of feedback received extensive scientific study directed toward the development of self-regulating systems and devices for the control of military equipment. Out of this work came the technology that made automation possible. In the November 1946 issue of *Fortune,* two physicists, E. W. Leaver and J. J. Brown wrote about the coming revolution in cybernetics. "Nowhere is modern man more obsolete than on the factory floor," they prophesied. "Modern machines are far more accurate and untiring than men."[20] In 1947 a Ford executive coined the word "automation" to describe the replacement of human workers by machines in the production process. What would become of the worker automated out of a job? This was not the concern of the engineers who created the new technology or the corporations who employed them.

Up until the early twentieth century, engineers came directly out of the workplace; an ingenious and highly motivated mechanic or craftsman could rise out of the shop floor into a position in management, especially in new fields like the auto, chemical, electrical, and aircraft industries where inventiveness was required. As the fields became more complex, however, large corporations helped establish technical schools and, through financial grants, encouraged existing universities to establish engineering curriculums. And the corporations had a profound influence on the way engineering was taught. Just as agricultural scientists in the state universities were paid to solve the problems of agribusiness, engineers were encouraged to work with the technological needs of the corporation rather than the public needs of the broader society. More than technical priorities were involved. Through professional societies, the influence of their teachers, and the career choices open to them, engineering students were encouraged to see themselves as future managers, not as part of the working class.[21]

Throughout the twentieth century, as assembly line techniques, mechanization and finally automation evolved, knowledge and therefore control of the workplace passed from the skilled worker through the engineer into the hands of corporate management. The resulting technology benefited the corporation while often reducing workers to the performance of boring, mindless, and repetitive tasks, hour after hour, week after week. The unions suffered too. Between 1948 and 1961, the number of production workers in manufacturing industries declined by about 1.5 million, while the number of white collar workers in those same industries increased by about the same number. While total union membership did increase somewhat in the postwar era (from 14.3 million in 1945 to 18 million in 1964), as a percentage of the labor force, it declined. Having no input into management affairs, weakened by internal strife, having purged or silenced its most militant members, the labor movement could only respond to automation defensively, fighting a rear-guard struggle to salvage jobs while management completed its hegemony over the shop floor.

The inability of the unions to counter management prerogatives in the workplace led to an outbreak of wildcat strikes, most notably in the auto industry from 1953 to 1955 as workers resisted a corporate decision to speed up production of cars from 48-50 an hour to more than 60.[22] The rash of unauthorized work stoppages was an indication that the labor bureaucracy—even in the UAW, which was one of the more democratic unions—was losing touch with the rank-and-file worker. Bureaucracy, perhaps, was inevitable as the unions became entrenched in their various industries. But the decline of labor militancy also contributed to the growth of an unresponsive hierarchical labor establishment. The importance of the shop steward declined. In the formative days of the labor movement, the shop steward, who was popularly elected by co-workers, collected dues and argued employee rights directly on the factory floor. The check-off system, in which union dues were deducted like social security from the employee's pay check, diminished personal contact between steward and rank-and-file worker. An elaborate system for adjudicating grievances stripped the steward of his power to speak up for the worker on the shop floor.

Labor coped with automation in different ways. The railroad firemen, for instance, insisted that their members remain on the trains even though machines did their work and they were along merely for the ride. Negotiations, commencing in 1959, allowed firemen to go along on 10 percent of all trips. This kind of featherbedding greatly increased railroad costs at a time when the government subsidized trucking industry was becoming the dominant form of transportation, and it also demoralized railroad workers, those once heroic figures of the American past.

More constructive was an agreement reached by Kaiser Steel and the United Steelworkers of America that resulted from a 113-day strike in 1959. This enabled employees to share in the savings from automation and increased productivity, and created an employment pool that employees who were automated out of jobs would belong to while receiving full wages. Another result of automation was a move for a shortened work week from 40 to 37 or 35 hours, which many workers began to get in the 1960s with no cut in their weekly pay.

Some unions, like the United Mineworkers, attempted to adjust to mechanization. In 1948, UMW President John L. Lewis won from the coal operators a royalty of 5 cents a ton to be used for hospitals and pensions. Later, the royalty rose to 40 cents a ton and the union built modern hospitals throughout the coal fields of the Eastern United States. Lewis also encouraged mechanization in deep mine and strip mine procedures, investing union money in corporation-owned mining operations. There was much to be said for Lewis' policy, for coal mining was hard dangerous work. Moreover, with the increase of imported Middle Eastern oil, the market for coal was declining in comparison with the tremendous increase in petroleum use. Lewis figured that it would be advantageous to have fewer men doing easier work at better wages than to have a larger workforce doing dangerous pick-and-shovel work at the risk of life, limb, and ultimate layoff.

But Lewis, who had little accountability to the rank-and-file, made a number of tragic miscalculations. As automation increased and miners were laid off, the UMW lost its membership base. No provision was made to find jobs for the unemployed miners. The corporations felt no responsibility for bringing in new industry and retraining ex-miners, and the federal government, until President Johnson's War on Poverty, also refused to intervene. Moreover, strip mining carved up the topography of the Appalachian coalfields, destroyed the ecology, and made even subsistence farming (a traditional sideline of Appalachian miners) impossible. Like the poor farmers of the black South, these mostly white miners were forced to migrate to urban areas where they created their own ghettos and were forced into low-paying jobs. As the demand for coal lessened, the Appalachian economy fell apart. Gradually, the UMW had to cut back on its welfare services and deny free hospital care to the unemployed miners who were no longer on its books. Eventually, in the early 1960s, the UMW had to abandon the hospitals, which in many areas were the only places where working people could get medical treatment, and the coalfields of Appalachia became symbols of poverty.

Whither the Working Class?

What became then of working people? The better paying unionized jobs, such as in auto and steel, offered security and a measure of middle-class affluence at the price of workaday boredom. Many workers, of course, wanted out of factory work, but the traditional alternatives, small business and farming, were increasingly closed to them. It took too much capital to start a farm, and small businesses were being squeezed out by supermarkets and other corporate retail establishments. So most workers hung on, waiting for their pensions if they were lucky enough to have them, biding their time: "thirty years and out" as the saying went. Meanwhile, what Stanley Aronowitz described as "the suppressed desire for work" continued to spill out in dozens of creative ways. The "do-it-yourself" craze in the working-class suburbs, the tinkering on cars, the care of backyard gardens and lawns—these expressed the continuous search to find expression and satisfaction in meaningful work.[23]

All the while, the labor movement continued to atrophy. Union members appreciated the economic standing it helped them win, but there was no call to rally the troops to fight for other social reforms or even organize the unorganized. The Landrum-Griffin Act of 1959 was conclusive evidence of labor's decline. Landrum-Griffin gave the federal government the power to intervene in union affairs for the purpose of combating corruption. Besides prohibiting criminals from holding union office, the law required labor to file regular financial reports and spelled out the rights of rank-and-file members that the leadership had to respect. For all its good features, Landrum-Griffin confirmed the diminished power that labor held within American society. For there was no equivalent law that allowed the government to meddle in corporate affairs and to routinely seek out corporate corruption. The few laws against monopoly and illegal trading practices were old and musty. The businessmen in the Eisenhower administration were opposed to their use, and the Democrats understood that corporate power had become so institutionalized that an authentic trust-busting campaign would destroy the economy. Against the awesome might of the big corporations, labor in the postwar period succeeded in winning economic security for a select number of member-workers. But its power as an independent force for social reform and economic justice throughout the whole society was lost in the process.

Chapter Ten

> *The stabilities of the family and the neigh-*
> *borhoods are the basic sources of all higher*
> *forms of morality, and when they are*
> *lacking, the whole ediface of civilization is*
> *threatened.*
>
> —*Lewis Mumford in*
> The Urban Prospect, 1962

> *The modern American family is the small-*
> *est and most barren family that ever*
> *existed. Each newly married couple moves*
> *to a new house or apartment—no uncles or*
> *grandmothers come to live with them.*
> *There are seldom more than two or three*
> *children. The children live with their peers*
> *and leave home early. Many have never had*
> *the least sense of family.*
> —*Gary Snyder in* Earth Household, 1969

"Americans tend to regard the small conjugal unit of husband, wife, and children so characteristic of our society, as perfectly 'natural,'" wrote sociologist Robin M. Williams in 1960, "but it is very special. In most simpler societies the kinship unit is a larger group, often including several generations and various collateral branches and having much greater family continuity than in our society."[1] The modern nuclear family evolved along with modern industrial society. As such, it was shaped by the demands of industrial society, which, in turn, developed to fit the requirements of the larger corporations.

Large corporations benefited from the nuclear arrangement because in stripping the family of its historical continuity and reducing it into an isolated fragment in time, it opened the family up to the introduction of a commodity culture that could be shaped through advertising and media models. Except on the family farms and in small business (which were also victims of this corporate drive), the family became primarily a consuming unit. Its economic value, as well as its social standing in the community, came not from what it produced, but from what it spent and the products it bought. Isolated in time, the nuclear family existed tenuously in the present, for however long the husband and wife stayed together. It had no tradition, no past, and no values of its own to convey to future generations.[2] Vulnerable to any message that offered it a sense of security and historical meaning, the nuclear family was susceptible to the corporate message of status, affluence, privatism, and consumerism which filled an ideological vacuum in the changing social environment.

Before the war, it was not uncommon for relatives to live near one another, in the same neighborhood or the same town. The rush to the suburbs, urban renewal, the disappearance of small towns and family farms all disrupted this familial pattern. Americans have always been mobile, but in the postwar era mobility became more the rule than the exception. And as individual nuclear families broke free from the web of more extended familial relationships, isolation and insecurity tended to increase.

An exaggerated sense of privacy, especially among the new affluent and middle classes, encouraged this feeling of insecurity which often bordered on paranoid fear. In a sense, this represented the national neurosis brought home to roost. Insecurity in international affairs led to a reliance on a gigantic military machine and nuclear overkill. Instead of ameliorating insecurity, however, this only added to it. The prescription for its cure was more weapons, hence more fear. In the family, isolation and an engrossment with privacy bred a similar fear of the outside world. Behind closed doors of a car or home, the world seemed threatening. The competition ethic, the status syndrome, the emphasis on personal wealth—all enhanced the importance of private property in the narrowest sense and added to this insecurity. Each family dwelling became a safe harbor in a hostile world, a fortress against strangers and the unfamiliar. The remedy? Not to venture forth into the world to examine the source of fear, but more locks on windows and doors, more privacy, further isolation.

Yet this was unnatural, not only to Americans, but for the human spirit. Left to their own organic development, people tend to be cooperative, to seek out and get along in group situations. In times of natural disaster or in commonly perceived emergencies, people act on this instinct and rally together. They need no coaxing or outside leadership. Mutual aid is spontaneous, leadership emerges. Floods and hurricanes have always brought out the best in the American people, allowed their natural generosity to take social form. People often remember times of disaster with a certain nostalgia. In everyday life, this spirit of sharing is stifled. For cooperation runs counter to the rugged individualism of a competitive capitalist culture. The isolated nuclear family, viewing the world with abnormal distrust, became the perfect counterpart of a materialistic society.

Fragmentation of Family Life

The family has always been the bedrock of a stable, harmonious society. When the family unit starts to break apart, it is an indication of grave social disorder. Families, tribes, and clans of the preindustrial age reflected a balanced way of life that unified the economic function within the social fabric. In an agrarian society, the sharing of work bound the family together; the same was true of localized cottage industry and the communal enterprise of large clans and tribes. Large families were obviously desirable and the household that included an assortment of relatives of various ages had an advantage. The individual roles may have been rigid and were certainly bound by sexist perimeters. But there was a unity to the way each member of the family contributed that need not have been abandoned in the development of more equal and diversified social roles. Aging was a process of life, and everyone contributed something to the family unit, young and old. Kids did the simple chores and were educated by any number of people each teaching the skills s/he knew best. Elderly members had more sedentary tasks, even if these were just to give advice. Age was not a handicap and old folks were not put out to pasture at too early an age to waste slowly away.

In a society of slowly evolving technological advancement that is not wedded to the idea of inevitable progress, old people are valued for their experience and their recollections of past events. In that way, ancient wisdom and collective experience are not rendered obsolete, but are valued as an important part of contemporary knowledge. In postwar America, however, old folks had no useful role.* Youth was idealized, and everything was advertised as new or better. Socialization to American values meant a rejection of the immigrant past or the native rural past with their emphasis on thrift, hard work, and family life. The pace of change made it hard for old people, used to more simple lives with fewer gadgets, to keep up. So, during the postwar period, the older generation began to be farmed out into old age homes, where they came under professional if indifferent help, or to live in clusters of retirement homes in Florida or the Southwest.

This is but one example of the fragmentation of family life—especially among the white middle class—that became so marked during the postwar years. The nuclear concept, celebrated by the media as a symbol of social strength, was but a thin

---

*Except in politics, where the entrenched position of old men is not due to any acquired wisdom that comes through the process of aging, but from the accumulation of power that increases with time and becomes unshakable with age.

disguise for society's atomization; its particles—mother, father, children—steadily splitting apart, finding support in their separate worlds: father at his place of work, children with their peers, mother from the media, which alone gave her some sense of importance. And to compensate, people yearned for an all-embracing idea, a concept that could deny reality and give them the illusion of the community that was not there. Just as a comedian may crack jokes to hide sadness, Americans fastened onto the idea of "togetherness" to deny loneliness.

The Myth of Togetherness

In 1954, the editors of *McCall's* magazine were batting around editorial ideas for improved promotion and increased circulation. Eureka! They came up with the word "togetherness" which, introduced in the May 1954 issue, described what the editor and publisher, a man named Otis Lee Wiese, called "the Life of *McCall's*." Women today "are not a sheltered sex," he wrote. They are marrying earlier, raising larger families, and sharing in unprecedented affluence. Women have greater opportunities in life than ever before. "But the most impressive and the most heartening feature of this change is that men, women and children are achieving it *together*. They are creating this new and warmer way of life not as women *alone* or men *alone*, isolated from one another, but as a *family* sharing a common experience."[3]

The *McCall's* theme struck a vital chord among the white middle class, and "togetherness" soon became a catchword, caricatured in *New Yorker* cartoons, discussed earnestly in Sunday sermons, and hashed out daily by media psychologists and advice-to-the-lovelorn columnists. "For a time," wrote Betty Friedan, togetherness "was elevated into virtually a national purpose."[4] As a verbal concept, togetherness neatly bridged what was real with what was missing. It represented a concern with material comforts, affluence, security, familial well-being. The public duty of the average citizen to be informed on public issues and to take part in the political life of the nation, which until now had been an essential part of the American myth, was discredited. The emphasis now was on the family and its internalized needs. But words could not create what contemporary culture was destroying. The nuclear family, as a basic unit of society, just would not hold.

The fragmentation of the family accelerated in the United States with the decline of agriculture, small towns, and neighborhood life. But the postwar years intensified the process. There is no statistical measure for this disintegration. Divorce rates, which spurted upward immediately after the war and then leveled off to between two and three per thousand, do not take into consideration the unhappy marriages that remained intact for the sake of the children, fear of social pressure, the convenience of habit, or religious sanctions. During the 1950s divorce was still a serious matter, and a sign of personal failure. It was only in the 1960s that the marriage bond loosened up and divorce rates skyrocketed. By the 1970s, serial monogamy had become commonplace in many segments of society.

A better indication of family disintegration, one which cannot be measured by statistics but which is obvious to any observer of the American scene, was the alienation of the young and their rebellion against the life that they grew up under during the postwar years. The beatniks and the teen-age juvenile delinquents of the 1950s were an advance warning of a generation gap to come. The way of life that developed in the postwar era, that was touted as being the best possible way to live, remained unchallenged for just one generation. The more creative children who grew up as part of it did not like the experience and chose to experiment with new ways of living as they came of age. Millions followed.

Fragmentation was generated by the suburban experience, a social revolution that the rhetoric of togetherness could not undo. The first people to move to the suburbs, as we have seen, were the younger, upwardly mobile white professional and executive classes. In leaving the old neighborhood or town for the treeless tracts of suburban sprawl, they left behind a carefully evolved set of family and neighborhood living patterns that had constituted the fabric of their immediate world. This culture remained behind to wither. Friends and relations did not move to the same suburban neighborhood or at the same time. The older people, perhaps, remained behind in their old neighborhoods, now on the decline, while younger relatives and neighbors scattered all across the suburban landscape. Old ties fractured and families drifted apart.

In the old neighborhoods, the family looked outward and was part of a dynamic culture. In the suburbs, community gatherings for the family as a whole were few and far between. Children had their activities, men had their organizations, women had charitable and service clubs all their own. When the family met together as a social unit it gathered alone. Usually it was to watch television. A way of life that had guided people for generations, that had provided them with their only sense of roots in the transient American experience, had come to an abrupt end.

Patriarchy and the Corporate Community

The head-of-household breadwinning male provided the suburban family with its framework of existence. The family basked in *his* success or was left behind in the race for status by *his* failure. Charged with the responsibility of being a good provider and thereby giving the family its definition was an ulcer-producing, coronary-provoking, death-inviting task.* The man had few household chores and almost nothing to do with child raising except on weekends when he was supposed to exert his authority as titular head. His life revolved almost entirely around his work—so much so that the values of work were often brought into the home. Public relations, as Norman Podhoretz noted in 1953, was the essential characteristic of the father's role.[5] Ralph Kramden and Archie Bunker—as working class husbands—were allowed to express authentic emotions, to get angry at other family members; but not Robert Anderson of the white middle class. What a price men paid for their authority! But despite the difficulties of living up to the expected masculine role, men sought it eagerly. If nothing else, it gave them identity and purpose. It also provided an illusion of potency that reinforced their belief in patriarchy. And the supremacy of the male animal and his "natural right" to rule was something that men would not give up willingly, no matter what its cost.

---

*Between 1949 and 1961, the life expectancy for white males at birth rose hardly at all, from 66.31 years to 67.55. By contrast, figures for white women were 72.03 and 74.19 years.

But the patriarchy of the postwar years was an illusion, and men often became petty as they strived to act as patriarchs. The father, oppressed by his job, got his potency back by oppressing the family. But the oppression served no social function. It could last only as long as women collaborated, and that collaboration, so definitive during the 1950s, was destined to end. There is no greater despot than the king who feels shaky on his throne. The postwar middle-class male, locked into the expectations of his corporate life, saw his natural domain, the family, retreating from his grasp. Anxious, he fought to get it back. Women during the post-war years would suffer most from the desperation of this male-perceived failing. The feminist ideal of women in their own right becoming self-fulfilled human beings retrogressed to conditions that resembled the anti-female ideology of the late nineteenth century.

Anti-Feminism

The anti-feminist ideology of the postwar period was an arbitrary reversal of the process of historic evolution. Independent women, admired during the 1930s and during the war, were now looked upon as neurotic freaks. A woman's place was in the home, dependent on her husband, passive and "femme". In one respect the experience of women during this time paralleled that of the small farmer and the blue-collar worker. At a time when technology was becoming available to take back-breaking labor out of agriculture and industry, the independent farm family was forced off the land and the skilled worker enslaved to the assembly line. Modern appliances, in theory, freed women from household drudgery. Technological advance encouraged independence; ideology alone kept women locked at home.

Myths like togetherness could not mask the fact that women bore the brunt of the middle-class doldrums. More so than at any time since the Victorian Age, women were to define themselves through a patriarchal vision intended to uphold male privilege. Feminism itself came under vicious attack; as a movement it was virtually wiped out. Like anti-Communism, anti-feminism became orthodoxy. If leftist ideas had the taint of treason to them, feminist beliefs were dismissed as neurotic. Women were not only expected to accept a male definition of themselves; they were expected to like it as well. Progress, which was a religion to Americans in every other area of life, ceased when it came to women. Proof of male superiority was in the Bible or, for secularists, went back to the Old Stone Age, as described by male anthropologists. For those few women who rebelled and demanded for themselves an independent life, a patriarchal psychological establishment, using the authority of science, was ready to pronounce them antisocial and maladjusted.

The feminist counter-revolution began, as we have seen, with the ending of the war emergency and the rising din of an all-male chorus insisting that women should leave the workplace and find happiness in the home. This economic demand received a boost in 1947 with the popularity of the book *Modern Women: The Lost Sex*, by Ferdinand Lundberg and Marynia F. Farnham. The goal of female sexuality, proclaimed the authors, is "receptivity and passiveness, a willingness to accept dependence without fear or resentment, with a deep inwardness and readiness for the final goal of sexual life—impregnation." Those women who do not accept this idea of femininity "constitute the array of the sick, unhappy, neurotic, wholly or partly incapable of dealing with life....They have always been known and dimly recognized for what they are—the miserable, the half-satisfied, the frustrated, the angered." What is more, the authors contended, hitting below the belt with an assertion that had no foundation in any scientific study (and was convincingly refuted by the Kinsey Report of 1957), feminists of an earlier day, "when they came to perform the sexual act found that they were frigid." Not content to threaten liberated women with an unsatisfactory sex life, the authors also equated feminism with Communism and warned that "although the Russians in recent years will have nothing of feminism, the political agents of the Kremlin abroad continue to beat the femininst drums in full awareness of its disruptive influence among the potential enemies of the Soviet Union" the aim being "to promote the theories of feminism and what it can of neurotic disorder on the already highly neurotic capitalist world."[6]

Between World War II and the publication of Betty Friedan's *Feminine Mystique* in 1963, only two feminist books appeared in print to offer an alternative vision of women's place in the world. In 1947 Ruth Herschberger in *Adam's Rib* argued that because a society teaches women to be passive and to repress physical desire, it conditions them to be sexually frigid and emotionally frustrated. *Adam's Rib* received little critical attention. *The Second Sex*, by the French author Simone de Beauvoir, appeared in English translation in 1953, sold widely, and was much discussed. *The Second Sex* described the subjugation of women in all spheres of life. A few critics agreed with its basic premise; most did not. "It always borders on the paranoid," wrote a reviewer in the *Atlantic Monthly*, while the liberal *Nation* warned that "because of certain [leftist] political leanings, Mme. de Beauvoir has to be read with critical caution."[7] For the psychiatric establishment, Dr. Karl Menninger described *The Second Sex* as "a pretentious and inflated tract on feminism. Hence, it is intrinsically tiresome....and not good scientific writing."[8] Nevertheless, the book had a profound impact on the women who read it and for whom it confirmed the unarticulated desperation they felt in their own lives.

These two books were but a ripple in a sea of relentless propaganda to the effect that a woman's place was in the home, that her normal role was nurturing children and caring for her husband, and that any show of independence, ambition or artistic spirit represented "penis-envy," a "masculine complex," and a neurotic hatred of self. The point of the togetherness myth was to give the housewife the aura of importance. Instead of encouraging women to create lives of their own, it attempted to make the home life the most vital point of existence and to claim that the male head of the household really yearned for this kind of domestic bliss.

The intensity of the attack on feminist ideas contrasted boldly with the image of womanhood during the Depression and the war when the media accepted the idea of strong, independent women. Radio soap opera, for example, consistently offered listeners images of career-oriented women. In a time of economic scarcity, a country cannot afford to place its women on a pedestal as sex objects or as clotheshorses for the latest fashions. Hence: "Dr. Kate," a serial about a woman doctor; "Her Honor, Nancy James," a woman judge; "Hilda Hope, MD"; "Joyce Jordan, Girl Intern," who after four years on the air graduated in 1942 to "Joyce Jordan, MD"; "The Life and Loves of

Dr. Susan"; "Portia Faces Life," about a woman lawyer; "The Romance of Helen Trent," about a fashion designer whose lovers invariably end up meeting mysterious, violent deaths; "Bess Johnson," about the female superintendent of a boarding school called Hilltop House; "Mary Marlin," who was a U.S. Senator; a western soaper called "Valiant Lady, A Woman of America"; "Prudence Dane," the editor of a newspaper whose serial was subtitled "Woman of Courage"; and "Ma Perkins," the operator of a small town lumber yard, which began on WNBC in 1933 and lasted through 7,065 broadcasts until television did it in after 27 years.[9] Even the comic books had a feminist orientation. Wonder Woman, with her matriarchal Amazonian society, began in 1941 and inspired Nyoka, the Jungle Woman, the female equivalent of Tarzan; and Mary Marvel, the high-flying little sister of Captain Marvel, who was himself fashioned after the most popular comic book hero of all time, Superman.

Heroines in prewar and wartime women's magazines were usually young women pursuing adventures or careers. But in the postwar period, the content of the influential women's magazines like the *Ladies Home Journal, Redbook,* and *McCall's* accurately reflected the new values. Earlier, they had published frequent articles on politics and world affairs. But by the 1950s, political concerns were limited to Princess Margaret's love life, the comings and goings of the Duchess of Windsor, and the way Mamie Eisenhower was decorating the White House. Instead of quality fiction, a new generation of popular magazine writers ground out stories on topics such as "Feminity Begins at Home," "Do Women Have to Talk So Much?," "What Women Can Learn From Mother Eve," "Really a Man's World, Politics," "Cooking to Me Is Poetry," and "The Business of Running a Home." Even actresses, who during the 1950s were the most obvious examples of independent women, were domesticated by the print media. Their art was often disparaged, if not ignored. Typically, Judy Holliday, the brilliant comedienne, was described in a 1957 story in *Redbook* as having "strong feelings of inadequacy as a woman" because of a recent divorce. Her career was taken for granted. "It is a frustrating irony of Judy's life that as an actress she has succeeded almost without trying, although, as a woman, she has failed."[10]

Despite the growing demand for professional people and

scientists, the number of female college students, in relation to male students, dropped from 47 percent in 1920 to 35 percent in 1958, and more than half of their number dropped out before graduation to support husbands or become housewives.[11] A 1956 study at Vassar College emphasized how completely female students had adjusted to their designated roles. Vassar was an elite school with a strong tradition of feminism and political activism. Its intellectual standards were high and its students usually had the financial independence to pursue any goal in life. But instead of seeking adventure, careers, or a life of their own, they opted for what Betty Friedan called the feminine mystique.

> Strong commitment to an activity or career other than that of housewife is rare. Many students, perhaps a third are interested in graduate schooling and in careers, for example teaching. Few, however, plan to continue with a career if it should conflict with family needs....As compared to previous periods, e.g., the "feminist era," few students are interested in the pursuit of demanding careers, such as law or medicine, regardless of personal or social pressures. Similarly, one finds few instances of people like Edna St. Vincent Millay, individuals completely committed to their art by the time of adolescence and resistent to any attempts to tamper with it....[12]

Life magazine's image of happy college graduates in 1956 were women "recently married to boys still studying for advanced degrees. These girls are surely neither dissatisfied nor grumbling. Instead, they are cheerfully working in bookshops or libraries, business firms, or hospitals, or even in part time domestic service, to help pay the bills until their husbands can finish their study or research."[13]

Women played an equally servile role in the political world. "Their work is mostly, and indispensably, at the grass roots level," said *Life*. "In the fever of campaigns they do at least as much as men to process mail, collect money, get out the vote and watch the polls."[14] In other words, what *Life* meant was, they do shitwork. Speaking to the graduating class of Smith College in 1956, Adlai Stevenson, with his usual wit, summed up the importance of women in public affairs. "Once they wrote poetry," he said. "Now it's the laundry list. Once they discussed art and philosophy until late in the night. Now they are so tired they fall asleep as soon as the dishes are finished." But the situation was not hopeless. Stevenson was encouraging. "Women in the home" can "have an important political influence on man and boy," he said. "I think there is much you can do about our crisis in the humble role of housewife. I could wish you no better vocation than that."[15]

The Humanist Challenge

In *The Feminine Mystique*, Betty Friedan wrote that just as "Victorian culture did not permit women to accept or gratify their basic sexual needs, our culture does not permit women to accept or gratify their basic need to grow and fulfill their potentialities as human beings."[16] But the will to self-fulfillment is irrepressible. In the postwar years, a humanist school of psychology began to place traditional psychoanalytical theory under social and political scrutiny and provide clinical support for society's non-conformists, including young people and women. Carl Rogers, Kurt Goldstein, Wilhelm Reich, Gordon Allport, Rollo May, Erich Fromm, Paul Goodman, Fritz and Lore Pearls, and especially Abraham Maslow were important in the development of this Third Force psychology.* Though their psychoanalytical techniques differed and they tended to emphasize different aspects of the human condition, all shared the important insight that in a mass society, rebellion, dissent and nonconformity could be taken as a positive sign of mental health and that the burden of psychological problems did not necessarily rest with the individual but could be traced directly to the workings of society.

Until this time, the hold that the Freudian psychoanalytical establishment had on American thought was complete. The problem was not so much the writing of Sigmund Freud. Just as some American leftists took the work of Karl Marx and turned it into a rigid body of sacred thought, American psychologists turned Freud's pioneering inquiries into the functioning of the human mind into a scientific dogma that could not be questioned.

*Freudianism was the first force; behaviorism the second.

Except for the equally doctrinaire behaviorists, the Freudians had little opposition. As Hobart Mowrer, a former president of the American Psychological Association put it, "Anyone who reached adulthood prior to 1950 knows how perversely Freudian theory and practice dominated not only in the specific field of psychotherapy, but also education, jurisprudence, religion, child rearing, and art and literature, and social philosophy."[17] At a time when psychoanalysis was for the first time available to the middle class, Freud's impact was pervasive.

Freudian psychology emphasized the darker aspects of humanity. According to Freud, human beings were driven by base, animal instincts. Hatred and aggression were the primary qualities of human conduct. The function of civilized society was to provide strictures against humankind's barbaric conduct. "Culture," wrote Freud, "has to call up every possible reinforcement to erect barriers against the aggressive instincts of men...."[18] Culture, as the American neo-Freudian determined, was meant to keep people in line. Thus, the psychologically healthy person was the one who repressed base desires and conformed happily to the social requirements of American society. As the standards of society define what is normal, any deviation from the norm becomes a symptom of psychological disorder.

The war experience, as it reinforced the Freudian view that humankind was instinctively murderous, also brought into question the nature of civilization and what exactly constitutes a normal, healthy society. The question begged asking: in an evil society like that of Nazi Germany, what does the "good" German do? Does s/he conform to the expectations of that society or become a misfit, a non-conformist, a rebel? Was a well-adjusted Nazi a healthy individual? Was a nonconforming anti-Nazi neurotic? What does it mean to be well adjusted to a corrupt society? Humanist psychology suggested answers that emphasized individual responsibility against societal consensus. While the established Freudians considered the inability (which was often a refusal) of women to adjust to their limited role as a symptom of neurotic behavior, humanist psychologists, viewing the same situation, reversed the perception. They saw unhappy women trying to adjust to repressive customs, denying their own human potential in order to fit in. The healthy response in this situation, they felt, was to encourage rebellion and to view non-conformity as a sign of health. To the humanists, the onus was on society; women (or anyone else) struggling for their own psychological survival were on the right track.[19]

During the late 1950s, it became obvious that the American housewife who supposedly had the best of everything was frustrated and unhappy. The myth of togetherness was soon forgotten, and the focus of women's magazines began to shift to women's problems and the increasing evidence of female discontent. In 1957 Betty Friedan, on a writing project to discover what had become of the members of her own graduating class of Smith College 15 years earlier, began to perceive a pattern of frustration and failure. "There was a strange discrepancy between the reality of our lives as women and the image to which we were trying to conform, the image that I came to call the feminine mystique," she wrote later.[20] In expanding her research into book form, Friedan uncovered a nation of unhappy women, a situation that by 1960 had begun to surface even in the national media. As *Newsweek* wrote in March 1960, the American woman:

> is dissatisfied with a lot that women of other lands can only dream of. Her discontent is deep, pervasive, and impervious to the superficial remedies which are offered at every hand....A young mother with a beautiful family, charm, talent and brains....is apt to dismiss her role apologetically. "What do I do?" you hear her say .... "Why nothing. I'm just a housewife."[21]

The response of the media was to acknowledge this problem, but also to disparage it. Said *Newsweek*, "All admit to being deeply frustrated at times by the lack of privacy, the physical burden, the routine of family life, the confinement of it. However, none would give up her home and family if she had the choice to make again." And *Redbook* Magazine, seizing upon this new awareness, ran a contest in their September 1960 issue, offering $500 for the best account of "Why Young Mothers Feel Trapped." More than 24,000 women responded.[22]

By 1960 there was ample evidence of growing social discontent. What was happening to the nuclear family and causing disaffection among women was being felt by young people as well. There was a loosening of bonds, a sense of desperation, a feeling of despair. But despair is a prerequisite of growth. Acknowledging that there is a problem is a first step toward its solution. The clamor for self-fulfillment, for community, for the chance of a happy, meaningful life, could not be repressed forever. What was troubling women was endemic to society; with the organization man who sold himself for the illusory security of belonging to an organization in which he was merely a cog; in the kids who were bored by suburbia and resisted growing up in their parents' image; in the blacks who would no longer shuffle for survival; in the working class "greasers" who saw no future in dead-end working-class jobs and so opted for the immediate gratification of an early marriage and a souped-up car; in all the rootless people who yearned for that security that comes from a sense of place. The imposed order of the postwar era was beginning to crack.

Chapter Eleven

Waitress: "What are you rebelling against?"
Marlon Brando: "Whattaya got?"
—The Wild One, *1954*

A primary concern of the adult world is to educate the young to the values of the existing society and make them collaborators in an unchanging future. The burden of education—at home, in the media, and in the schools—is to initiate young people to the current orthodoxy and to instill in them a belief in all the traditions and mythologies that bind a society together.

Before the war, young people shared adult perceptions of a benevolent America. Even during the "Roaring Twenties," when the young introduced a hedonism that grated against the dominant puritan morality, their rebellion lacked political vision. Responding to premature signs of affluence that affected a small upper and upper-middle class elite, flappers and shieks set the style for the so-called "Jazz Age." But their understanding of America was not that different from the expectations of older Americans. They were merely the first to realize what was in every American's dreams.

In the postwar years, friction between the two generations seemed to have no root cause. To be alive and an American at the end of World War II was to have the best of everything. Middle class, white young people, in particular, seemingly had it made. Affluence was their inheritance, and their parents, scarred by the memories of the Depression, were committed to working themselves to the bone so that their children would never have to be economically insecure. Higher education became a middle class right and opened the door to professional and white collar jobs that translated into status, respectability, and economic security.

Yet there was another reality to postwar life. Alongside this new middle-class affluence was the fear of nuclear holocaust, the possibility of going to bed one night and never seeing daylight, of sleeping through the end of the world. Of course, fear of the bomb cut through generation lines. But adult America was used to dealing with crisis. The years between 1929 and 1945 had been one challenge after another, and the country had come through with flying colors. The threat of nuclear war could be met in the best Amerian tradition of courage, pragmatism, and business enterprise: air raid shelters, civil defense programs, a resurgence of patriotism, ideological conformity, and a powerful military machine that would deter others from making war. One Air Force general estimated that more than 10 million people would be killed instantly in a nuclear war. But he was confident that the U.S. would respond in kind, destroy the enemy, and win the war.[1] Young people lacked this confidence. Their future was open before them but it was completely out of their control. Moreover, they had missed the spirit of unity and accomplishment that older generations had experienced during the war. As the postwar years progressed, old mythologies began to fade—not only the ones that came out of the war, but also the venerable ones set forth in the history texts. The past was beginning to lose its hold and a new consumer-oriented mythology was being fostered in its place. But the new values were fragile. What was the meaning of life when it could be snuffed out on a moment's notice? What did affluence mean in the face of nuclear death? What good was postponed gratification when there might not be a tomorrow? Why work hard for a respectable career when in nuclear war even the spectacular glass office buildings would be reduced to rubble? These were not metaphysical abstractions. Who, growing up in the postwar years, did not have fears or nightmares about nuclear war death?

The Juvenile Delinquent as a Generational Hero

A rising rate of juvenile delinquency, along with a growing cult of violence, was the first indication that the socialization of young people was not going well. Or, put another way, it was going *too* well, and the young were learning the underlying values of postwar society while ignoring the glossy suburban image that supposedly represented the real thing.

Of course, juvenile delinquency was not new to the American scene; indeed it is present in almost every urban, industrial setting. But before the war, delinquency was closely connected to adult crime, and in the ethnic ghettos where it flourished it had a certain legitimacy. As the Little League was to organized baseball, teenage gangs were to organized crime: a minor league tryout camp for youthful prospects. Criminals, gangsters, and juvenile delinquents of this period were not so much alienated from society as they were barred from it. Before the war, positions of wealth and importance in all but a few specific fields (e.g. sports, entertainment, big-city politics, the garment industry) were reserved for WASPs. Ambitious and enterprising members of ethnic minorities often turned to criminal activities such as bootlegging, gambling, and drugs as outlets for their talent and energy. Many of them had considerable standing within their immediate community. Like the philanthropists of the corporate world, they were often generous with their money, supporting local charities and becoming pillars of their local church or synagogue. And just as young WASPs worked hard to impress potential benefactors in the corporate world, ghetto kids engaged in petty crime in order to show *their* potential employers, the leaders of the local crime syndicates, that they had the stuff for a successful career. A good job in crime, like an executive's career, was a sure path to the American dream, if only more risky. This was the context of delinquency in the prewar world. Whatever form it took— stealing, numbers running, narcotics dealing, or neighborhood battles with rival street gangs—it served a purpose within its immediate culture. It signaled no disrespect for adults or their authority; rather it reflected a desire to enter into the materialistic mainstream of American society.

Juvenile delinquency increased during the war, declined in the period between 1945 and 1950, and after 1950 proliferated to a national crisis.[2] The nature of this delinquency differed from the prewar. More and more it became intra-generational (teenage gangs fighting each other) or targeted against symbols of authority (young people joining together to attack the icons of adult society). Though only a small number of teenagers were ever actually involved in gang warfare or crimes of violence, delinquency was viewed as a national problem that cut across geographic, racial, ethnic, and class lines. Police in New York estimated that the number of dangerous delinquents in the city was no more than eight or nine thousand, but that another hundred thousand tottered on the brink of serious crime. It was not a matter of isolating a few bad apples. Writing about a gang called the Cobras in Brooklyn's Bedford Stuyvesant ghetto, journalist Harrison Salisbury of the *New York Times* noted that "the pattern of anti-social activity set by gangs like the Cobras casts a dark shadow over an ever-widening area of the nation— good neighborhoods and bad, small cities and large, New York, San Francisco, and Chicago." And, what gangs like the Cobras do today, he said, "teenagers in Great Neck, Long Island, or Beverly

Hills, California [two of the most affluent suburbs in the country] will consciously or unconsciously imitate and reflect tomorrow."³ The testimony of a police official of a small city in Washington state bore this out. "Gang warfare reared its ugly head in our community," he said, "and already reports have reached our ears of a number of beatings having taken place. Numerous weapons, inluding zip guns made from battery cables and car fan belts, along with a large collection of assorted knives and a homemade .22 caliber pistol or two have been seized from juveniles."⁴ Newspaper headlines told the extent of the crsis. TWO TEEN THRILL KILLINGS CLIMAX CITY PARK ORGIES. TEEN AGE KILLERS POSE A MYSTERY—WHY DID THEY DO IT? POLICE WONDER. YOUTH CONFESSES OHIO GIRL KILLING. 22 JUVENILES HELD IN GANG WAR. TEEN AGE MOB RIPS UP BMT TRAIN. CONGRESSMEN STONED, COPS HUNT TEEN GANG. These were only a few of the headlines in one year, 1954.⁵

Magazine articles like "Why Teenagers Go Wrong?" became commonplace and youth "experts" came into demand to provide answers. Working mothers were often blamed for its wartime outbreak, but this was a propaganda ploy to get women back into the home. As a political issue, liberals blamed slum housing and poverty, but the new housing projects made teenage crime even worse, and the suburbs had their share of delinquency too. Conservatives blamed disrupted family values, which was more to the point, and a breakdown in law and order. But, at the same time, they supported the consumerism and corporate values that were so baneful to family life. Their only remedy was more police. One psychiatrist, Fredric Wertham, made a career for himself as an anti-comic book crusader. The gory pictures and the emphasis on violence and crime, he insisted, encouraged kids to become delinquent.⁶ In Congress, Richard Clendenen, executive director of the Senate Subcommittee on Juvenile Delinquency, made much the same point:

> There is a very real possibility that these so-called comic books that are sold and read in this country at the rate of 22 million copies per month may be exerting an imponderable but delinquent producing influence upon a large number of relatively stable children.... Heavy exposure to violence and human suffering, even in

printed form, may lead to callous normal sensibilities and enable a person to engage in violence somewhat more readily.[7]

In self-protection, the comic book industry adopted a code that strictly regulated the degree and types of violence that could be depicted. The code also decreed sexual prudery in the comics. Some observers agreed with Wertham and Clendenen that media depiction of violence could lead to a breakdown in social order. But rather than limiting their critique to the printed word and movies as well, they pointed to the example of international violence and in particular the threat of nuclear weapons. Bertram Beck, the director of the Special Juvenile Delinquency Project of the Children's Bureau, wrote in 1954 that "the positive correlation between the rate of delinquency and war and cold war cannot be ignored. It is hard to instill those built-in controls of hostile behavior when children are being reared in a world that reeks of hostility and in which the whole economy is geared to the ultimate expression of hostility—death and destruction."[8]

Gang warfare certainly did mirror international affairs. Young people carved up their cities into little neighborhood-states for security and self-defense. Within each neighborhood a kind of patriotism was strong. A gang might feel about the local candy store hangout the way a country might feel about its capitol building. The threat of its desecration by an alien power would invariably lead to war. When gangs rumbled, they fought over control of "turf." As such, gang warfare had, within its own logic, a purpose as serious as World War II. Borders were carefully marked off: a street-corner here, a schoolyard there—every gang member knew where he or she (girls were organized into auxilieries and often served as weapons carriers in combat) was safe, and a gang member on alien turf had no more rights than a person traveling in a foreign country without a passport. Gangs were even structured on the government model with a president, vice-president, a minister of war who planned tactics and secured weapons, and a minister of state who negotiated with other gangs over boundaries, treaties, mutual security pacts, alliances, and cease-fires in time of war. As a form of combat, "rumbling" (or "bopping" as it was known in the black ghettos) differed little from the accepted methods of war.[9] The availability of weapons was the only crucial distinction. For rumbles, teenagers in postwar America chose from an arsenal of zip guns, shivs, leather garrison belts with razor sharp buckles, knucks, switchblades, knives, sticks, pipes, and occasionally a homemade pistol.* Otherwise, the structure of combat was the same. In time of "war," gangs even drafted neighborhood kids who were not actual members and served harsh punishment on those "draft dodgers" who chose to resist. Occasionally, however, a bright youth who was aloof from the gang, but whom everyone respected because they knew he was destined to make good and escape their environment, was deferred. The way gangs conducted their affairs indicated that their leaders, at least, were youngsters of high intelligence who understood perfectly the world around them. But their abilities were either unrecognized by adults in authority or, more often, not being put to positive use.

Gangs also fascinated the small minority of young people who liked to read. Among the first adult books that young people read during this time (often putting fake covers on them and reading them surreptitiously in school) were Irving Shulman's *Amboy Dukes* and *Cry Tough*, Harold Robbins' *A Stone for Danny Fisher* and *59 Park Avenue*, and Mickey Spillane's Mike Hammer dectective series that emphasized machismo, sex, violence, blood, and gore. *The Amboy Dukes*, a novel about a teenage gang in the Brownsville section of Brooklyn during the war years whose hero was serving his apprenticeship in crime, was published in 1946 and in its cheap paperback edition sold over 2 million copies. Shulman's follow-up novel, *Cry Tough*, had a paperback press run of 1,150,000 books between its first printing in March 1950 and its sixth printing in August 1951. In 1949, Hollywood released a movie version of *Cry Tough* entitled *City Across The River*. It made a profound impression on the young people who filled the neighborhood theatres every Saturday afternoon, and it anticipated the success that *Black-*

---

*The presence of homemade guns in the arsenal of many gangs suggests a mechanical ingenuity and gift for invention that was disappearing in other sectors of society and receiving little encouragement or support from the local schools, whose manuel trade classes were where schools dumped all the kids not headed for college.

board Jungle enjoyed in 1955 with the same urban gang-warfare themes.

Danny Fisher, which appeared in paperback in 1953, was to New York Jewish culture what James T. Farrell's earlier *Studs Lonigan* was to Irish Chicago. It chronicled the coming to age of a rather decent, moderately ambitious Brooklyn boy whose only way out of the web of poverty was to accept employment in organized crime. *59 Park Avenue*, about a call-girl ring in New York, was, for many, a basic primer on sex. Though the scenes were not at all explicit, the pages with the "hot parts" were folded down and worn out from over use. Who read these books? Not the gang members and juvenile delinquents themselves. For they didn't read. And except for *Danny Fisher*, none of these books gained much critical attention from the adult literary world. These low-cost paperbacks became, instead, cult books among the young. By some invisible grapevine that linked young people all across the country, white middle class youth with a literate bent, few of whom would dream of being in gangs themselves (they were too intimidated), knew about these books and identified with the characters.

In *Growing Up Absurd*, published in 1960, Paul Goodman argued that delinquency was predictable given the conditions of corporate society and the fact that there was nothing constructive or exciting for young people to do. Employment opportunities were directed at college-bound kids. They alone could foresee a future, though the world that awaited them held little attraction and led many to adopt a "rock" or "greaser" identity as a means of expressing their rejection. For the working-class young there was no evident way out of their situation. Work on an assembly line or some other blue collar and therefore low status job was all they could look forward to. Meanwhile, as teenagers there was little that was constructive to do. Changing urban patterns had made even the traditional after-school job difficult to find, and in the country there were fewer farms and therefore fewer chores to perform. In the cities, chain-store managers often did not live in the neighborhood where they worked; not knowing the kids on the block they could not hire them informally for odd jobs when their help was needed. The same held true in other fields. Fewer newspapers meant a cut-back in street vendors and home delivery jobs. Laws restricting adolescent employment, which were necessary to protect children from business exploitation, became stricter and better enforced. Craft unions demanded that workers hold union cards and this made it difficult for young people, especially those in minority groups, to learn a craft or a skilled trade. The adult world seemed a conspiracy aimed at denying the young responsibility. "I assume that the young *really* need a more worthwhile world in order to grow up at all," said Goodman, "and I confront this real need with the world they have been getting. This is the source of their problems. *Our* problem is to remedy the disproportion."[10]

Greasers and Rocks

Juvenile delinquency as a pose was as much a threat to society as were the incidents of gang warfare. The wierd style of "The Rock"—or in some parts of the country the "greaser," for his greasy haircut and his fondness for souped-up cars—that the young cultivated was seemingly aimed at mocking the organization man's crewcut and his unspectacular shirt, tie, and suit. Rocks had slicked-down ducktail haircuts (DAs), with each strand of hair kept in place by a greasy bottled hair tonic; pegged paints; tight-fitting shirts with the collar turned up in back and sleeves rolled tightly around the biceps to emphasize muscles in the same way that tight sweaters showed off girl's breasts; and taps on the shoes (heel and toe) to serve as an advance warning system. You could hear a rock approaching a block away from the metallic click of his feet on the pavement. This gave you time to prepare your own image. Every meeting between two rocks was an encounter, a confrontation like that of peacocks preening themselves for superiority in demeanor. The rock presented himself to the world as hard, cold, and tough. Emotion was sissy stuff, for girls. A rock who showed fear was no longer a rock and therefore lost his identity. Fear was the way of life, and the rock was always on stage. In a tension-filled, emotionally charged situation, he had always to deny his feelings. The rock could not even breathe properly (and consequently could not talk but had to mutter) because breathing allowed emotions to flow. The rigidity of this studied pose represented the rejection of the warm, social instincts of humanity. Disavowing natural feelings, the rock had to construct himself in the image of a cold, emotionless machine, primed at all times to respond to other people with calculated, unfeeling violence.

Gang warfare, and with it the rock sensibility, began to fade in the mid-1950s. Social workers had begun to move into areas of heavy teenage crime, hang out with the gangs, gain the confidence of their leaders, and steer them whenever possible to more legitimate pursuits. Rock'n'roll, after 1955, was a socializing influence. In the black ghettos, heroin did most to pacify the gangs. As the black writer Claude Brown has noted, heroin, distributed in black neighborhoods by the Mafia with the help of the police, "was one way of putting down bopping."

When you were on horse, you didn't have time for it. And in Brooklyn [where Brown was hanging out] a lot of cats were using horse to get away from bopping. It gave them an out, a reason for not doing it, and a reason that was acceptable. Nobody could say that you were scared or anything like that; they would just say that you were a junkie, and everybody knew that junkies didn't go around bebopping.[11]

In Harlem, Bedford-Stuyvesant, and other black communities, heroin swept in like a plague. "Drugs were killing just about everybody off in one way or another," Brown wrote. "It had taken over the neighborhood, the entire community. I didn't know one family in Harlem with three or more kids between the ages of fourteen and nineteen in which at least one of them wasn't on drugs...."[12]

Given the hold that the media had on youthful imagination, it is possible to trace the development of the rock ethos and the growing sense of generational consciousness through a series of Hollywood movies that focused on the "problem" of juvenile delinquency. *The Wild One* (1954), with Marlon Brando and Lee Marvin as rival leaders of two motorcycle gangs terrorizing a California town, set the style for teenage juvenile delinquency even as it reflected a problem that was already in existence. The movie was based on a 1947 incident when motorcycle gangs took over and terrorized the town of Hollister, California, until the police intervened. By design, the movie cast the two gang leaders in the most disagreeable light: Marvin as a drunken bully with no redeeming qualities, and Brando as an inarticulate punk unable to relate to anyone or anything other than his cycle. With no sense of personal honor, Brando steals a motorcycle trophy and then attempts to pass it off as something he won. The heroine, Mary Murphy, a waitress whose father is the town constable, is attracted to him, but he is unable to respond to her warmth and interest. Clad in a leather motorcycle jacket, motorcycle cap, and big storm-trooper boots, Brando is an emotional cripple. The rigidity with which he carries himself, the tension of his face, the way he mumbles, his overall uptightness should have made him repellent to the audience. Yet, like Mary Murphy, the teenage audiences empathized with Brando's character. His leather motorcycle outfit became the rage. Movie exhibitors complained that apprentice hoods, clearly aping Marvin and Brando, would congregate in front of the theater and rough up passersby, just as they had seen in the movies. A liberal critic offered that Brando's "orientation with the cyclists and against the town was part of the adolescent protest against a society in which it cannot take part" and left it at that.[13] More accurately, Brando and his friends did not want to take part. As crudely drawn as Brando's character was, he was moviedom's first white hipster. In one scene, Mary Murphy asks Brando where he and his friends are going. "Oh man," Brando mutters, "we just gonna go."

The Wild One won no critical awards and was generally forgotten by the movie critics after it dropped out of the neighborhood circuit. But along with Rebel Without a Cause (1955), it was probably the most influential picture of its time. Rebel, with James Dean, Natalie Wood, and Sal Mineo in the feature roles, placed juvenile delinquency in a middle class suburban setting. Like The Wild One, Rebel described the intra-generational conflict by pitting Dean, the new kid in town, against the local rocks. Dean shared Brando's alienation but he was more capable of human expression. Whereas Brando was emotionally dead, Dean was simply confused. As the star-crossed lovers, Dean and Wood captured the imagination of the youthful audience, if not the adult critics. By assigning blame to the parents for a lack of understanding, the movie made identification with the two teenagers easier, but conflict with parents was by then taken for granted. What was important in Rebel was the way Dean, Wood, and the parentless outcast Sal Mineo, related to one another. There was a softness in these teenage characters that was absent in *The Wild One*. They were still acting tough and looking cool and creating postures to mask their emotion. But their alienation clearly worried them; they were no longer sure. In *Rebel*, the hipster outsider was seeking a way back—but to what? The mainstream society of middle-class America remained repellent. There is a beautiful scene in an abandoned mansion where Dean, Wood, and Mineo take refuge from the police, from their parents, from the other teenage toughs tracking them down. In the mansion, Mineo is like a lost puppy, looking for a home. He seizes upon Dean and Wood as surrogate parents and they accept the role. Before the climax when the police surround the mansion and unnecessarily shoot Mineo, the three runaways pretend they are, like children, playing house. They are warm, understanding, honest, tender, and sensitive to one another, manifesting every decent quality that their parents are shown to lack. The unintended message of the picture reinforced the feeling of generational solidarity. However awful parents are, James Dean and Natalie Wood were a sign that given the chance to grow up the young would do better.

The Horny Fifties

Preoccupation with sex is often an indication of boredom. Americans during the postwar era spent a good part of the time fantasizing about sex—which is to say that Americans were bored much of the time. Sexual customs during this period also reflected a gap between reality and expectations. The well-ordered customs that in earlier times guided young people through adolescence and puberty into marriage and child rearing lost their hold. The old ways may have been backward and repressive, but only in retrospect. A healthy sexuality is one in which there is a balance between what one experiences and what one expects. Puritans who didn't have much sexual opportunity but didn't expect much can only be considered repressed by the standard of contemporary society, where sexual expectations are artificially inflated.

As in other areas of life, there was no continuity between the old sexuality and the new. As the old standards eroded, people found themselves confused, in a moral vacuum. New social customs did not evolve out of personal experience but were imposed, synthetically, by the media. Not surprisingly, the new message prescribed sex as a commodity, and social relations as a competitive process involving status and power. With tradition fast fading, the objectification of sex became pervasive. To walk down a street, to see a movie, or to turn on the television was to be met by a thousand and one suggestions of the promise of available sex.* For sexually precocious teenagers, expectations far outstripped reality. To be young in postwar America was to be perpetually horny.

In suburbia, young people began to date at earlier and earlier ages. There wasn't much else to do. Twelve-year-olds, who in the country would have been wandering through the fields or raising 4-H cattle, and who in the city might have been playing stickball or tag were now taking dancing lessons and being primed by anxious parents for the social whirl. For girls growing up at this time, there was little else to do.

A girl's life depended on her success with boys. "To be skillful," the editors of *Seventeen* magazine advised in 1957, "a woman has to have certain basic attributes; they include loving the male involved, having a sense of humor, good taste, and common sense, and a very feminine ability to look prettily bewildered and helpless while plotting and achieving a goal she thinks is important...." Social relations had all the subtleties of Oriental diplomacy. "In dealing with a male, the art of saving face is essential. Traditionally he is the head of the family, the dominant partner, the man in the situation. Even on these occasions when you both know his decision is wrong, more often than not you will be wise to go along with his decision—

---

*One study of movie advertisements in newspapers found that the use of sex appeal before the war never rose higher than 50 percent as an advertising device. In 1951, 70 percent of all movie ads emphasized sex (and ads emphasizing violence rose 8 percent to 17 percent in the same period). But whatever the promise, Hollywood never came across. The Production Code assured that even in the bedroom comedies the bed was a prop that was never used. The lesson of these films was not sensuality, but seduction: girl tempts boy by making sexual promises; sex is not something to be consumated and enjoyed; its function is simply to trap the boy into marriage.

temporarily—until you find a face-saving solution." In other words, even when he is wrong he is right.[14]

For a girl who was interested in a profession, a hobby, or a career, or in just growing up to be independent, the entire conditioning process was a warning sign that told her she was on the wrong track. Make a "double column of everything you can think of that each sex is allowed to do in your town," the author of one text on family living suggested to her students in 1955. For starters, the author listed these activities: "Girls can polish their nails, curl their hair, talk endearingly to each other, pretend to be ill, wear either skirts or slacks." Boys can, on the other hand, "stay out later, shave their faces, use rough talk, ask a girl for a date, swim in a pool without a suit."[15] Everything in a girl's life revolved around looking pretty. This was the road to social status, marriage, children—fulfillment. "The outer you is a reflection by which all other persons measure the inner you," *Seventeen* advised. "You will want to remove underarm hair and perhaps hair on your legs...."[16]

Some girls rebelled. They fought to retain their humanity in the only ways open to them. They became beatniks and didn't wear makeup or they fantasized themselves in careers rather than as wives and mothers. Some didn't go out on dates, others went to the other extreme and slept around as an act of rebellion. A few, if lucky, found other girls and boys like themselves in the same dilemma and became friends, clinging together outside the mainstream of teenage society. For this they felt isolated and were thought of as neurotic. Their parents, if they could afford it, sent them off to be psychoanalyzed where the cure was usually worse than the problem. The presumption was, at all times, that society was right and the well-adjusted person conformed to its expectations.

If girls defined themselves by their popularity with boys, boys, in part, gauged their masculinity by their success with girls. The dynamic of social relationships was based on making out. Boys boasted of their accomplishment in competitive baseball terms. A kiss was getting to first base; sexual intercourse was a home run, scoring, or going all the way. In this regard, adolescents were only reflecting adult preoccupations. The immensely popular Kinsey reports on male (1948) and female (1953) sexual behavior were pioneering attempts to study the sexual practices of the American people. They were based on almost twenty thousand personal interviews. These studies improved human understanding by showing standard sexual practices to be so diverse that few could be considered neurotic or even abnormal. But as an approach to sexuality, the studies reflected statistical achievement and not the qualities of human relationships. In the popular perception of the Kinsey Report, sex was a phenomenon to be studied as something separate from the whole of life.

At least until the introduction of birth control pills in 1960, and for some time thereafter, sex for teenagers was more thought about than practiced. Indeed, the existential questions of the postwar years—"should I or shouldn't I"—often referred to the mundane problem of a goodnight kiss. For girls, there was controversy over the correct line. *Seventeen* approved of kissing, but that was the limit. *Scholastic* magazine, more prudish and directed at a less sophisticated audience, shut the door on even that. "If you do kiss the boys goodnight," it advised in 1955, "you're running the risk, of having yourself footnoted as 'an easy number.' "[17]

The double standard was accepted without question by both sexes. This was oppressive to girls and confusing to boys. Consider: a boy who made out with a different girl every Saturday night would not be considered a "slut." He'd be considered a Don Juan, an "ass man," to be envied or admired by almost everyone. The opposite was true for girls. There were girls who "did it" and there were girls who were virgins (or "cock teasers" as they were often called) whom a boy could marry. It was all right to "do it" with girls who "did it," but these girls were not the ones you'd be serious about.

Making out was the preoccupation of teenage romance. Relationships could rarely be anything more than superficial. Kids went steady when they might have been happier playing ball, or pursuing artistic interests and hobbies. Given the political climate of the Cold War years, intellectual discussion was suspect. Except for school elections, there was no place for the young in politics anyhow. But it was equally difficult to talk intimately about dreams, fantasies, the future, because none existed. Adult responsibility and participation in the workaday world were things to be postponed, not talked about in eager anticipation. And, because of the need to be always super-cool, it was impossible to talk about personal fears and problems. Emotionally detached, cut off from the past and intimidated about the future, the young could not be fazed by anything except perhaps failing marks at school. If you were slated for a factory job, grades didn't mean anything, but for the white middle class, good grades were the check-points of success. Without good marks the road to the future that society had all mapped out was jeopardized, and what else was there but this road? The young were trained for nothing in life but what the adult world assigned them.

PART THREE:
"This Little Light..."
(for allen hoffman, 1943-1971)

...the only people for me are the mad ones,
the ones who are mad to live, mad to talk,
mad to be saved, desirous of everything at
the same time, the ones who never yawn or
say a commonplace thing, but burn, burn,
burn like fabulous yellow roman candles
exploding like spiders across the stars....
—*Jack Kerouac in* On The Road, *1957*

Prologue: The Kerouac-Ginsberg-Cassady Karass

...the beat generation, by whatever name it is called, is the natural expression of our times, international in character and deeply rooted in the chaos of our society. For all his faults, the hipster is a hero of our times because he has rebelled against a society which is only rational but no longer sane, a society which, because it has divorced man from his intuitive self, can talk calmly of waging nuclear war. The hipster's ability to act spontaneously in a society which demands conformity is in itself an affirmation of the ability of the human being to will its own actions.

—*David McReynolds*, We Are Being Invaded by the Twenty-First Century, *1970*

Jack Kerouac spent the final weeks of the war in his mother's house in Ozone Park, a quiet, all-white working class neighborhood of residential houses in Queens, New York. During the day, he worked as a soda-jerk in the neighborhood drug store. At night, he got high on benzedrine and wrote stories that he could not get published. Kerouac, who had grown up in a French-Canadian and Catholic working-class family in Lowell, Massachusetts, won a football scholarship to Columbia University, but quit the team and dropped out of college in 1941, during his sophomore year. According to Lou Little, the Columbia coach, "Kerouac left the team because he is tired."[1]

After abortive stints in the merchant marine and the navy, Kerouac returned to New York and began hanging around the Columbia campus. There, in 1944, he became friends with a pre-law student named Allen Ginsberg ("A spindly Jewish kid with horn-rimmed glasses and tremendous ears sticking out," Kerouac first described him) and William Burroughs, Jr., a scion of the Burroughs business machine family.[2] Kerouac and Ginsberg both wanted to be writers. Burroughs, who had been to Harvard, had become a junkie, a connoisseur of hard and soft drugs. It was he who turned Kerouac on to bennies, which were then popular in the New York drug culture. Harry "the Hipster" Gibson, a familiar character around the bop scene that summer, even sang a song entitled, "Who Put the Benzedrine in Mrs. Murphy's Ovaltine?" that was an underground rage among the hipster aficionados.[3]

Through Burroughs and Ginsberg, Kerouac met Herbert Huncke, a petty thief, junky, and storyteller who served as their guide to New York's hipster underground. This was a world cut off in every way from the mainstream culture of 1940s America. According to Huncke, the hipster outcasts were *beat*, not in the sense of being beaten, but as in beatific; their retreat from the dominant society was not a negative act but a courageous attempt to create new space and new lives. The hipster withdrawal was total. Unlike intellectuals, they did not despair of society; nor would they criticize it or torment themselves because they didn't fit in. Hipsters were the first urban American drop-outs; in effect, they had pulled the plug and cut themselves off from the postwar American dream.

The hipster world that Kerouac and Ginsberg drifted in and

out of from the mid-forties to the early fifties was an amorphous movement without ideology, more a pose and an attitude; a way of *being* without attempting to explain why. Hipsters themselves were not about to supply explanations. Their language, limited as it was, was sufficiently obscure to defy translation into everyday speech. Their rejection of the commonplace was so complete that they could barely acknowledge reality. The measure of their withdrawal was their distrust of language. A word like "cool" could mean any number of contradictory things—its definition came not from the meaning of the word but from the emotion behind it and the accompanying nonverbal facial or body expression. When hipsters did put together a coherent sentence, it was always prefaced by the word "like," as if to state at the onset that what would follow was probably an illusion. Words in themselves, removed from emotion, were suspect. There was neither a future nor a past, only a present that existed on the existential wings of sound. A Charlie Parker bebop solo—that was truth. "Peace is our business," said the professionals of war. "Oo bop sh'bam" was the hipster response.

The hipster's worldview was not divided between the "free world" and the "Communist bloc," and this too set it apart from the then current orthodoxy. Hipster dualism, instead, transcended geopolitical lines in favor of levels of consciousness. The division was *hip* and *square*. Square people sought security and conned themselves into political acquiescence. Hipsters, hip to the bomb, sought the meaning of life and, expecting death, demanded it now. In the wigged-out, flipped-out, zonked-out hipster world, Roosevelt, Churchill and Stalin, Truman, McCarthy, Stevenson and Eisenhower shared one thing in common: they were square.[4]

Most intellectuals dismissed the hipster ethos as a nihilistic sulk. Norman Mailer was one of the few to see in their withrawal a positive rebellion. Political radicalism was dying, so a new motor-force was needed to energize change. The hipster, said Mailer, signified the coming together of the bohemian, the juvenile delinquent, and the Negro—"the first wind of a second revolution in this century, moving not forward toward action and more rational equitable distribution" (as in the traditional Marxist approach) "but backwards toward being and the secrets of human energy."[5]

Kerouac, Ginsberg and their circle of friends were one of the many groupings who together were creating a resurgent bohemia out of the hipster sensibility. In the middle 1950s, hipsterism, now dubbed the beat generation, would burst upon the American scene and, Pied-Piper-like, make a pitch for the young. The Kerouac-Ginsberg clique might even have remained an anonymous part of this underground subculture had Kerouac not met up with Neal Cassady, a cross between the irreconcilable urban hipster and the mythical cowboy, who brought a new vision of America out of the frontier West.

Cassady grew up in the Denver slums. He hung out in poolhalls and libraries, stole cars, did time in reformatories, and lived with an intensity that—to those who knew him—still remains a wonder. He drew people to him like a supercharged magnet. Whether burning out an engine in a nonstop dash across the continent, capping tires, working as a railroad brakeman, or as "the most fantastic parking-lot attendant in the world," or rapping all day and all night eyeball-to-eyeball with friends, Cassady committed himself completely to the experience. His frantic energy dominated every scene; moving in a circle of writers, he would inevitably be the one person others would write about. As Dean Moriarty and Cody Pomeroy, Cassady was the hero of Kerouac's most important books. In the 1960s, after serving time in prison on a marijuana rap, he reappeared as a Merrie Prankster, driving Ken Kesey's psychedelic bus and turning on a new generation of youngsters to what would become a more political version of the hipster vision.[6]

In Cat's Cradle, Kurt Vonnegut, Jr., described the teachings of a fictitious wise man named Bokonon. A basic tenet of Bokonism is the existence of the "karass." Explains Vonnegut, "If you find your life tangled up with somebody else's life for no very logical reason, that person may be a member of your karass. Humanity is organized into teams, teams that do God's Will without ever discovering what they were doing."[7] The team of Kerouac, Ginsberg, Cassady (later to include Gary Snyder and others) was an authentic "karass." Throughout the late forties and early 1950s, in the doldrum days of the postwar years, these three were traveling back and forth across the continent, linking up various parts (most of them unknown to one another) of the hipster and bohemian subculture, energizing whatever scene they were in. The publication and notoriety of Ginsberg's poem "Howl" in 1955 and the publication in 1957 of Kerouac's *On The Road* (some six years after it was written) marked a historic turning point for the hip subculture. The media honed in on Kerouac's "karass" and publicized the idea of a "beat generation." The subsequent popularity of the beat writers and the enthusiasm with which a sector of white middle class youth grasped the beat ethos and style was an early indication of the youth rebellion to come. Out of the postwar hip and beat subcultures emerged the counter or alternative culture movement of more recent years.[8]

Chapter Twelve

"Against the ruin of the world, there is only one defense—the creative act."
—*Kenneth Rexroth in* Disengagement: The Art of the Beat Generation, *1957.*

Intellectual life in the postwar era was haunted by the vestiges of the past. The established intellectuals were under the sway of the New Critics, a group of poets and academicians committed to formalism, scholasticism, and opposition to political activism and ideology. Their influence dominated important little magazines like the *Partisan Review, Commentary, The New Leader*, the *Kenyon* and *Swanee* reviews, the major publishing houses in New York, and the English departments of the most respected universities. The New Critics viewed literature, like all art, as something removed from the turbulence of life. Some had been radicals during the 1930s, but their encounter with Stalinism left them in despair. They no longer believed in the possibility of a socialist revolution that would uphold their own humanist values.

Other New Critics in this scholarly alliance were conservatives (like Allen Tate and John Crowe Ransom) bent on preserving a remnant of what they believed to be the superior and civilized standards of their own parochial world. Like cloistered monks, yielding to the moral and spiritual breakdown of the contemporary world, they retreated to the academy in order to preserve their elitist tradition against mass culture. Their orientation was exclusively European and white. They were the defenders of highbrow culture and virtually anyone outside their genteel circles was dismissed as anti-intellectual.

Into this complacent academic scene ambled a new generation of artists and writers. Inspired by the hipster ethos, but committed to new forms of artistic expression, these younger musicians, artists and writers wanted to express their alienation from the intellectual pretensions of the New Critics and from the stifling, conformist values of middle-class America. But while the hipsters were retreating from American society, these new intellectuals were drawn towards it, groping for a new vision of American life, one that was spontaneous and humane, not dependent upon acquisitive wealth and power. In an era of cold-war repression, it should not be surprising that their rebellion would be expressed in artistic rather than political terms.

Creative Currents in the Arts

At the same time that black jazz musicians were developing bebop, abstract expressionist painters in New York, including Jackson Pollack, Willem de Kooning, Mark Rothko, Franz Kline and Robert Motherwell, were rebelling against the formal aesthetics of the established art world. Influenced by European surrealism and encouraged by the emigration to the United States of a number of important refugee artists, these "action" painters were reacting not only against the social realism and regionalism of 1930s art, but against the carefully delineated abstractionism of an earlier avant garde. Earlier abstract painters, though subjective in approach, created from objective reality. Only as the object passed through their own filtered perception did it become abstracted or distorted. The new school of action painters went one step further to deny the necessity of an objective reality. Their inspiration was wholly subjective, their work was turned inward, the act of creating became a way of describ ng the emotion of the moment. Technically, this represented ı breakthrough in form and structure. The artist created his or her own aesthetic logic as an expression of immediate creative need. By doing away with external criteria and with all rationalized form, the action painter was risking a step into the unknown and assuming full responsibility for the result. In a society where passive acceptance of the imposed order was the rule, the act of painting became heroic defiance. The artist stood alone, creating as s/he felt, unconcerned, as was the bop musician, with public taste or whether it would sell.

Action painting found its literary parallel in a new strain of American poetry, as a large number of young writers began to rebel against the formalistic and obscure style of poetry that was favored by the New Critics, and under their influence, published and taught in the schools. The younger poets wanted to turn poetry into a living art. With their rebellion came a poetry revival and an entirely new audience.

If the new poets had a model, it was William Carlos Williams, a family physician in New Jersey who was considered a minor poet by the reigning critics. Williams wrote about direct experience ("no ideas but in things" was his method) and by taking literature out of the ivory tower he made it a tool for understanding everyday existence. Williams, said Ginsberg, was "writing the way he talks...trying to say something, for real...not just making a lot of pretty words...."[1] Independent of Williams and unknown to Ginsberg, Charles Olson was moving in the same direction. The dominant figure at the experimental Black Mountain College after 1948, Olson advocated a poetry that was "energy transferred from where the poet got it, by way of the poem itself, all the way over to the reader."[2] Projective verse was poetry to be spoken with lines created to fit the human breath, and words meant to communicate directly with the listener or reader, not to provide critics with fodder for textual analyses. Olson's poems and his essay on projective verse reflected what other poets and writers were thinking about, that poetry should be read in public, to be communicated directly with a live audience.

In New York, Jack Kerouac was going through the same development. Influenced very much by jazz, he saw the written line as an improvisation with the phrasing reflecting the rhythm and structure of a jazz solo. Kerouac, Allen Ginsberg has said, "was the first writer I ever met who heard his own writing, who listened to his own sentences as if they were musical, rhythmic constructions, and who could follow the sequence of sentences that make up a paragraph as if he were listening to a little jazz riff...."[3] Ginsberg, who had studied at Columbia and come under the influence of New Critics like Lionel Trilling, Jacques Barzun, and Mark Van Doren ("The General Staff of the Enemy," Kenneth Rexroth called them),[4] was writing conventional verse until he came under the influence of Kerouac. Ginsberg's *Howl*, written in 1955, was the first popular example of modern American poetry meant to be read aloud to communicate energy as well as meaning.* *Howl* was arranged like a jazz solo, with what Ginsberg called "a Hebraic-Melvillian bardic breath" and "long saxophone-like chorus lines." The "who" that appears at the beginning of virtually every breath unit is meant to keep the beat. Thus, the poem was written not to look proper on paper but to fit Ginsberg's vocal abilities, to communicate a

---

*The Welsh poet, Dylan Thomas, was making frequent American tours during this period. His poems were also written to be spoken and celebrated the magic of existence possible in everyday life.

body rhythm with its verbal message.[5] Even if the descriptive passages and the apocalyptical references were obscure to the young people who were its first audience, the way the poem sounded when read aloud was as familiar as a screaming tenor saxophone chorus on a 1950s rock 'n' roll record, and just as easily understood.

Both abstract expressionism and the new poetry were intimately connected with jazz. The New York abstract expressionists hung out at the Five Spot and other Greenwich Village jazz clubs. In San Francisco, poets Lawrence Ferlinghetti and Kenneth Rexroth experimented with merging poetry and jazz. Jazz itself was building upon the advances of the early bopsters. Charlie Parker died in 1955, but the other bop pioneers carried on, influencing some of the better swing musicians and a generation of youngsters, notably John Coltrane, Horace Silver, Sonny Rollins, Clifford Brown. While jazz of the 50s generally adhered to bebop forms, within that discipline black musicians were able to explore their cultural roots. Only after they had fully incorporated the feeling of gospel, funk, and soul into the structure of bop, were jazz musicians ready to take the further step of abandoning the structure—which, after all, had been borrowed from white, European music—altogether. In 1958, Ornette Coleman began to attract attention with a white plastic alto saxophone and a music that, though steeped in the blues, refused to adhere to arbitrary limitations (pre-established chord progressions, bar lines, etc.) in the improvisatory act. Like the poets, Coleman wanted his music to be an extension of human feeling and speech, to convey directly, without reliance on formal structures, emotions and feelings that would describe his inner self. Like abstract expressionism, Coleman's music bordered on anarchy and, in the hands of less talented artists, descended into chaos. But Coleman and others like him had a sense of what they wanted to say in music and were willing, like the action painters, to take responsibility for creating form as they created music. Like the abstract expressionists and the poets, Coleman was attacked by the critics and the established musicians in his field. Jazz critics called his music anti-jazz and other musicians complained that he played out of tune. Despite this opposition, the new generation of poets, artists, and jazz musicians gradually found an audience. And it was an audience that responded actively to the challenge of the artists by trying to discover means, in their own lives, to take responsibility for the world around them and not to passively accept the inherited rules.

Bohemian Life

The new forms of artistic expression revitalized bohemian life. In the postwar years, this was centered in New York's Greenwich Village and San Francisco's North Beach, but little bohemias existed in most major cities and on the campuses of such progressive liberal arts colleges as Antioch, Bennington, Black Mountain, Chicago, and Reed. Socialist Michael Harrington, coming of age in St. Louis during the late 1940s, recalled his port of entry to the bohemian life at a bar called the Little Bohemia on a little street just off a levee lining the Mississippi River. There, with "the painters and other regulars in the back of the room," he shared talk "about art and psychoanalysis and the motherland of Greenwich Village," a conversation that must have been going on concurrently in dozens of other little bohemias.[6]

The bohemian way of life, which had first become identifiable as a unique subculture in Greenwich Village before World War I, represented a rebellion against Babbitry, philistinism, materialism, and the conformity of American middle-class life. In a nation of businessmen, bohemia was where the arts could flourish untainted by mass taste and commercial values. It was a hotbed of radical politics, the cultural avant garde, and experimentation in new lifestyles. Until the emergence of the beat generation in the late 1950s, bohemia was small enough so that everyone knew or knew of everyone else, and between artists, writers, political organizers, and philosophers of all stripes there was a continuous cross-fertilization of ideas.

Pre-beat bohemia was more than anything else a working community, though the hipster influence brought an influx of young people who saw themselves as experimenting with life rather than producing writing, crafts, or art. Despite its radical orientation and a tendency to stick its tongue out at the square bourgeois, early postwar bohemia made no pretense of being a social movement or proselytizing beyond its embattled bounds. Nevertheless, its existence was correctly perceived by middle-class America as a threat to its young. One of the best-selling novels of the 1950s, Herman Wouk's *Marjorie Morningstar*, described the lure of bohemia upon middle-class youth. The parents of middle America heaved a collective sigh of relief when Marjorie resisted the glamour represented by her bohemian lover and settled for the virtuous security of the middle class, as the wife of a nice Jewish lawyer. But a lot of teenagers who read the book wondered if Wouk had not given his heroine a raw deal.

Because bohemian life flourished in a few isolated artistic ghettos, the authorities were usually tolerant of its nonconformist conduct. Besides, a thriving bohemia provided a veneer of excitement for urban life that as a tourist attraction and seedbed for popular culture had economic value. However much bohemians shunned material wealth, success was a preoccupation of their lives, and during the affluent 1950s money began to filter down even to the bohemian basements. Wealthy dilettantes and powerful moguls of corporate culture hovered about the fringe waving the prospect of fame and fortune at any struggling artist who showed potential for commercial success. Indeed, many of these promoters had been bohemians themselves; the intellectual and artistic establishment of the postwar world was full of bohemians of an earlier generation who had made "good." Like retired generals and admirals who hired out to the defense industry as emissaries to the Pentagon, this older generation gave the media an inroad into creative America. Lacking a sense of itself as a political force or social movement, bohemia was continuously fighting for its integrity against the bourgeois world. And, since bohemians had no collective alternative to the dominant business culture, there was only a minimum amount of social pressure (much of it simply personal jealousy) against those about to go commercial and "sell out."

If bohemia was embattled with surrounding capitalism and mass culture, it put up no struggle against the sexism of that same culture. Sanctions against creative women were as pervasive within bohemia as anywhere else. The boundaries of the sexual revolution were narrowly defined by the bohemian patriarchy in order not to threaten male prerogatives. The bohemian lifestyle, remember, grew out of the requirements of creative work; there was nothing escapist or drop-out about it except on its hipster fringe. Bohemians lived cheaply because their only asset was the time they had to devote to their art. For this reason they shunned time-consuming careers and favored, as part-time work, menial or physical labor that left their minds free for thought. Creative work is also solitary work. After a day alone at a typewriter or in front of a canvas, there is a need to unwind and relax with convivial company and to share and challenge each other's ideas. Hence, an informal communalism and the famous bar scenes of the 1950s and the incessant party-going. But these were predominantly male scenes; a place for men to hold court, discuss their work, and argue politics. Michael Harrington, who left St. Louis to become a Village regular, described the New York bar scene as a "gregarious, potentially erotic release from a disciplined existence." Each bar had its own crowd of regulars. "Pretty girls could enter it rather easily," he noted, "men much less so, and the faces changed slowly."[7] Women were welcome because they brought with them the excitement of erotic potential, not because they were expected to add to the conversation.

Women often came to bohemia with the same creative ambitions as men. But there were few women role-models to provide support and few men took them seriously enough to encourage their creative work. The only niche available to women in the bohemian subculture, as in the dominant culture, was the nurturing or supporting role. Besides ego-support (which young struggling artists usually need in abundance), women provided male artists with income (often with the kind of compromising office job that no "principled" male bohemian would ever accept), cooked, cleaned house, and raised babies. In bohemia, as in the middle-class suburbs, the man was the dominant figure and the functions of the society were arranged for his needs.*

Just as the corporate society imposed the ideology of

---

*In his novel *Making Do*, Paul Goodman accurately described the sexual structure of bohemian life:

> To exist in decent poverty a *man* had to meet strict require-ments. He had to have a refined taste for the highest things, which alone do not cost money. He had to be doing something so worthwhile that he did not need intrinsic rewards. He had to choose his vices very carefully and healthfully. *His wife had to respect their way of life so highly that she did not need to keep up with the Joneses.* They had to be able, in a pinch, to live on bread and water. (Italics added.)

"togetherness" on the American housewife to give her an illusion of importance, bohemia boasted about its commitment to the sexual revolution. The premise of the sexual revolution was that women had the same sexual rights as men. And at that time, the idea that women had the right to choose and discard lovers with the same freedom as men was very daring; to listen to the way the middle class reacted to this "free love," it was the most dangerous idea that bohemians had. The bohemian sexual revolution did strike a blow at this sexist morality and pointed the way to more honest social relationships. But as an ideology, it also served to deflect a more generalized feminist challenge against the bohemian patriarchy. Feminism, as male bohemians defined it, was limited to the bedroom and to what men could adapt to for their own advantage.

Why was there no overt female resistance to this over-whelming oppression, a vasselage that virtually destroyed an entire generation of creative women? For one thing, male artists, in reaction to the effete and academic style of the older generation, adopted the macho pose of the wild holyman, a religious shaman whose art is a magical expression, the gift of the gods. Given the religious orthodoxy of the time, that the divinity was by definition male, this was a conceit that women could not successfully adapt to, even if they had wanted to. Moreover, during the postwar period, being a bohemian, next to being a leftist (and the two were often the same) was the most daring life a person could lead. Women especially risked being disowned by their families and condemned by the double standard on moral grounds. And bohemia itself, being small, isolated and without political power, existed on the defensive. Understandably, the difficulties of bohemian life in the postwar era were sufficiently risky to discourage a more far-reaching rebellion against male domination that may ultimately have threatened the well-being of the entire community itself. Besides, as we have seen, feminism, like all radical ideology, had been suppressed. Even among the politically sophisticated and the cultural vanguard there was insufficient encouragement from within the bohemian culture to sustain such a feminist challenge.*

---

*This is not to say that there were no women poets, writers, and artists.

The San Francisco Renaissance

Poetry was to San Francisco what abstract expressionism was to New York: the creative center of the bohemian scene. A continent away from the New York publishing world, Bay Area poets were not intimidated by the promise of commercial success. In San Francisco, there was a tradition of small literary magazines, and the New Critics and the heavy intellectualism of the *Partisan Review* were scorned. In 1947 Ruth Whit started the San Francisco Poetry Center, which featured readings by local poets in a friendly communitarian environment. "Public poetry" was reborn in San Francisco, Bay Area poet and critic Kenneth Rexroth said, and "a tribal, preliterate relationship between poet and audience" took hold.[8] This, of course, reinforced the poet's self-image as shaman and holy man. But it also led to the creation of a magical, spiritual-like feeling of *community* that set the Bay Area apart from the rest of American culture. Among the poets active in postwar San Francisco besides Rexroth were Philip Lamantia, William Everson, Robert Duncan, Lawrence Ferlinghetti, Lew Welch, Jack Spicer, and later Gary Snyder and Michael McClure.

Throughout the early fifties, the Bay Area and New York's Greenwich Village were in a creative ferment, with the Kerouac-Ginsberg-Cassady karass the transcontinental connection. In the summer of 1955, the many divergent bohemian scenes began to gel. In June, Viking Press in New York, agreed to publish Kerouac's second novel, *The Beat Generation*, which would

---

Among the better known abstract expressionists were Jean Freilicher, Elaine deKooning, Joan Mitchell, Grace Hartigan, and Marisol, and in New York in the late 1940s there was even one all-woman art gallery. Female poets had a more difficult time, especially in comparison with the present, when women poets have become the most important voice within the feminist movement (much the same way as men poets articulated the spirit of the beat movement). Donald Allen's *The New American Poetry* (1960), which is the basic poetry anthology of this period, includes just four women among the forty-five entries. Denise Levertov, Barbara Guest, Muriel Rukeyser, Adrienne Rich, Anne Sexton and Sylvia Plath (not listed in the anthology) were the most important poets of this time. In jazz, except for female vocalists, there were few women musicians of the first rank. Marian MacPartland and Mary Lou Williams, both pianists, were the most prominent. Trombonist Melba Liston was the only woman to find regular employment in a big band.

appear two years later retitled *On The Road.* Written and
rewritten between 1949 and 1956, *On The Road* put the beat
generation on the map. But in 1955, it provided Kerouac with
money to travel, first to Mexico and then, at Ginsberg's behest, to
San Francisco. Before leaving Mexico, Kerouac wrote Ginsberg,
"Let's shout our poems in San Francisco streets—predict earth-
quakes!"[9]

Ginsberg himself had settled in San Francisco and began
overthrowing the final vestiges of his academic New York past:
abandoning straight work, coming out as a homosexual, and
experimenting with drugs. He became a central figure in the
local poet's scene, which now included Gary Snyder, who had
arrived in Berkeley from Reed College. When Ginsberg first met
him, at Rexroth's suggestion, Snyder was living in a small hut in
Berkeley preparing to travel to Japan to study Zen. It was
Ginsberg who introduced Kerouac to Snyder, and their time
together became the subject of Kerouac's most political and
prophetic book, *The Dharma Bums.*

In Gary Snyder, the different strains of political radicalism,
Eastern mysticism, poetry, ecological consciousness and the
importance of native ground came together. Kerouac's description of Snyder (Japhy Ryder) in *The Dharma Bums* captured the
range of his subsequent influence: Ryder, he wrote,

> was a kid from Eastern Oregon brought up in a log
> cabin deep in the woods...from the beginning a good
> boy, an axman, farmer, interested in animals and
> Indian lore so that when he finally got to college...he
> was already well equipped for his early studies in
> anthropology and later in Indian myth and in actual
> texts of Indian mythology. Finally, he learned Chinese
> and Japanese and became an Oriental scholar and
> discovered the greatest Dharma Bums of them all, the
> Zen lunatics of China and Japan. At the same time,
> being a Northwest boy with idealistic tendencies, he
> got interested in old fashioned IWW anarchism and
> learned to play the guitar and sing old worker songs to
> go with his Indian songs and general folklore
> interests.[10]

By the time Kerouac arrived in the Bay Area in 1955,

Ginsberg was well along in the planning of a poetry reading to be held at the Gallery Six, a cooperative gallery run by abstract expressionist painters. The scheduled readers were Michael McClure, Gary Snyder, Philip Whalen, Philip Lamantia, and Ginsberg. Rexroth was to introduce the poets, and a handbill, mimeographed by Ginsberg, announced, "Remarkable collection of angels all gathered at once at the same spot. Wine, music, dancing girls, serious poetry, free satori. Small collection for wine and postcards. Charming event." Over a hundred people turned out for the reading, which gave birth to the San Francisco Poetry Renaissance. The high point was Ginsberg's first public reading of his poem *Howl*. As Kerouac recalled in *The Dharma Bums*,

> Everyone was there. It was a mad night. And I was the one who got things jumping by going around collecting dimes and quarters from the rather stiff audience standing around in the gallery and coming back with three huge gallon jugs of California burgundy and getting them all piffed so that by eleven o'clock when Alvah Goldbrook [Ginsberg] was reading from his poem "Wail" (*Howl*) drunk with arms outspread everybody was yelling "Go! Go! Go!" (like a jam session) and old Rheinhold Cacoethes [Rexroth] the father of the Frisco poetry scene, was wiping tears in gladness....

> Meanwhile scores of people stood around in the darkened gallery straining to hear every word of the amazing poetry reading as I wandered from group to group, facing them and facing away from the stage giving out little wows and yesses of approval and even whole sentences of comment with nobody's invitation but in the general gaiety nobody's disapproval either. It was a great night....

As Rexroth remembered, years later, "All of a sudden Ginsberg read this thing that he had been keeping to himself all this while, and it just blew things up completely."[11]

The Beat Generation

1955 marked the beginning. In the summer, Ferlinghetti began publishing his Pocket Poetry series with poems by Kenneth Patchen, his own *Pictures of a Gone World*, and Ginsberg's *Howl and Other Poems*. When police busted Ferlinghetti for publishing and purveying obscene literature, *Howl* became a sensation. A celebrated civil liberties trial, with a lineup of respectable academicians to attest to its literary merits, boosted sales. The *New York Times, Mademoiselle*, and the *Village Voice* publicized Ginsberg as poet and prophet. Appearing in Venice, California, Ginsberg was asked what he meant by the phrase "naked values," and in response, disrobed.

By 1956, however, the beats—as a literary and social movement—were scattered. The experience narrated by Kerouac in *On The Road* took place in the period immediately after the war, and the major beat figures by now had moved on to other things. Cassady spent most of the fifties working as a railroad brakeman in California, a family man. Kerouac, stuck with the reputation, "King of the Beats," tried futilely to live down the past. Ferlinghetti kept his bookstore and publishing venture going and continued to write poems of an increasingly political nature. His book *Coney Island of the Mind* (1958), became one of the best selling poetry books in the history of publishing, with 600,000 copies in print by 1974. Snyder, in Japan during most of the furor, escaped notoriety and emerged in the 1960s as a major figure in the ecology movement and the counterculture. Ginsberg traveled, exploring Eastern mysticism and psychedelic drugs. He too would emerge in the 1960s as a leader of the counterculture and anti-war movement.

Nevertheless, the beat generation had become a fad. Newspapers and magazines sent reporters into the bohemian enclaves to titillate their readers with reports of "beatnik" life. Tourist buses in San Francisco made the beat enclave of North Beach a regular stop on its sightseeing routs. (The beats returned the attention by renting a bus and touring suburbia with wide-eyed amazement at the kind of lives people led there.) Were it not, in fact, for the media's insatiable search for hot copy, the beat phenomenon might easily have passed without making the impact it did. But there was something vital in the movement that begged attention.

Paul O'Neil, writing in *Life* in 1959, zeroed in on the lifestyle of San Francisco's North Beach, which he described as being in pitiable rebellion against the "seeping juices of American plenty and American social advance...." Heaping scorn on what he called "the only rebellion around," O'Neil wrote that "beat philosophy seems calculated to offend the whole population." Beat spokesmen, he continued,

> in the course of what may be described as the Six Year War against the Squares, have raised their voices against virtually every aspect of current American society: Mom, Dad, Politics, Marriage, the Savings Bank, Organized Religion, Literary Elegance, Law, the Ivy League Suit and Higher Education, to say nothing of the Automatic Dishwasher, the Cellophane-wrapped Soda Cracker, the Split-level House and the clean, or peace-provoking (sic) H-bomb.[12]

But what O'Neil and others like him refused to see was that the beat rejection of the split-level, nuclear, mass-consumption existence of middle-class America was not the same thing as rejecting all of America. The beat's rejection was the other side of spurned love. They were searching, perhaps naively (was it ever really there?), for the spiritual America of Walt Whitman's dream, a romantic vision of a democratic society with its magic and innocence still intact. Beat heroes were people close to the earth, who were intimate with the earth's rhythms, life's magical forces. The yeoman past that the big corporations were ruthlessly trying to destroy hung on tenaciously in beat literature. The independent farmer, for instance, victimized by the policies of the USDA, lived on in *On The Road*. Stopping for lunch at a "homemade diner," Kerouac

> heard a great laugh, the greatest laugh in the world, and here comes this rawhide oldtime Nebraska farmer with a bunch of other boys into the diner; you could hear his raspy cries clear across the plains, across the whole gray world of them that day. Everybody else laughed with him. He didn't have a care in the world and had the hugest regard for everybody. I said to myself, Wham, listen to that man laugh. That's the West, here I am in the West. He came into the diner calling Maw's name,

and she made the sweetest cherry pie in Nebraska, and I had some with a mountainous scoop of ice cream on top. 'Maw, rustle me up some grub afore I have to start eatin myself or some damn silly thing like that.' And he threw himself on a stool and went hyaw hyaw hyaw. 'And throw some beans in it.' It was the spirit of the West sitting right next to me. I wished I knew his whole raw life and what the hell he'd been doing these years besides laughing and yelling like that. Whooee, I told my soul....[13]

Romanticized, yes; elementary populism, for sure; but as a distorted stereotype of the Western Farmer, how vastly different it was from both the backward hick of the urban media and the farmer-in-a-business-suit image favored by agribusiness spokesmen. If Kerouac the hipster rejected mainstream society he found reconciliation in the yeoman types of the American past.

In addition, the beats emphasized the kind of friendly communalism that the middle-class nuclear family, isolated in suburbia, had left behind. One of the key aspects of bohemian life was the continent-wide network of friends and acquaintances whose homes were always open to travelers with the appropriate introductions. In *Earth Household*, Snyder described the evolution of this underground family:

> I remember sitting down to Christmas dinner eighteen years ago in a communal house in Portland, Oregon, with about twelve others my own age, all of whom had no place they wished to go home to. That house was my first discovery of harmony and community with fellow beings. This has been the experience of hundreds of thousands of men and women all over America since the end of World War II. Hence the talk about the growth of a new society. But more; these gatherings have been people spending time with each other— talking, delving, making love. Because of the sheer amount of time "wasted" together (without TV) they know each other better than most Americans know their family.[14]

The fact that the beats did find an audience and that this audience often consisted of the most sensitive members of the student generation, should have been reason to take their message seriously. Instead, commentators disparaged the movement as a passing fad or an aberration composed of outcasts, misfits, and the most neurotic members of the affluent society. According to Dr. Francis J. Rigney, a San Francisco psychiatrist quoted in *Life*, at least 60 percent of the North Beach beatniks with whom he communicated "were so psychotic or so crippled by tensions, anxieties and neuroses as to be incapable of making their way in the ordinary competitive world of men...."[15] In a sense, of course, he was right. The beats could not comfortably adjust to "the ordinary competitive world of men" which they, echoing Rigney, considered insane. When the beats began to drop out of society, it was like rats leaving a sinking ship; their frenzied activity—as Ginsberg described in *Howl*—"yacketa-yakking screaming vomiting whispering facts and memories and anecdotes and eyeball kicks and shocks of hospitals and jails and wars." It was a premonition of the youth rebellion of the 1960s. But the beats were too few in number and their antics too far-out to make an impact on a public that tolerated its outsiders only for the entertainment they provided. The popular media made light of the beat rebellion, adopted the image of beard, sandals, beret, and bongo drums as caricature, and let the message go by. Television even created its own loveable beatnik character in Maynard Krebs of the "Dobie Gillis" situation comedy show. Harmless Maynard, with his pathetic goatee, his dirty sweatshirt (everyone else on the program wore sweaters and button-down shirts), and his ersatz hip talk could easily have passed for an updated version of Jughead, the familiar comic-strip fall guy. But uncertainty about the meaning of the beat attraction lingered beneath the surface of self-assurance.

"Whoever heard of rebels so pitiful, so passive, so full of childish rages and nasty masochistic cries?" asked O'Neil in 1958. And a critic in the *Wall Street Journal*, obviously taken by Kerouac's characterization of Gary Snyder, predicted confidently that Japhy Ryder would soon sell out. "He'll live in Palo Alto or Winnetka or Westport," wrote the reviewer. He'll become "an account executive or a book editor with a too-expensive family, a white Jaguar, a collection of Maxwell Bodenheim poems, a Hammond organ, a hi-fi set and a mild delusion he is somehow shaping the future of the world."[16] By 1960, John Ciardi, the poetry editor of *Saturday Review*, was hopefully, but prematurely, writing an "Epitath for the Dead Beats." He insisted that "as rebellions go, this Beat jazz really wasn't much fun. As a literary movement it began and ended just about nowhere. As a set of antics, it still has a bit of mileage in it.... But if the Beats had any sort of rebellion going once, there seems to be little enough left of it now beyond a fad for hip-talk and blare-jazz in crummy dives. That's dead enough, as the man said waving away the buzzards, let's bury it."[17]

By every indication, the beat generation should have run its course. The beats were preaching voluntary poverty to a generation spoiled by affluence. They seemed to be rejecting politics at a time when Adlai Stevenson—the first authentic liberal hero since Franklin Roosevelt—was making intelligent political dialogue possible again. They were pushing esoteric Eastern religion in the face of a well-publicized religious revival that featured splendid new churches and synagogues with gymnasiums and swimming pools. And beats expressed themselves best in poetry; as any English teacher of that time could testify, kids hated poetry. In 1957, Rexroth said that "the youngest generation is in a state of revolt so absolute that its elders cannot even recognize it."[18] But where was his evidence?

Actually, the young teetered on the brink between acquiescence and activism. The vast majority chose the life that the older generation had laid out, clinging to it with a tenacity that belied their insecurity. A few rebelled and in the beats found the model that previous generations had lacked. America's political rhetoric, the bluster, the militaristic stand, the desperate concern with being number one made no sense to a generation that had to cower under school desks in civil defense drills in helplessness and fear. John Wayne, the mythical adventurer, had opened the West and had created a society in his own pioneering image. But the future of the fifties generation was planned out; there was nothing that society would allow young people to create for themselves. At a time of political silence, the beats were, in actuality, the only rebellion around. Moreover, they were expressing those very values that corporate society denied.

Chapter Thirteen

Hey, kids, the cops don't want you to have a good time.

—Alan Freed, Boston, 1958

Clearly what will be called personality problems depends on who is doing the calling. The slave owner? The dictator? The patriarchical father? The husband who wants his wife to remain a child? It seems quite clear that personality problems may sometimes be loud protests against the crushing of one's psychological bones, of one's true inner nature. What is sick then is not to protest when this crime is being committed.
—Abraham Maslow in Toward a Psychology of Being *1968*

The postwar years finished off Tin Pan Alley. An era of popular entertainment came to an end as family listening fractured along generational lines. What adults enjoyed bored the hell out of kids, and parents hated rock 'n' roll. By the middle 1950s, a generation of brilliant and sophisticated songwriters— the Gershwin brothers, Rodgers and Hart, Cole Porter, Irving Berlin, Dorothy Fields, Jerome Kern, Harold Arlen, Johnny Mercer and many, many others—were either dead or past their musical prime. As a group they had brought the popular song to a creative peak.[1] But few young white composers were coming up to take their place. During the postwar era, white musicians with any imagination played modern jazz.

Very few popular standards came out of the postwar era. The great melodies and lyrics—the songs that become vintage with age and are reinterpreted by every new generation— belonged to an earlier time. Hits of the 1950s like "Oh My Papa" and "Lady of Spain" (Eddie Fisher), "Doggie in the Window" (Patti Page), "Come on-a My House" (Rosemary Clooney), "Catch a Falling Star" and "Round and Round" (Perry Como), and "Mule Train" and "Jezebel" (Frankie Lane) have mostly been forgotten. But the older songs like "Embraceable You," "Stardust," "Don't Blame Me," "I Got Rhythm," "Funny Valentine," and "Old Black Magic," remain as standards. Significantly, Frank Sinatra, the most brilliant pop singer of all time, reached the nadir of his singing career during this period. When he made his comeback, it was as an actor and as a singer of old standards. Fresh material of high quality was not available.

A music as lifeless as 1950s pop led to a regression in dancing. The loosely improvised rhythms of the jitterbug gave way to the regimented dance steps taught by Kathryn and Arthur Murray and their numerous dance studio competitors.* Popular dancing became formalized and artificial. New steps were introduced to the public like the latest car models—on schedule. Dancers ceased being innovative; they became consumers, waiting for the Murrays to introduce the latest dance craze. And the new steps were sufficiently unnatural to require schooling. Dancers couldn't just feel the rhythm and start to boogie. They

---

*The Murrays ran a chain of ballroom dance studios and they were a popular fixture in television's early days.

had to learn the basic steps, like a military drill, movement by movement. The Murrays became commissars of social dancing.

Music and Generational Consciousness

At the same time that pop music was losing its vitality, young people were beginning to feel the effects of the new affluence. Allowances were up; advertisers began to discover that adolescents were a lucrative market (valued at $9 billion in 1956) and potential disciples of name brands. In 1952, the first transistor radios began trickling into the stores. Soon kids would be able to listen to the radio even while hanging out on the street corner. But radio stations, like the record companies, were out of touch with what young people wanted. Rock historian Charlie Gillett has written:

> Faced with a continuous broadcast of melodrama/ sentiment/trivia over the major radio networks, the more adventurous members of the popular music audience had been twiddling their dials in search of something better for several years. And in many areas of the country they had been rewarded with one and sometimes two spectacular stations, playing either country and western music or rhythm and blues, each recorded mainly by independent companies. In both cases, the music was so different from the standard styles that it often satisfied the need of the refugees from the popular music stations.[2]

Hillbilly music of the rural south began to infiltrate the mainstream culture in the late 1940s. Hillbilly's appeal, until then, was to a small, regional audience, mostly rural. The urbane sophisticates who favored the more classically-oriented pop music of Tin Pan Alley disparaged hillbilly as "shitkicking music," for uneducated rubes. But in 1948 a popular singer named Patti Page covered "Tennessee Waltz," a stately mountain tune that had had a modest success on the hillbilly circuit. "Tennessee Waltz" quickly rose to the top of the hit parade; within six months almost five million copies were sold.

Page's success served notice that hillbilly could attract a national audience, and record executives began to pay more attention to the popular music of the rural South. In 1949, singer-composer Hank Williams recorded "Lovesick Blues," his first big hit. Between 1949 and his death in 1953, Williams had eleven gold records. Though his music was steeped in the southern rural tradition, Williams' songs were adopted by such Tin Pan Alley artists as Tony Bennet, Frankie Laine, Jo Stafford and Theresa Brewer.* But in addition to his success with pop musicians, he was beloved by his hillbilly audience. About the same time that Williams became a regular on the Grand Old Opry—the most listened to radio program in rural America— segments of the Opry began to be broadcast nationwide. And hillbilly, as it broadened its appeal, began to be called by the more respectable sobriquet, "Country and Western."[3]

In the early 1950s, the music of black America began to achieve even greater popular acceptance. As outsiders, blacks had developed a popular culture of their own outside the mainstream. Jazz, especially bebop, was an attempt by blacks to assert their own identity. But this was difficult music, appealing to an educated audience. More popular in the black communities was rhythm and blues with its elementary harmony, its simple melodic lines, its screaming tenor sax or funky blues guitar, its unvarnished lyrics and—most important—the heavy rhythmic back beat so superb for dancing. Numerous small independent record companies scoured the ghettos and the rural countryside for local talent. The resulting "race" records (only in the postwar era did they become known as rhythm and blues) were marketed exclusively to a black audience and were featured on white owned black radio stations that few whites knew existed. In 1951, the year of such shlock pop hits as "I Saw Mama Kissing Santa Claus," a white Cleveland disc jockey named Alan Freed began featuring rhythm and blues. His show became an instantaneous hit with news of it spreading through the streets and schools of Cleveland. In March, 1952, Freed produced the country's first live rock'n'roll concert, with all black performers. Thirty-

---

*Hank Williams' songs include "Your Cheating Heart," "Cold Cold Heart," "Half As Much," "Hey, Good Lookin'," "Ramblin' Man," and "Kaw Liga." These, and other songs, have become popular classics, no less than the Tin Pan Alley standards of Porter, Carmichael, Berlin, Kern, Loesser and the like.

thousand fans, most of them white, showed up at the 10,000 seat auditorium, and Cleveland experienced the first rock 'n' roll riot. In 1954 Freed was signed by WINS in New York and his nightly rock'n'roll party, directed specifically at a teenage audience, became the most popular program on radio. Disc jockeys in other cities quickly followed the same formula, and rock'n'roll became a nationwide teenage craze.

Alan Freed's coming to prime time radio in 1954 as an uncompromising champion of black popular music helped prepare the way for the white participation in the civil rights movement that was soon to come. Freed introduced young white America to black culture. Teenagers after the mid-1950s did their homework to black music, necked to black music, and joined together as a generation conscious of itself to the beat of black music. White adults were outraged. Their carefully wrought plans for the young were being flaunted. The young were dancing to the rhythm of an unexpected drummer.

From the pulpit, from educators, from psychologists, and from experts on adolescent life came denunciations. The *1955 Yearbook of the Encyclopedia Britannica* huffed, "The rock'n' roll school in general concentrated on a minumum of melodic line and a maximum of rhythmic noise, deliberately competing with the artistic ideals of the jungle itself."[4] *Variety*, the newspaper of the entertainment trade, attacked the music for its allegedly suggestive "lear-ics," forgetting that composers like Cole Porter excelled at sexually suggestive double entendres.[5] And in the *New York Times* "a noted psychiatrist" labeled rock 'n'roll "a communicable disease" and "a cannabilistic and tribalistic kind of music."[6] Mostly, though, adults pretended that rock'n'roll was a passing fad and that their children would come back to the fold.

The large record companies did everything possible to destroy the music. Before rock, five large corporations—Decca, Columbia, RCA Victor, Capital, and MGM—controlled distribution and therefore monopolized the popular music market. Most rock hits, however, were on small local labels that were started after World War II to record music at the grass-roots level. Imperial, Specialty, Alladin, RPM, and Flair came out of Los Angeles; Chess/Checker and Vee Jay out of Chicago; King out of Cincinnati; Duke and Peacock out of Houston; Savoy out of

Newark; Sun out of Memphis; and Herald/Ember, Rama, Gee, Old Town, and Atlantic (the one independent to become a major) out of New York. These companies had direct connections with the ghettos where rock music was first created. Rock 'n'roll proved the efficiency of decentralized industry. Between 1953 and 1959, record sales increased from $213 million to $603 million, in large part because of rock'n'roll.[7] Most of the biggest selling popular hits were on independent labels.

Unable to stop rock'n'roll, the major companies worked to destroy its creative integrity. With no access to the source, they began covering rock hits with bleached, toned-down versions by white artists. At first this worked. Fats Domino's "Ain't That a Shame" became a national hit when sung by clean-cut Pat Boone, who wore a sweater and white bucks. Bill Haley took Joe Turner's "Shake, Rattle, and Roll" out of the bedroom and into the kitchen and won first place on a number of charts. The McGuire Sisters converted the Moonglow's hit, "Sincerely," (with its intricate harmony of "hoot-hoot whoos" and "shoo-doobedoos" that parodied its own sentimentality), into a saccharine version that treated the trivial emotionalism of the lyrics seriously. And when Georgia Gibbs recorded LaVerne Baker's "Tweedle Dee" and "Dance With Me Henry" her renditions were so obviously stolen from the originals that Baker called for a Congressional investigation.

It was not until 1956, with the discovery of Elvis Presley, that the major companies began to beat back the independent challenge and co-opt black music. Presley, from Southern white working-class origins, was discovered by Sun Records, an independent label in his home town of Memphis. Memphis, unlike Nashville (where country music was strong) was a blues town, and Presley had an uncanny grasp of the rawest black music. The owner of Sun Records, Sam Phillips, was looking for a singer like Presley. "If I could find a white man," he supposedly said, "who had the Negro sound and the Negro feel, I could make a billion dollars." And he was right. Presley's first records for Sun, including "Hound Dog" and "Heartbreak Hotel," were nationwide sensations. A white singer had never sounded so black before, and yet by adding a country flavor of his own, he did not sound a carbon copy. According to musicologist Henry Pleasants, Elvis "heralded a metamorphosis of popular music, a new phase in the interaction of white and black musicality" merging "all the musical currents of America's subcultures: black and white, gospel, country and western, rhythm and blues."[8]

Presley touched off the biggest pop craze since Glenn Miller and Frank Sinatra. In 1956 alone, his records sold 10 million copies, more than 10 percent of the year's total for all popular artists. *Life*, as always, abreast of the latest fads, noted that his style "was deeply disturbing to civic leaders, clergymen, some parents. He does not just bounce to accent his heavy beat. He uses a bump and grind routine usually seen only in burlesque. His young audiences unexposed to such goings-on, do not just shout approval. They get set off by shock waves of hysteria, going into frenzies of screeching and wailing, and winding up in tears."[9] Wherever Presley appeared, he brought controversy. On Ed Sullivan's popular Sunday night television show, the camera focused from his waist up so as not to expose the television audience to his frenetic movements. In Jacksonville, Florida, a judge threatened him with a warrant for impairing the morals of minors; but Presley insisted, "I don't do no dirty dancing."[10] The more the adults criticized his style, the more the young loved him.

Presley brought rock'n'roll into the mainstream of pop culture. His synthesis of black rock and white country was duplicated by other singers, bringing the era of classic rock'n' roll to a premature close. RCA Victor, which bought Presley's contract from Sun, set about to tame his style, saddling him with ballads and love songs that—though they were hits—lacked the creative force of his early records. As Presley set the artistic pace, other artists followed; even the independents abandoned rhythm and blues for second rate Presley imitations. But in Presley, young whites experienced the soul power that they never imagined they had. He gave them a sense of energy that had seemingly been lost, but that had been preserved—in isolation— in black culture. Presley, more than anyone else, gave the young a belief in themselves as a distinct and somehow unified genera- ation—the first in America ever to feel the power of an integrated youth culture.

Throughout the 1950s rock'n'roll was central to the ado- lescent experience. Even as incidents of juvenile delinquency declined, there were still teenage riots, and most of them had to do with rock'n'roll concerts. Many cities banned the concerts. Rock riots, however, differed from earlier rumbles in that instead of fighting each other, the young were testing out their new found energy, often beyond the limits that adults would tolerate. In May, 1958, Alan Freed was directing a rock'n'roll party in Boston. Kids were screaming and dancing in the aisles as usual; in the middle of the concert, police turned on the lights and announced that the concert was over. Taking the microphone, Alan Freed reportedly told the audience, "Hey, kids, the cops don't want you to have a good time." The result was a teenage riot that spread throughout the city.[11] Freed was charged with anarchy and incitement to riot, and his career collapsed as he lost his job on WINS. But the vitality that rock'n'roll engendered continued to grow, and more and more kids began to understand the acumen of Freed's commentary.

Underground America

The same restlessness that led young people to rhythm and blues and country music led many of them to look for other kinds of off-beat entertainment. Often they ignored the prime-time programs offered on network TV and the more popular mass audience disc-jockey shows for the obscure jazz and "soul" stations beaming into black audiences. Jocko, Hal Jackson, and "Symphony" Sid Torin were big in New York. The Hawly show from Baltimore, presenting jazz at midnight, could be heard on a good radio throughout the East, while Daddy-O Daylie had a following in Chicago and Detroit. Mort Sahl had a midnight show in San Francisco that could be picked up in Alaska. Phil Kernan (father of the Grateful Dead's Pigpen) broadcast from Berkeley, "Wolfman Jack" Smith from Shreveport, Dewey Phillips from Memphis, and Jean Shepherd from Cincinnati—and after 1955, from WOR in New York, midnight to 3 a.m.

Jean Shepherd was the most important of these late-night radio personalities. With WOR's 50,000 watt transmitter, Shepherd's voice blanketed the Northeast, but his reputation reached much farther as homemade tape recordings of his monologues were passed around the country from friend to friend. A denizen of Greenwich Village and an original contributor to the *Village Voice*, Shepherd divided the world into day people, who "lived in an endless welter of train schedules, memo pads and red tape," and the night people listening to his program. Day people lived in an illusion of efficiency; night people saw its absurdity. "Creeping meatballism" was the great social disease plaguing the nation, Shepherd told his listeners. This represented the passive acquiescence of people who surrender to the demands of the consumer culture, who collaborate in their own manipulation. Against this, Shepherd described the position of the night people who, even though they cannot win, at least take a stand and are able to laugh at day people's folly.[12]

There was another side to Shepherd that, in its subtlety, may have had a more subversive effect on his audience than his cultural analysis. "I'm this kid, see..." Shepherd would begin a program and then go off on a long, improvised monologue about growing up in prewar Chicago. A superb storyteller with an eye for detail and an uncanny ability to verbalize the ambiance of an earlier age, Shepherd would re-create a time when kids roamed free in the city or lived near enough to farmland to gorge themselves in a midnight raid on a cantaloupe field. The Shepherd family seemed to include a bevy of zany uncles and crazy aunts, and Shep and his friends knew everyone in their neighborhood. By contrast to the life Shep described, the kids tuning in had nothing adventurous to look forward to except the draft and a job. In Shepherd, these kids found reinforcement for inarticulated despair. There were other ways to live, there were better ways to grow up.

The opening into hip consciousness offered the adventure-some other underground attractions that most Americans were unaware of. In the mid-1950s, jazz began to reach a wider public. If rock'n'roll represented an introductory course to black culture, jazz represented a graduate seminar. Jazz was American society turned upside down. All its major figures and its cultural heroes were black, and its inspirations came from the black experience. Jazz stood racism on its head. Though white musicians tended to gain greater popular acceptance, it was the blacks who got the most respect. At a time when the country was going through the first pains of creating an integrated society and its endemic racism was being publicly exposed, jazz *was* an integrated society with cultural standards that were overwhelmingly black.*

*In jazz, a widely held belief, dubbed Crow-Jim, insisted that blacks were

For many, rock'n'roll led also into the American folk tradition of blues, bluegrass, traditional ballads, work songs, and political broadsides. The folk tradition had long been cultivated by the American Left. While some folk singers simply wanted to collect and perform music from the country's past, others saw it as a way of weaning people away from the synthetic popular culture and showing them a people's history chronicled through song. During the late 1930s, for instance, Pete Seeger and Woody Guthrie were part of the Almanac Singers, writing and performing music about the CIO organizing drives and other current events. The Almanac Singers, along with bluesmen Huddie Ledbetter ("Leadbelly") and "Big" Bill Broonzy, often performed at union rallies and left-wing fundraisers. While their records never made the "top 40," they did succeed in reaching a fairly wide audience. After the war, Pete Seeger and other veterans of the Almanac Singers were reunited as the Weavers and in 1948 began to perform nonpolitical folk songs that brought folk music into the mainstream of pop culture. Having made the "Hit Parade" with such folk hits as Leadbelly's "Goodnight Irene," "Tzena Tzena," and "Wimoweh" ("The Lion Sleeps"), the Weavers became victims of the blacklist. Seeger was subpoenaed by HUAC and offered to talk about his music and perform for the committee so they would know the kinds of songs he sang; but, citing the First Amendment, he refused to talk about his politics. Even after his conviction for contempt of Congress was overturned by the higher courts, Seeger was effectively blacklisted from the mass media until 1967.

Throughout most of the 1950s, after the Weavers were blacklisted, the audience for folk music was limited to left-wing and bohemian circles and some college campuses. Then, in the late fifties, sophisticated black singers like Harry Belafonte began recording calypso and traditional folk ballads, while a few older bluesmen such as Sam "Lightning" Hopkins, John Lee Hooker, and "Mississipi" John Hurt began appearing in coffee

inherently better jazz musicians than whites. Right or wrong, Crow-Jim challenged the customary way that white America viewed race. Only in jazz did whites want to integrate with blacks. In a decade when civil rights was first becoming an explosive issue, this represented a fresh, consciousness-raising way of looking at the world.

houses and on campuses. In 1958, a group of white college students called The Kingston Trio, hoping to duplicate the success of the Weavers, hit paydirt with a recording of an old Southern folk tune entitled "Tom Dooley." These events sparked a folk revival, and the music that Seeger and musicians like him had been performing all along suddenly found a new youthful following.

Out of this folk revival came a renewed interest in folk history and native traditions, those same life-giving qualities that the commercial media were trying to bury. This fascination for authenticity in human experience meshed with the beat rejection of middle-class life. In addition, because the Left had done the most to keep folk music alive, the new generation of folk enthusiasts inherited a repertoire of politically assertive folk songs. College students who were not taught about farmer-labor movements or about the CIO organizing campaigns in their history courses learned about them through the songs of Seeger, Guthrie, and the Almanac Singers. Not surprisingly, student activism, as we shall see, began to revive itself about the same time as folk music became popular. The impact of the beats, the popularization of the hip subculture, the interest in jazz, country music, and traditional blues were all part of the same ferment that was beginning to manifest itself on college campuses.

Sick Comics or a Sick Society?

The postwar decade was a good period for comedy. But very few comedians had a political perspective. Or, when they did, as with Bob Hope and Fred Allen, the jokes were very much within an acceptable frame of reference. Hope—and this was true of other comedians like him—identified completely with the corporate world and became with his success its house comedian. Through most of the fifties about the only visible sign of political iconoclasm besides Walt Kelly's comic strip, "Pogo," was the comic book *Mad*.

Mad began as a 10-cent comic in 1952, and became a magazine rather than conform to the standards set by the industry's comic book code. Ostensibly directed to an adolescent audience, *Mad* was the most satirical and irreverent mass publication on the market. In *Mad*, Miss Rheingold became

"Miss Potgold," G.I. Joe was transformed into G.I. Shmoe, and Walt Disney's "Mickey Mouse" became "Rickey Rodent." In *Mad*'s takeoff on "Howdy Doody" (called "Howdy Dooit"), the popular children's program was shown to be one continuous plug for brand-name products. In one sequence, Buffalo Bill, (Howdy's human foil) asks one member of the "peewee gallery" "what would you like to be when you grow up?...A police Chief?...A fireman?...An Indian?...Or (hot-dog) maybe a JET FIGHTER PILOT? Huh?" The kid replies:

> Please, Buffalo Bill...Don't be juvenile! If one had the choice, it would probably be soundest to get into a white-collar occupation such as investment broker or some-such. Of course...advertising and entertainment are lucrative fields if one hits the top brackets.. Much like Howdy Dooit has! In other words... What I want to do when I grow up, is to be a hustler like Howdy Dooit! I want to be where the cash is...the green stuff... moolah...pound notes...get it? MONEY![13] (Ellipses in the original)

The strip ends with a child waving a pair of scissors at Buffalo Bill, who falls to the floor in a disjointed heap.

With the easing of Cold War tensions in the late 1950s, political satire and commentary became part of comedy routines. In 1958, Paul Krassner began publishing *The Realist*, a magazine that attacked Eisenhower, advertising, anti-Communism and other icons of American life. Krassner also peddled a red-white-and-blue poster that said, "FUCK COMMUNISM." Although it expressed the essence of American postwar political ideology, by postal standards it was deemed obscene and not fit for the mails.

In 1958 Mort Sahl, the Berkeley radio monologist, toured the country as a stand-up comedian and became the first hip comic to become well known. By the standards of that time, Sahl seemed very far out, the first comedian to stand outside of the political mainstream and make jibes at the establishment from a vaguely defined radical orientation. Being in favor of all the "right" things (peace, integration, ban-the-bomb, sexual liberation, etc.), he had President Eisenhower, the archetypal square, to serve as his foil. But when Kennedy became President, he lost the easy target. Like the early hipsters who were overly fascinated by style, Sahl was taken in by the young president. In the style of Bob Hope, Sahl became court jester to the new administration. He could make barbs at its expense, but it was all for fun; the outsider had become the insider and the liberal establishment had become his friends.

Sahl was one of a group of comedians that *Time* in 1959 dubbed "sickniks."[14] Others in the school were Shelly Berman, Dick Gregory, Elaine May and Mike Nichols, Bob Newhart, Lenny Bruce, and Jonathan Winters. In addition to political routines and social commentary, these comedians, along with *Village Voice* cartoonist Jules Feiffer, probed the interpersonal relationships of the hip, affluent middle class. This too represented a break with the comedy of the past. Sex, in American humor, had always been bawdy and risque. Humorous commentary about personal relationships was outside comic bounds. By creating *schticks* about the difficulties of sex and interpersonal relationships, the new comedians were bringing these problems into the open. This meant, in effect, that they no longer had to be concealed as embarrassing failings, but could be shared in a light-hearted context as hang-ups common to everyone.

By calling these young comedians "sick." *Time* was describing a basic area of confrontation between the dominant culture and the hip subculture. In totalitarian societies, psychology is often used as a weapon of repression. Dissenters are often classified as psychotic and confined to mental hospitals "for their own good." In this way, the state avoids having to deal with its rebels on political grounds—because they are "crazy,"their dissent is not worth listening to. In America, the media's dismissal of Sahl, Bruce, et al. as "sick" comics had the same effect. It was also part of a recurring postwar pattern, in which any kind of rebellion was dismissed as symptomatic of mental illness. Juvenile delinquents were maladjusted, independent women were sexually frustrated and neurotic, beats were sadsack characters who could not make it in the *real* world, homosexuality was a social disease, passivity was a quality endemic in women but "unmanly" in men. Likewise, "sicknik" humor, in the words of *Time*, represented a "personal and highly disturbing hostility toward all the world." The comedians, because they had an audience and were part of a growing, self-aware "underground" community, fought back. They insisted that their humor was not sick, but that the society that they were satirizing was sick. And by exposing the absurdities of this unhealthy society, they were making people aware of the sickness and thus creating possibilities for a cure.

If society is corrupt, should the individual rebel? The psychologist Abraham Maslow speculated that rebellious behavior could be a sign of mental strength. "Perhaps," he said, "it is better for a youngster to be *unpopular* with the neighboring snobs or with the local country club set." He questioned the merit of being "well adjusted." "Adjusted to what?" he asked:

> To a bad culture? To a dominating parent: What shall we think of a well-adjusted slave? A well-adjusted prisoner? Even the behavior problem boy is being looked upon with a new tolerance. Why is he delinquent? Most often it is for sick reasons. But occasionally it is for good reasons and the boy is simply resisting exploitation, domination, neglect, contempt and trampling upon.[15]

And so, the youthful dissidents of the postwar years, the restless progeny of the hipsters and beats, were slowly developing a culture of their own. And, in the wake of this ferment and in a context of Cold War thaw, intellectual currents in politics and the social sciences were providing positive support for this rebellious mood.

The Beginnings of a Counter-Culture

Juvenile delinquency was on the wane. James Dean was dead, and Elvis Presley—the most obvious symbol of youthful rebellion—was about to be drafted willingly into the army. The major record corporations were reasserting their dominance over popular music.* Dick Clark's "American Bandstand" on

*In 1955, classic rock's golden age, Bill Haley's "Rock Around the Clock" was the best-selling record. Of the next twenty-four hit records, twenty were by black artists, including Johnny Ace, The Platters, Chuck Berry, The Penguins, Fats Domino, the Moonglows, Ray Charles, Etta James, The Charms, Little Walter, Bo Diddley, The Five Keys, Al Hibber, and the

network TV with its following of white teenagers, had replaced Alan Freed as the most important showcase of musical talent. Yet something was happening to young people all across the country. In Minnesota, Bobby Zimmerman, a high school student in the iron-mining town of Hibbing, was playing guitar and piano in imitation of black bluesmen. In 1959 he'd start hanging out in Dinkytown, Minneapolis' version of Greenwich Village, change his name to Bob Dylan, and start copying Woody Guthrie. In Port Arthur, Texas, Janis Joplin, an outcast in high school, was fancying herself a beatnik, reading books that were not assigned in class, and hanging out in local roadhouses soaking up black music. In Palo Alto, California, Kepler's bookstore and a local peace center, both run by World War II CO's, were the hangouts for a coming generation of hippies, including the nucleus of the band that would later become the Grateful Dead.

From Westport, Connecticut, to Winnetka, Illinois, similar scenes were taking shape; kids were pestering their parents for guitars and bongo drums and passing around copies of Ginsberg's *Howl* and Ferlinghetti's *A Coney Island of the Mind* in the same furtive way that an earlier generation handled *The Amboy Dukes*. On weekends, San Francisco's North Beach, despite police harassment, would be flooded with young people from suburbia, all in beatnik "uniform" of workshirts and dungarees, and many with books of poetry (or copies of Walter Kaufman's book on existentialism, which was then the "in" thing to have, but which nobody read) sticking out of their pockets. In Greenwich Village, teenagers were flooding the streets on weekends, turning Macdougal Street into Coney Island and causing the local residents to complain. Sunday afternoon, baby beatniks from the Bronx and Long Island gathered with guitars in Washington Square Park to sing songs about hard times and hard traveling although most of them had never done more than commute to the city from their comfortable middle-class

---

El Dorados. The white artists on the list were Mitch Miller, mambo king Prez Prado, Bill Hayes (singing "The Ballad of Davey Crockett"), and Tennessee Ernie Ford. By 1958, of the twenty-five tunes, only the Silhouettes (with No. 9), The Elegants, The Platters, and the Coasters represented the nitty-gritty black rock styles.

homes.* The *Village Voice*, the first underground newspaper, articulating both bohemian and radical ideas, was gaining a youthful readership on college campuses across the country. In Boston, Joan Baez was appearing barefoot in tiny coffeehouses. In a veterans hospital in Palo Alto a young novelist named Ken Kesey volunteered himself as a guinea pig so that doctors could learn the effects of LSD. In Liverpool, England, high school kids like John Lennon, Paul McCartney and George Harrison were organizing rock'n'roll bands and listening to the kind of American blues that were rarely heard on the top 40 radio stations in the United States.

All this was happening to a small minority of young people in isolated places all over the country. It could not, then, be classified as a "movement." The kids involved felt isolated and strange; they did not know that other kids were going through similar experiences elsewhere. In the declining years of the 1950s, America seemed to have hurdled the darkness; John Kennedy was in the wings, young, vigorous, handsome, in-augurating—or so he said—the coming to power of a new generation.

---

*In a sign of things to come, New York City's park commissioner, Newbald Morris, banned singing in Washington Square Park during the summer of 1958. But the folk singers refused to move, causing a confrontation with the police and a number of arrests. Older bohemians living in Greenwich Village, rallied to the folk-singer's cause. Old militant union songs, like "We Shall Not Be Moved," took on meaning for a new generation of militants, not working-class assembly line workers, but white, middle-class kids from Long Island, Teaneck, Westchester County, and the Bronx.

Chapter Fourteen

We are people of this generation, bred in at least modest comfort, housed now in universities, looking uncomfortably to the world we inherit.

When we were kids the United States was the wealthiest and strongest country in the world; the only one with the atom bomb, the least scarred by modern war, an initiator of the United Nations that we thought would distribute Western influence thoughout the world. Freedom and equality for each individual; government of, by, and for the people—these American values we found good, principles by which we could live as men (sic). Many of us began maturing in complacency.

As we grew, however, our comfort was penetrated by events too troubling to dismiss. First, the permeating and victimizing fact of human degradation, symbolized by the Southern struggle against racial bigotry.... Second, the enclosing fact of the Cold War, symbolized by the presence of the Bomb.... We might deliberately ignore, or avoid, or fail to feel all other human problems, but not these two, for these were too crushing and immediate in their impact, too challenging in the demand that we as individuals take the responsibility for encounter and resolution.

—Students for a Democratic Society, the Port Huron Statement, 1962

Hiroshima and Nagasaki brought a moral urgency to American politics. The advent of the nuclear age led many people to evaluate their view towards war as an acceptable instrument of national policy. Humankind seemed to be at a crossroads. "The one thing that the atomic bomb has achieved, besides the horror of Hiroshima," wrote an editor in the pacifist newspaper *The Conscientious Objector*, "is a decided simplification of the issues before us, our choice now being a regenerative humanity or literal extinction."[1] In the immediate aftermath of the war, with the horror of the bombings still fresh in mind, popular opinion momentarily agreed. *Life*, in its first editorial on the Atomic Age, noted that the concept of strategic bombing had led inevitably to Hiroshima, and this progression presented a potential breakdown of civilization and moral law. "Our sole safeguard against the very real danger of a reversion to barbarianism," said *Life*, "is the kind of morality which compels the individual conscience, be the group right or wrong. The individual conscience against the atomic bomb? Yes. There is no other way."[2]

Life quickly abandoned its flirtation with individual responsibility and the politics of conscience. For the government and its supporters, the bomb became a guarantor of peace; the threat of its use would make other governments think twice before giving their citizens marching orders. As one scientist recalled, "It was not an altogether unrealistic hope that mankind could be reasoned—or frightened—into entering a new, peaceful world."[3] But this presumption rested on the idea of a Pax Americana; what was good for the United States was good for the rest of the world. And it assumed a commitment to the status quo despite the revolutionary fervor sweeping the colonial possessions of the faltering European empires. The only threat to world peace, according to this, the dominant view, came from the Soviet Union. Colonial people would themselves not revolt to seek independence or national liberation, unless ordered to do so by the troublemakers within the Kremlin. By using the bomb to intimidate the Soviets, the U.S. could keep order throughout the world.

In opposition to this nuclear-edged Pax Americana, was the view that war was no longer a practical instrument of foreign policy, because a nuclear war would be suicidal for all, with neither victors nor survivors. Nuclear pacifism, as this position was sometimes called, had its adherents in the scientific community. In late 1946, educator Robert Hutchins told the pacifist leader A. J. Muste that "a movement is gaining ground among scientists...against working on anything that looks like a weapon." Norbert Weiner, the father of cybernetics and a missile expert for the U.S. government during the war, stated that "the policy of government...during and after the war, say in the bombings of Hiroshima and Nagasaki, has made it clear that to provide scientific information is not a necessarily innocent act. I do not expect to publish any future work of mine which may do damage in the hands of irresponsible militarists." To which Albert Einstein commented, "Non-cooperation in military matters should be an essential moral principle for all true scientists."[4]

Meanwhile, out of the mainstream, a handful of committed radical pacifists were experimenting with nonviolent tactics. Many of them had served time in prison during World War II as noncooperating conscientious objectors (CO's). Many were followers of the Reverend A. J. Muste, a longtime socialist labor leader who had become a Christian pacifist in the late 1930s. Muste urged an active nonviolence that, while being anti-capitalist, would base itself on a principled morality—the key, he felt, to revolutionary change. The pacifist minority addressed itself to the problem, expressed by Niccolo Tucci in *Politics* magazine in 1945, of "not how to get rid of the enemy, but rather how to get rid of the last victor. For what is a victor but one who has learned that violence works. Who will teach *him* a lesson?"[5] As soon as the United States began its postwar testing of atomic bombs in 1946, nonviolent activists began demonstrations aimed at raising the issue to public consciousness.

The Radical Dilemma

One of the new pacifism's more important adherents was Dwight Macdonald, who, from 1944 to 1949, edited a small radical magazine called *Politics*. A former writer for *Fortune* magazine, an ex-Trotskyist, and a respected member of the *Partisan Review* circle of intellectuals, Macdonald moved during the war to a quasi-anarchist pacifist position that recognized as the major problem facing the postwar world the issue of power and how to diffuse centralized political authority. Outside of the tiny pacifist press, *Politics* was the only publication to criticize American bombing tactics during the war and to speak about the moral implications of a strategy that increasingly resembled that of the enemy.[6]

Radical nonviolence formed the kernel of the ideas that Macdonald was moving toward. "Anyone who follows the CO press," he wrote in June 1945, "must be struck with how serious and original thinking is being done by CO's these days. Unlike the routinized Socialist and Trotskyist press which...just plods along month after month in the old treadmill, the CO's seem to be examining their basic ideas in the light of experience.... This new kind of CO thinking is...more politically conscious in that it sees the coercive power of the state as a major problem...."[7] In this spirit, *Politics* tried to articulate a third-camp ideology that looked neither to the Soviet Union nor to the United States as a model, but considered that the power each of these two giants wielded in the unstable postwar world was a source of trouble. Sensitive to the problem of power and its misuse, Macdonald also broke with the old radicalism by challenging the notion of progress. In an essay, "The Root is Man," he argued the distinction between "Progressivism" and true "radicalism." Progressives, he said, "see the present as an episode on the road to a better future"; they "think more in terms of historical process than of moral values." Progressives also believe "that the main trouble with the world is partly lack of scientific knowledge and partly the failure to apply to human affairs such knowledge as we do have." Above all else, Progressives "regard the increase of man's mastery over nature as good in itself...." "Radical," on the other hand,

> would apply to the as yet few individuals...who reject the concept of Progress, who judge things by their present meaning and effect, who think the ability of science to guide us in human affairs has been overrated and who therefore redress the balance by emphasizing the ethical aspects of politics. They, or rather we, think it is an open question whether the increase of man's mastery over nature is good or bad in its actual effects

on human life to date, and favor adjusting technology to man, even if it means—as may be the case—a technological regression....[8]

Macdonald, however, ran aground on the dilemma of the Cold War.The magazine, as its readers were aware, existed in a moral vacuum, a result of the war. "Except for a small group who as I do read *Politics* each month," wrote one subscriber, "all my friends and acquaintances have become zombified. This numbification I know to be general."[9] *Politics* represented ideology as an abstraction; there was no movement in existence to experiment with its ideas. Himself uncompromisingly anti-Stalinist, Macdonald was befuddled by the postwar conflict with the Soviet Union. The U.S., he felt, could not be trusted; but Stalinism had to be stopped at all costs. "There are only two factors in the political world today," Macdonald said, "the Kremlin and the State Department, and if one doesn't choose one, one must choose the other."[10] The Cold War had made independent politics impossible, and in 1949 *Politics* folded.

The radical intellectuals never recovered from World War II. As Mills wrote in 1951,

Few intellectuals rose to protest against the war on political or moral grounds, and the prosperity after the war, in which the intellectuals shared, was for them a time of moral slump. They have not returned to politics, much less turned left again, and no new generation has yet moved into their old stations. With this disintegration has gone political will; in its place there is hopelessness.[11]

The Cold War and the ensuing repression contributed to the left's defeat. But a contributing factor was the left's failure to comprehend the resiliency of the capitalist system, especially in the context of the postwar pax America. At the end of the war, the left was confident that a new depression would revitalize the class struggle and bring about a return to the revolutionary conditions of the 1930s. Corporate leaders, in and out of government, fearing the same possibility, took measures to avert it. The economy boomed. Anti-communism (within the left it took the form of anti-Stalinism) gave credence to first Truman's and then Eisenhower's military and foreign policy goals. Labor militancy was softened by affluence and destroyed by a bureau-cratic and sometimes corrupt union leadership. The radicals of the 1930s were middle-aged. Their economic predictions had proven wrong. Many opted for the financial success that the postwar economy offered. Some abandoned politics for oppor-tunities in business. Many became secure in academia; others "made it" in the literary world. Disillusioned because their own flirtation with idealism had led to the Stalinist nightmare, they were ready to abandon the socialist vision and make peace with the American dream. "The intellectual knows now," wrote Arthur Schlesinger, Jr., in a 1952 issue of *Partisan Review,* "that the chief hope for survival lies in the capacity of the American government and the strength of American society." "The love long repressed," wrote Max Lerner in the same issue, "is now being released."[12]

The Civil Rights Movement

Black Americans gained little by the American victory in the war. Segregation was a way of life in 1945 as it had been before the war. Throughout most of the war, the American military remained completely segregated. In the army, where all-black units (whose ranking officers, however, were white) distinguished themselves in combat, less than 1 percent of the officer corps was black, although 10 percent of the enlisted men were. In the navy, blacks served as messmen and did little fighting.[13]

At home, the mobilization that ended the Depression had helped blacks least. Just as they were the first to be fired when the economy failed, they were the last to be hired when military contracts led to economic revival. The jobs that opened up in 1940 after President Roosevelt designated the U.S. "the arsenal of democracy" were filled on a white-first basis. Only after a threat in January 1941 by A. Philip Randolph of the Brotherhood of Sleeping Car Porters to lead a march on Washington for equality in employment, did the administration move to remedy the situation. In June 1941, Roosevelt issued executive order 8802 forbidding "discrimination in the employment of workers in defense industries or government because of race, creed, color, or national origin." Even then, the Fair Employment Practices

Commission (FEPC) that he established had no powers. Yet, in the immediate postwar years, barriers of segregation were beginning to fall. Returning black veterans and those industrial workers with union experience were more assertive. The stereotype of Negro passivity began to disappear. Though in the South, racism was as virulent as ever and terrorism against black people was as commonplace as before, many Americans began to feel shame about racial atrocities that in the past they readily chose to ignore.

In 1948 Jackie Robinson broke the racial barrier in major league baseball. The aggressive second baseman for the Brooklyn Dodgers, ignoring the provocations of racist players and fans, quickly established himself as a baseball star. With Robinson's success, racial barriers in professional sports fell and black athletes like Willie Mays in baseball, Jimmy Brown in football, and Bill Russell and Wilt Chamberlin in basketball became national heroes, emulated by young athletes of all races.

As an indication of events to come, the Congress of Racial Equality (CORE), which had been organized by pacifists in 1942 in order to experiment with nonviolent tactics against racial segregation, succeeded after the war in desegregating movie theatres in Denver, restaurants in Detroit, the Palisades Amusement Park in New Jersey, the Euclid swimming pool and amusement park in Cleveland, playgrounds in Washington, D.C., the downtown shopping area of St. Louis and Woolworth lunch counters throughout the north. The victories were small and the South considered too tough to crack. Yet, despite harrassment during the anti-Communist scare that almost destroyed the organization, momentum was building. Equally important, CORE trained hundreds of people in the techniques of nonviolent action, instruction that proved decisive in later years.[14]

CORE, with its small, interracial, activist membership was the cutting edge of the civil rights movement. The two major civil rights organizations, the Urban League and the National Association for the Advancement of Colored People (NAACP) had broader membership and more moderate programs. The Urban League, funded by the philanthropy of wealthy whites, sought to open up job opportunities for blacks, especially as they moved North. But the jobs it provided were on the menial level, of the kind its wealthy backers thought "fitted" the black mentality. As a service organization, it remained aloof from political struggle. Even organized labor was too hot for the Urban League to support; such backing would have alienated its corporate source of money. Of the unions, for that matter, the AFL was a bastion of white supremacy and its skilled-craft unions continued throughout the 1950s to prevent blacks from learning the trades. The CIO, on the other hand, had an excellent record in battling for the rights of its black members.

The NAACP, founded in 1910, was distant from the day-to-day struggle of black Americans. With a membership drawn mostly from the black middle class and sympathetic whites, and an organizational structure that centralized power in a small, unchanging leadership body, the NAACP eschewed militancy, direct action, and efforts to build a grass-roots movement, concentrating instead in political lobbying and, through its Legal and Defense Fund (headed throughout this period by future Supreme Court Justice Thurgood Marshall), on winning court battles and establishing legal precedents for Negro rights. This it did with singular success, even though many of the legal victories proved unenforceable without a politically conscious movement to back them up. Among the NAACP's victories were the outlawing of segregation on interstate buses in 1946, in state universities and graduate schools in 1950, the outlawing of segregation in Washington, D.C. in stores and restaurants, in 1953, and—most spectacularly—in public schools in 1954.

School segregation, which in 1950 was sanctioned by custom or law in twenty-one states plus Washington, D.C., was considered the key aspect of the civil rights struggle. In 1951, NAACP lawyers helped Oliver Brown bring suit against the Topeka, Kansas, Board of Education; his eight-year-old daughter had to cross a railroad grading and travel twenty-one blocks to an all-black school, instead of being allowed to attend an all-white school just five blocks from her home. On 17 May 1954, the Supreme Court unanimously voted in Linda Brown's favor and struck down the "separate but equal" doctrine, in effect making integrated public education the law of the land. This decision, which discussed the psychological and sociological effects that discrimination had on black people, proved to be the opening wedge in the contemporary civil rights struggle.

Brown vs. Topeka Board of Education brought the struggle against Southern racism to the public. The Supreme Court backed off from requiring immediate compliance, however, and in a 1955 follow-up decision called merely for "all deliberate speed." By 1961, only 7 percent of the South's public schools were integrated, and this figure included Washington, D.C., where compliance was complete.[15] In the Deep South, resistance was absolute. The Ku Klux Klan began to re-emerge for the first time since the 1920s, and White Citizens Councils were organized everywhere to give racism the veneer of middle-class respectability. One hundred southern congressmen issued a statement in 1956 declaring their support for those states that "have declared the intention to resist forced integration by any lawful means...." In this spirit, southern legislatures passed a maze of laws aimed at delaying compliance for decades if not forever. President Eisenhower refused to support the Supreme Court ruling publicly, other than to speak generally of respect for the law, and the Democratic leader Adlai Stevenson, urged that civil rights be approached cautiously, with moderation. Meanwhile, where its legal defense failed, the white South resorted to violence. Between 1955 and 1958, the peak years of the anti-integration movement, at least six blacks were killed in school-related incidents. Other casualties included eighteen people shot, forty-four beaten, five stabbed, thirty homes bombed, one church bombed, and four Jewish temples bombed.[16] There were also a number of unrelated lynchings. The most spectacular, in the summer of 1958, involved a young black from Chicago named Emmett Till who was in Mississippi visiting relatives. For allegedly whistling at a white woman in a rural country store, the youngster was kidnapped and murdered. In this case, local police arrested the perpetrators, but an all-white jury refused to convict them of any crime. More commonly, local law enforcement officials refused to curb this violence as long as it was directed against blacks and the small white minority that supported civil rights. And the FBI, busy chasing down subversives, insisted that it had no power to protect the victims of white racism.

The beginning of each school year focused national attention on school integration. In 1955, Clinton, Tennessee, was the center of violent white resistance. In 1956, the attempt of nine black students to integrate the high school in Sturgis, Kentucky, led to white rioting and the calling out of the Kentucky National Guard. In 1957, Little Rock, Arkansas, became the focal point as Governor Orval Faubus, vowing that no black children would enter Central High School, called out the National Guard to bar the entrance of eight black teenagers. This open defiance of federal law, sanctioned by the governor of a state, was a challenge that Eisenhower could not ignore. When, on September 23, a mob of whites prevented the children from attending school, the President ordered 1,000 members of the 101st Airborne Division into Little Rock to uphold the law. Even then, in a television address, Eisenhower refused to discuss the moral issue of black rights. Instead, he defended his action on narrow legal grounds. "The very basis of our individual rights and freedoms," he said, rests upon the certainty that the President and the executive branch of government will support and insure the carrying out of the decisions of the federal courts, when necessary, with all the means at the President's command. Unless the President did so, anarchy would result."*[17] A white boycott and the daily gathering of angry whites outside the school forced the soldiers to remain in Little Rock through May 1958, while the eight black students attended school with only a handful of whites. The next year, Faubus again attempted to close the school and it was not until the start of school in 1959 that token integration was allowed to proceed peaceably. By this time, Little Rock had become an international scandal.

On 1 December 1955, a black seamstress named Rosa Parks refused to give her bus seat to a white man, as required by law, in Montgomery, Alabama. "I don't really know why I wouldn't move," she said later. "I was just tired from shopping. My feet hurt."[18] (Her motivation was probably more conscious than she would let on. Rosa Parks represented a new generation of politically active Southern blacks. A former official of the

---

*Many liberals wanted Eisenhower to personally go to Little Rock, take the black children by the hands, and lead them through the mob into school, thus placing the Presidency morally behind integration and the new law. Mort Sahl, noting that the President's main interest in life seemed to be golf, insisted that the basis for his refusal rested with his indecision about which golfing "grip" to use when holding the children by the hand.

Montgomery NAACP, she had on occasion attended programs at the Highlander Folk School, a small alternative school in the hills of Tennessee that had been organized by radicals in the 1930s and remained a center for labor and civil-rights activists.) The night of her arrest, an ad hoc committee of black women met to decide on a plan of action. The leaders of the entire black community, including Martin Luther King, Jr., the new minister at the Dexter Avenue Baptist Church, were consulted and it was decided to call a bus boycott to begin the next Monday, the first day of the working week. On Sunday, black ministers spread the word of the boycott from their pulpits and King and the others spent the weekend grinding out mimeographed instructions for the city's 50,000 black residents. Right from the start, the boycott was almost 100 percent effective. In *Stride Towards Freedom*, King described the excitement of the first day:

> All day long it continued. At the afternoon peak the buses were still empty of Negro passengers as they had been in the morning. Students of Alabama State College, who usually kept the South Jackson bus crowded, were cheerfully walking or thumbing rides. Job holders had either found other means of transportation or made their way on foot. While some rode in cabs or private cars, others used less conventional means. Men were seen riding mules to work, and more than one horsedrawn buggy drove the streets of Montgomery that day.
>
> During the rush hours the sidewalks were crowded with laborers and domestic workers, many of them well past middle age, trudging patiently to their jobs and home again, sometimes as much as twelve miles. They knew why they walked, and the knowledge was evident in the way they carried themselves. And as I watched them I knew that there is nothing more majestic than the determined courage of individuals willing to suffer and sacrifice for their freedom and dignity.

"A miracle had taken place," King went on. "The once dormant and quiescent Negro community was now fully awake."[19]

The first night, at a mass meeting, the black community

organized itself into the Montgomery Improvement Association with King as its president, and accepted a resolution calling for a continued boycott until courteous treatment by bus drivers was guaranteed. Other demands were that passengers be treated on a first-come, first-serve basis, with blacks seated from the back of the bus towards the front and whites from the front towards the back, and black bus drivers to be hired for black routes. The boycott lasted for more than a year despite continuous police harassment, arrests of the leadership (including King), and numerous bombings. The black community stayed together, organizing carpools, while NAACP lawyers pursued the issue of segregated buses through the courts. On 13 November 1956, the decision upholding Rosa Parks was announced, and on 21 December, after negotiations with white officials, Montgomery blacks ended their boycott and began riding integrated buses.

King, Ralph Abernathy, and other black ministers formed the Southern Christian Leadership Conference (SCLC) the next year. Like Northern-based CORE, SCLC was committed to nonviolence, a position that King had espoused before the Montgomery experience as a result of studying Gandhi and Thoreau and thinking about the strategy for gaining black rights. As was the case with the activists in CORE, there was nothing passive about King's pacifism. "For while the nonviolent resister is passive in the sense that he isn't physically agressive toward his opponent," King wrote,

> "his mind and emotions are always active, constantly seeking to persuade his opponent that he is wrong. The method is passive physically, but strongly active spiritually. It is not passive nonresistance to evil, it is active nonviolent resistance to evil."[20]

During the closing years of the 1950s, except for the battle over integrated schools and some small marches on Washington for integration, the civil rights struggle seemed quiet. Yet in 1957 a bus boycott in Rocky Mount, North Carolina, similar to the one organized in Montgomery, emerged triumphant. CORE began to move into the South and established an important student chapter in Nashville, while in 1958 and 1959, its list of financial contributors jumped from 4,500 to 12,000.[21] In August 1958, the Youth Council of the Oklahoma City NAACP carried out a lunch counter sit-in, though it received no publicity. In 1958 and 1959, Bayard Rustin organized two student marches on Washington for integrated schools that attracted, in 1959, 25,000 people, many of them students from the South. And the SCLC began setting up chapters around the region. King became a recognized national spokesman, an activist counterweight to the traditional national organizations, the Urban League and the NAACP. What happened in Montgomery the day Rosa Parks decided to assert her human dignity sent forth ripples throughout the country.

The Ban The Bomb Movement

By the late fifties the worst of the anti-communist crusade had passed and the "spirit of Geneva," encouraged by the Eisenhower-Khruschev summit meeting of 1956, had improved the political climate within the United States. But the continued testing of increasingly sophisticated nuclear devices by both countries did nothing to abate the climate of fear. In the United States, civil defense programs remained a high priority and air raid drills and take-shelter drills were routine. Nevertheless, the consensus over the arms race was beginning to fracture. From the scientific community, including the developers of the first atomic weapons, came opposition to the hydrogen bomb. Continual high-altitude nuclear testing was creating long-range environmental problems that the builders of the bomb did not anticipate and that proponents of the bomb tried to ignore. Most notable was the discovery of radioactive Strontium 90 in the food supply, especially milk. Radioactive nuclear fallout was monitored everywhere on the globe, including the polar regions, and evidence showed that the effects of nuclear weapons could not be localized to the target area. During the 1956 presidential campaign, Democratic candidate Adlai Stevenson proposed that both the U.S. and the Soviet Union cease testing hydrogen weapons as a first step to nuclear disarmament. His eloquent description of the dangers from radioactive fallout gave the subject legitimacy.

The radical pacifist movement in 1956 began publishing *Liberation* magazine, the first activist-oriented, pacificist inspired publication since *Politics*. With an editorial staff that has included at one time or another Muste, Dave Dellinger, Bayard Rustin, Paul Goodman, Staughton Lynd, Sid Lens, and Barbara Deming—all of them seminal figures in the new radicalism—*Liberation* took up the cause of civil rights, decentralization, nonviolent action, and a Third Camp foreign policy. The Third Camp position got its impetus from *Politics* and two publications of the American Friends Service Committee (AFSC): *The United States and the Soviet Union* in 1949, and *Speak Truth to Power* in 1955. The Third Camp idea rejected the power politics of both the United States and the Soviet Union. It looked instead toward a third and yet uncharted way that rejected the centralized nationalism and dependence on military power for security that both powers shared. Faith in technology, industrialization, and centralization for the sake of efficiency was rejected in favor of a "politics of the future." Emphasis would be placed on "the possibilities for decentralization, on direct participation of all workers or citizens in determining the conditions of life and work, and on the use of technology for human ends, rather than the subjugation of man to the demands of technology."[22]

If *Liberation* was the ideological voice of the budding movement, the Committee for Nonviolent Action (CNVA) was its activist arm. It began as an ad hoc committee to plan civil disobedience against a nuclear bomb test in August 1957. Eleven pacifists crossed into a prohibited area and were arrested. In 1958, CNVA became a permanent committee with Muste as its central figure, and a series of spectacular civil disobedience actions were taken in succeeding years.

One of the most successful of these projects was the attempted sailing of the *Golden Rule* into the nuclear bomb test area in the South Pacific. The ketch sailed from California to Honolulu on 2 May 1958 (with a crew that included George Bigalow, a commander of a submarine chaser in World War II) and then to Eniwetok, where the U.S. had scheduled bomb tests. The Coast Guard intercepted the vessel and the men were arrested and taken to Honolulu where they refused bail while awaiting trial for contempt. Their adventure caught the attention of the world, and with news of their arrest came announcements of support demonstrations in seven American cities, plus Montreal and London.

These early CNVA demonstrations were viewed by most people as being somewhat kooky and extreme. Respectable people didn't go to jail. National defense was a subject about which the government knew best. The bomb and the threat of nuclear annihilation were facts that the public had to bear up under. There was little the public could do but to vote when asked, and to trust those who it elected. But each CNVA demonstration moved a few people, inspired individuals to change their lives in what seemed at first like small meaningless steps but which led, in many cases, to a full-time commitment to peace and justice. The organization that benefited most by CNVA's agitation was SANE (The Committee for a Sane Nuclear Policy), formed in 1957 by many of the same people active in CNVA. SANE, more moderate then CNVA, was structured as a membership organization, with an educational purpose to join pacifists and non-pacifists together in the common effort to bring the arms race under control. The two organizations effectively complemented one another: CNVA's stirring demonstrations shook people out of their complacency and made them want to do something about the bomb. For those not ready to make the commitment that CNVA required, SANE was available to channel their energy. With chapters all across the country, it reached out especially to the white middle class, activating liberal Democrats, veterans of the Old Left, and young people who, until then, did not know that a politics of public of protest existed.*[23]

The Emerging New Left

In the late 1950s all the strands of an embryonic movement began to come together on the college campuses. The impetus was at first cultural. The Old Left student groups like the Socialist Party's Young People's Socialist League (YPSL) operated on the fringe of campus society, with never more than a few dedicated individuals in a handful of places.[24] More important

---

*In 1958, The Eisenhower administration, which had dismissed such proposals earlier as "catastrophic nonsense," agreed with the USSR to cease all above-ground nuclear testing. It was a step. For the first time since the beginning of the Cold War, radical ideas were filtering through to people with power.

was the influence of the beats, and their growing political awareness, represented by Gregory Corso's mushroom-shaped poem, *Bomb*, which fantasized what it was like to be both a bomb and its victim, and Lawrence Ferlinghetti's political broadside, "Tentative Description for a Speech to be Given on the Impeachment of President Eisenhower" (1959). Folksingers and jazz also had an impact. The *Village Voice, The Realist,* and the political commentary of the new comedians helped students view the world from a frame of reference that was not taught in school.

Ban-the-bomb and civil rights were the first issues to make a dent in student apathy. But they were still fringe issues. The silent generation of college students that dominated the campuses during the Cold War began to disappear only in the late 1950s. In 1957, *The Nation* magazine ran a symposium on what it called "The Careful Young Man." At college after college, it was noted that the overriding concern of the student generation was with personal security, and that the most important value was conformity to adult expectations. At the University of Michigan, college was described as a place where "with touching submissiveness, he (the student) accepts the remarks of lecturers and the hard sentences of text books as directives that will lead him to a job." At Yale, an English professor noted that the "present campus indifference to either politics or reform or rebellion is monumental." A student at the University of Washington attempted to put her generation in perspective, writing:

> What we all lack who are under thirty is some guiding passion, some moral vision, if you will. We are unable to wind the loose threads of our experience into some larger pattern, and we know it....If our revolt appears mild, it is because we have not found anything to promote.[25]

But change was in the wind. Compulsory ROTC was under challenge. A few avant garde English majors began writing papers on beat poetry, much to the consternation of their teachers. The anti-nuclear group, SANE, spawned a student affiliate, led in many places by children of Old Left families. In Chicago, a coalition of pacifists and socialists formed the Student Peace Union in 1959, and it spread rapidly. The *Monthly Review* magazine, an independent Marxist journal founded by political economists Paul Sweezy, Leo Huberman, and Harry Magdoff, and a small democratic socialist magazine, *Dissent*, founded in 1954 by, among others, Irving Howe, began to reach a university audience. Also in the late fifties, revisionist interpretations of the Cold War started to make their appearance. William Appleman Williams' seminal *Tragedy of American Diplomacy* was published in 1958. A professor of History at the University of Wisconsin, Williams helped start *Studies on the Left*, a theoretical journal that anticipated the development of the New Left, a few years later. By 1959, *The Nation* was calling attention to the "Tension Beneath Apathy" that was noticeable on univversity campuses.[26]

This Little Light...

On 1 February 1960, four freshman students at the all-black North Carolina A&T College sat in at an all-white Woolworth lunch counter in Greensboro. They sat there without being served until the store closed; during the next few days more students joined them, including whites from a nearby women's college. Not knowing how to sustain their action, they turned to a local NAACP official, Dr. George Simkin. Simkin knew of CORE's earlier experiments with nonviolent action and put in a call to CORE's regional office to ask for advice. Two organizers, Gordon Carey and James McCain, immediately set off for Greensboro to train the students in nonviolent tactics. In New York, two other CORE activists, Jim Peck and Marvin Rich, began negotiations with Woolworth executives to desegregate its lunch counters all across the nation. At the same time, CORE urged its members to set up local support demonstrations, the first of which took place at a Woolworth store in Harlem two weeks later. From Greensboro, the movement spread on its own momentum.[27] In Atlanta, black college students Ruby Doris Smith and Julian Bond responded to Greensboro by setting up similar demonstrations. In Nashville, James Lawson, a theology student and conscientious objector, organized a movement that included such future civil rights leaders as Marion Barry, John Lewis, Diane Nash, and James Bevel. Within two weeks of Greensboro, sit-ins took place in Rock Hill, Columbia, and Orangeburg, South Carolina; Chattanooga, Memphis, Knoxville, and Oak Ridge, Tennessee; Houston, Texas; Jacksonville, Florida; Frankfurt, Kentucky; Jackson and Biloxi, Mississippi—and that was just the beginning.

Non-violent organizers—many of them veterans of CORE—who had waited for years for such a moment, sped South to lend their experience. King put the reputation of SCLC behind the student activists and provided the money for the establishment of a coordinating body, the Student Nonviolent Coordinating Committee (SNCC). As the movement moved through the South, it touched upon the conscience of the student population in the North—white as well as black. Many dropped out of school or abandoned new careers. Bob Moses Parris—a young black teacher at an exclusive New York private school who would soon become one of the most influential organizers of SNCC—later recalled watching the Greensboro sit-in on television. "The students had a certain look on their faces, sort of sullen, angry, determined. Before, the Negro in the South had always looked on the defensive, cringing. This time they were taking the initiative. They were kids my age, and I knew they had something to do with my own life...."[29]

For whites, this was the first generation to feel intimately connected with the lives of their black peers. Rock'n'roll, baseball stars like Jackie Robinson and Willie Mays, cultural heroes like Charlie Parker, Chuck Berry, and Leadbelly—all had helped to bridge the racial gap. The once silent generation, restless and in search for something to believe in, had at last found its cause. Of course most students remained apolitical and apathetic. But thousands of young whites did rally to the support of these first sit-ins, writing letters to campus newspapers, raising money for bail funds and legal costs, and picketing their own local chainstores. Demonstrations were organized at over 100 college campuses and on most—as with the participants—it was a new experience. By year's end an estimated 50,000 people had taken part in the new movement, and there had been 3,600 arrests.[30] Going to jail, once a stigma, was now becoming a badge of honor.

The sit-in tactics were adopted for other issues. In May 1960, when HUAC staged hearings on supposed subversion in the Bay Area, hundreds of Bay Area residents gathered at San Francisco's City Hall in protest. Denied access to the hearing room, they refused to leave City Hall. The police then turned fire hoses on the demonstrators and dragged many of them down the stairs in view of reporters and television cameras. HUAC and the FBI immortalized the episode in a melodramatic, badly distorted film, "Operation Abolition," aimed at showing that the students had been duped by Communist organizers. The film was shown on college campuses and to local civic organizations. Off-campus, the film was generally taken at face value, but students around the country viewed it with scorn and took the side of the demonstrators. Rather than squelching campus opposition as the moviemakers intended, the film helped nurture the campus protest movement of the early 1960s. Never again would HUAC—or any other government agency—be able to silence people through intimidation, fear, or threats of repression.

The cultural dissidence of the post-World War II period now took on a political dimension. Though the corporate-government alliance would remain powerful and in power, and though the governing assumptions by which it ruled would remain intact, the popular consensus that had supported it, that had been forged by affluence (and, by apathy, acquiescence and velvet-glove coercion) would be broken. In the coming decades, the American people would begin to question and, in many cases, challenge the basic assumptions of postwar life. The long-awaited dawn of the sleepless night had come. The spark ignited at Greensboro spread its brilliance over the land: seeds long implanted began to sprout; the persistent stalks that would not die bent towards the light, took nourishment, and began to grow. The deadening days of the postwar era were over; the age old battle against darkness renewed. The struggle itself would last for decades and would not easily be won. But in the struggle comes victory; the struggle itself creates the light.

> This little light of mine, I'm gonna let it shine.
> This little light of mine, I'm gonna let it shine.
> This little light of mine, I'm gonna let it shine.
> Let it shine.
> Let it shine.
> Let it shine.[31]

FOOTNOTES

Part One—Prologue

1. *Song Hits Magazine*, November 1942 (Volume 6, Number 8), p. 30.
2. The essential bop recordings are: Dizzy Gillespie; "The Small Groups, 1945-1946," including "Oo-bop sh'bam" (Phoenix LP-2) and Charlie Parker, The Savoy Sessions (Savoy SJL 2201), as well as his Dial and Roost sessions available on an assortment of album reissues.
3. *Down Beat Magazine*, 1 August 1945.

Chapter One

1. *Wall Street Journal*, 4 April 1949; reprinted in *The World of the Wall Street Journal*, Charles Preston, editor (Simon and Schuster, 1959), p. 127.
2. *Business Week*, 11 August 1945, p. 9.
3. *Life*, 7 January 1946, p. 67.
4. *Life*, 25 November 1946, p. 49.
5. *Fortune*, October 1945, p. 125.
6. W. A. Swanberg, *Luce and His Empire* (Scribner, 1972), pp. 180-183.
7. Lawrence Wittner, *Rebels Against the War* (Columbia University Press, 1969), p. 99.
8. John Bagguley, "The World War and the Cold War" in *Containment and Revolution*, David Horowitz, editor (Beacon, 1967), p. 93.
9. Walter LaFeber, *America, Russia and the Cold War* (John Wiley & Sons, 1967), p. 19
10. William Miller, *New History of the United States* (Braziller, 1958), p. 412.
11. John Morton Blum, *V is for Victory* (Harcourt, Brace, Jovanovich, 1976), p. 122.
12. Norman Markowitz, *The Rise and Fall of the People's Century* (The Free Press, 1973), p. 167.
13. John Lewis Gaddis, *The United States and the Origins of the Cold War* (Columbia University Press, 1972), p. 224.
14. Markowitz, p. 186.
15. William Appleman Williams, "American Intervention in Russia" in *Containment and Revolution*, p. 34.
16. Gaddis, pp. 157-158.
17. D. F. Fleming, *The Cold War and Its Origins*, Volume One (Doubleday, 1961), p. 182.
18. Blum, p. 122.
19. Richard Barnet, *Roots of War* (Atheneum, 1972), p. 36. Blum, p. 122.
20. Bruce Catton, *Warlords of Washington* (Harcourt, Brace, 1948), p. 121.
21. Blum, p. 123.
22. Stuart Chase, *For This We Fought* (Twentieth Century Fund, 1946), p. 94.
23. Lloyd C. Gardner, *Architects of Illusion* (Quadrangle, 1970), p. 271.
24. David Halberstam, *The Best and the Brightest* (Random House, 1972), chapters 1-4. For more generalized studies of the corporate elite and its hold on American life, see: G. William Domhoff, *The Higher Circles* (Random House, 1970) and *Who Rules America?* (Prentice-Hall,

1967); C. Wright Mills, *The Power Elite* (Oxford University Press, 1956); Gabriel Koldo, *Wealth and Power in America* (Praeger, 1962) and *The Roots of American Foreign Policy* (Beacon, 1969).

25. Lloyd C. Gardner, "The New Deal, New Frontiers and the Cold War" in *Corporations and the Cold War,* David Horowitz, editor (Monthly Review Press, 1969), pp. 95-96.

26. For further discussion of the Open Door and its impact on American foreign policy, see: William Appleman Williams, *Roots of the Modern American Empire: A Study of the Growth and Shaping of Social Consciousness in a Marketplace Society* (Random House, 1969) and *The Tragedy of American Diplomacy* (revised edition, Dell, 1962); David Horowitz, *Free World Colossus* (Hill and Wang, 1971); Gabriel Kolko, *The Politics of War; The World and United States Foreign Policy, 1943-1945* (Random House, 1968). For a study of the Open Door and its importance to the corporate and domestic economy, see Harry Magdoff, *The Age of Imperialism* (Monthly Review Press, 1969).

27. Thomas R. Brooks, *Toil and Trouble* (Delcorte, 1964, 1971), p. 210.

28. Gardner, *Architects of Illusion*, p. 57.

29. Michael Tanzer, *The Sick Society* (Harper & Row), 1968, p. 77. William Appleman Williams, "The Large Corporations and the Cold War" in *Corporations and the Cold War*, pp. 95-96.

30. Magdoff, pp. 10, 20, 177.

31. Gardner, *Corporations and the Cold War*, p. 132.

32. Gabriel Kolko, *Main Currents in American History* (Harper & Row, 1976), p. 311.

33. Fred J. Cook, *The Warfare State* (Macmillan, 1962), p. 66.

34. Richard Barnet, *Economy of Death* (Atheneum, 1970), p. 69.

35. *Life*, 19 November 1945, pp. 32-33.

Chapter Two

1. *New York Times*, 27 December 1972, p. 46.

2. Martin J. Sherwin, *A World Destroyed: The Atomic Bomb and the Grand Alliance* (Vintage, 1973, 1975), p. 143.

3. Tanzer, p. 79.

4. I. F. Stone, *The Truman Era* (Vintage, 1953), p. 17.

5. Richard J. Walton, *Henry Wallace, Harry Truman and the Cold War* (Viking, 1976), p. 36.

6. Fleming, p. xii.

7. Fleming, p. 205.

8. Harry S. Truman, *Year of Decision, Memoirs,* Volume One (Doubleday, 1955), pp. 76-82. Gaddis, pp. 204-205.

9. Gar Alperovitz, *Cold War Essays* (Anchor, 1970), p. 110.

10. Sherwin, p. 223.

11. Sherwin, p. 224.

12. Truman, p. 87; Alperovitz, p. 70.

13. Thomas M. Patterson, *Soviet-American Confrontation* (John Hopkins Press, 1973), p. 35.

14. Patterson, p. 37.

15. Fleming, p. 339.
16. Dean Acheson, *Present at the Creation* (Norton, 1969), pp. 150-151. Gaddis, p. 300.
17. George Kennen, *Memoirs 1925-1950* (Atlantic, Little Brown, 1967), pp. 293-295, 547-599; LaFeber, pp. 64-66; Fleming, pp. 462-463.
18. *The Shaping of American Diplomacy: Readings and Documents in American Foreign Policy*, Volume Two, William Appleman Williams, editor (Rand McNally, second edition, 1970), pp. 398-399.
19. Gaddis, p. 339.
20. Review of the World Situation, 1949-1950, hearings held in executive session before the Committee on Foreign Relations, United States Senate, 81st Congress, first and second sessions (U.S. Government Printing Office, Historical Series, 1974), pp. 21-22; Acheson, p. 197.
21. Fleming, p. 444.
22. Ronald Steel, *Imperialists and Other Heroes* (Random House, 1971), p. 22.
23. Richard Freedland, *The Truman Doctrine and the Origins of McCarthyism* (Knopf, 1972), pp. 100-101.
24. Acheson, p. 219.
25. Todd Gitlin, "Counter-Insurgency: Myth and Reality in Greece" in *Containment and Revolution*, p. 144.
26. Steel, p. 22.
27. Legislative Origins of the Truman Doctrine, hearings held in executive session before the Committee on Foreign Relations, United States Senate, 80th Congress, first session, on S 938—a bill to provide for assistance to Greece and Turkey (U.S. Government Printing Office, Historical Series, 1973), p. 128.
28. Freedland, pp. 164-165.
29. Fleming, p. 478.
30. Freedland, p. 169.
31. Freedland, p. 186.
32. Freedland, p. 194, 196.
33. Freedland, p. 281.
34. Freedland, p. 275.
35. Stone, p. 26.
36. Acheson, p. 260.
37. *Review of the World Situation, 1949-1950*, pp. 205-207.
38. Acheson, p. 260.
39. Steel, p. 27.
40. Acheson, pp. 375, 378; LaFeber, pp. 97-100.
41. Harold G. Vatter, *The U.S. Economy in the 1950s* (Norton, 1963), p. 72.

Chapter Three

1. United States Relations with China, (The China White Paper), (Department of State Publication 3573, Far East Series 30, 1949), pp. 357, 970.
2. Theodore White, *In Search of History* (Harper & Row, 1978), pp.

205-210; Swanberg, p. 3.

3. *Life*, 7 October 1946, pp. 36-37.

4. *Review of the World Situation, 1949-1950*, p. 97.

5. Paul S. Holbo, *United States Policies Towards China* (Macmillan, 1964), p. 94.

6. William F. Fulbright, *The Crippled Giant* (Random House, 1972), p. 68.

7. Steel, p. 29.

8. Acheson, pp. 405, 535, 536.

9. *Review of the World Situation, 1949-1950*, p. 398.

10. I.F. Stone was one of the few critics of the U.S. position in the Korean War. His *Hidden History of the Korean War* (Monthly Review Press, 1952) was totally ignored by intellectuals, book reviewers, and other journalists. The CIA actually made an effort to buy up foreign editions. A highly regarded newsman, Stone was blacklisted by the mainstream press and so started his own newsletter, the famous *I.F. Stone Weekly*.

11. Acheson, p. 411.

12. Harry S. Truman, *Years of Trial and Hope, 1946-1952*, Volume Two (Doubleday, 1956), p. 339.

13. Stone, *Hidden History*, pp. 176-177.

14. Townshend Hoopes, *The Devil and John Foster Dulles* (Little Brown, 1973), p. 47.

15. Herbert S. Parmet, *Eisenhower and the American Crusade* (Macmillan, 1972), pp. 170-171.

16. Norman A. Graebner, *Cold War Diplomacy* (Van Nostrend, 1962), p. 63.

17. Parmet, p. 194.

18. Parmet, p. 197.

19. LaFeber, pp. 147-148; Hoopes, pp. 171-173.

20. LaFeber, p. 151; Parmet, pp. 278-279.

21. Parmet, p. 281.

22. Peter Lyon, *Eisenhower: Portrait of the Hero* (Little Brown, 1974), p. 653; Parmet, p. 406.

23. Tad Szulc, *Compulsive Spy* (Viking, 1974), pp. 26-27.

24. Andrew H. Berding, *Dulles on Diplomacy* (Van Nostrend, 1965), p. 63.

25. *Life*, 21 September 1953, pp. 59-62.

26. LaFeber, p. 163.

27. Dwight D. Eisenhower, *Mandate for Change* (Doubleday, 1962), p. 372.

28. The literature on the Vietnam War is vast. For the background to U.S. intervention, see *The Pentagon Papers; the Defense Department History of U.S. Decision-making in Vietnam*, Senator Mike Gravel, editor (Beacon, 1971, 1972) and Daniel Ellsberg, *Papers on the War* (Simon and Schuster, 1972).

29. Graebner, p. 88.

30. Harvey O'Connor, *The Corporations and the State* (Harper Torchbook, 1974), p. 171. See also Magdoff, *Age of Imperialism*.

31. Hoopes, p. 317.
32. Hoopes, p. 315; Graebner, pp. 92, 97.
33. Magdoff, p. 49.
34. Magdoff, p. 52.
35. Sam H. Schurr and Bruce Netschert, *Energy in the American Economy, 1850-1975* (John Hopkins Press, 1960, revised 1975), p. 86.
36. *Readers Digest*, March 1954, pp. 103-106.
37. Richard O'Connor, *The Oil Barons* (Little Brown, 1971), p. 324.
38. Michael Tanzer, *The Energy Crisis* (Monthly Review Press, 1974), pp. 27, 45-46; Anthony Sampson, *Seven Sisters* (Viking, 1975), pp. 110-111.
39. Robert Engler, *The Politics of Oil* (University of Chicago Press, 1961), p. 67.
40. Eisenhower, p. 159.
41. Harvey O'Conner, p. 185.
42. Lyon, pp. 588-589.
43. Eisenhower, p. 422; Lyon, pp. 589-592.
44. *Documents in American History*, Henry Steele Commager, editor (Appleton Century Croft, seventh ed., 1963), p. 613.
45. Eisenhower, p. 423.
46. Lyon, p. 614.
47. Howard S. Bierch, *The United States and Latin America* (Macmillan, 1969), p. 46; Robin M. Winks, *The Cold War from Yalta to Cuba* (Scribner, 1975), p. 212.
48. Herbert L. Matthews, *Revolution in Cuba* (Scribner, 1975), p. 130.
49. Matthews, p. 121.
50. Parmet, p. 560.
51. Parmet, p. 561.
52. *New York Times*, 1 May 1975, p. 8.
53. Gardner, *Corporations and the Cold War*, p. 135; Joseph Phillips, "Economic Effects of the Cold War," in *Corporations and the Cold War*, pp. 188-189; Magdoff, p. 198.

Chapter Four

1. Jeremy Brecher, *Strike!* (South End Press, 1977), pp. 226-227.
2. Stan Weir, "American Labor on the Defensive," *Radical America*, July-August 1975), pp. 178-181.
3. Markowitz, p. 202.
4. Markowitz, p. 276.
5. Markowitz, p. 242.
6. For a discussion of the Communist Party USA during this period, see: Joseph Starobin, *American Communism in Crisis* (University of California Press, 1972); Al Richmond, *A Long View from the Left* (Houghton Mifflin, 1972); Peggy Dennis, *The Autobiography of an American Communist* (Lawrence Hill, 1979); and Vivian Gornick, *The Romance of American Communism* (Basic Books, 1978).
7. Sidney Lens, *American Radicalism* (Crowell, 1966), p. 341.
8. Samuel Eliot Morison and Henry Steele Commager, *The Growth of the*

American Republic, Volume Two (Oxford University Press, 1962 edition), p. 785.

9. David Caute, *The Great Fear: The Anti-Communist Purge Under Truman and Eisenhower* (Simon and Schuster, 1978), pp. 280-282.

10. Truman, *Years of Trial and Hope*, p. 283.

11. Caute, p. 291.

12. Fred J. Cook, *The FBI Nobody Knows* (Macmillan, 1964), pp. 33, 40-41.

13. Bernard Devoto, "Due Notice to the FBI," *Harper's Magazine*, October 1949.

14. Freedland, p. 146.

15. Freedland, p. 233.

16. Markowitz, p. 257.

17. Markowitz, pp. 277-281.

18. James Aronson, *The Free Press and the Cold War* (Bobbs-Merrill, 1970), p. 43.

19. *New York Times*, 31 August 1947, p. E7.

20. Freedland, pp. 230-231.

21. Freedland, p. 237.

22. Freedland, p. 231.

23. *Teaching American History*, Bureau of Secondary Curriculum Development, N.Y. State Educational Department, 1955, pp. 248-255.

24. Harold J. Noah, Carl E. Prince and C. Russell Riggs, "History in High School Text Books: A Note," *School Review*, winter 1970, volume 70, no. 7, pp. 426-428.

25. Paul Samuelson, *Economics* (McGraw Hill, 1958 edition), p. 13.

26. Caute, pp. 70-71.

27. Caute, pp. 341, 549.

28. Caute, p. 85.

29. Siegfried Kracauer and Joseph Lyford, "A Duck Crosses Main Street," *New Republic*, 13 December 1948, pp. 13-15.

30. For studies of HUAC, Communism and Hollywood, see: *Thirty Years of Treason, Excerpts from Hearings Before the House Committee on Un-American Activities, 1938-1968*, Selected and edited by Eric Bentley (Viking, 1971); Stepfan Kanfer, *Journal of the Plague Years* (Atheneum, 1973); John Cogley, *Report on Blacklisting, Volume One, Movies* (The Fund for the Republic, 1956); Andrew Dowdy, *Movies are Better Than Ever* (Morrow, 1973), Chapter Two; and Caute, pp. 487-520, 557.

31. Charles Hingham, *Hollywood at Sunset* (Saturday Review Press, 1972), p. 50; Kanfer, pp. 60-61.

32. Kanfer, pp. 75-78.

33. Cogley, p. 23; Dowdy, p. 20.

34. Kanfer, pp. 77, 85.

35. For studies of the Hiss case, see: Allister Cook, *A Generation on Trial* (Knopf, 1950), which puts the trial in the context of anti-New Deal sentiment; Whittaker Chambers, *Witness* (Random House, 1952); John Cabot Smith, *Alger Hiss: The True Story* (Holt, Rinehard, Winston, 1976); and Allen Weinstein, *Perjury: The Hiss-Chambers Case* (Random House, 1979). Weinstein, especially, utilizing FBI documents released

under the Freedom of Information Act, declares Hiss guilty. But the FBI and other federal agencies involved refuse to release the most essential documents, so Weinstein's case, at best, is incomplete. Hiss continues to proclaim innocence and through the Freedom of Information Act is assembling documents to prove himself so.

36. Cook, *FBI*, p. 356.

37. Books on the Rosenbergs include a brief for their innocence written by their sons, Robert and Michael Meerpool, *We Are Your Sons, The Legacy of Julius and Ethel Rosenberg* (Houghton Mifflin, 1975); Alvin H. Goldstein, *The Unquiet Death of Julius and Ethel Rosenberg* (Lawrence Hill, 1975); Walter and Miriam Schneir, *The Rosenberg Case: Invitation to an Inquest* (Penguin, 1973); Louis Nizer, *The Implosion Conspiracy* (Doubleday, 1973); Jonathan Root, *The Betrayers* (Coward, McCann, 1963); and John Wexby, *The Judgement of Julius and Ethel Rosenberg* (Cameron and Kahn, 1955).

38. Acheson, p. 364.

39. Caute, p. 46.

40. Kanfer, pp. 101-103.

41. Kanfer, pp. 105-107.

42. Merle Miller, *The Judges and the Judged* (Doubleday, 1952), p. 92.

43. Miller, pp. 81-84.

44. Kanfer, pp. 186-187.

45. Aronson, pp. 22-23.

46. Aronson, pp. 97, 107.

47. *New York Times*, 24 February 1957, p. 1.

48. Letter to the Editor, *New York Times Sunday Magazine*, 2 February 1968.

Part Two—Prologue

1. David Riesman, *The Lonely Crowd* (Yale University Press, 1950), p. 11.

2. Joseph Bensman and Arthur J. Vidich, *The New American Society* (Quadrangle, 1971), pp. 125, 129.

Chapter Five

1. Vatter, p. 1.

2. *Life*, 25 November 1946, pp. 32-33.

3. Robert L. Heilbroner, *The Economic Transformation of America* (Harcourt, Brace, 1977), p. 215.

4. *Fortune*, October 1956, p. 128.

5. John Kenneth Galbraith, *The Affluent Society* (Houghton-Mifflin, 1958), p. 119.

6. *Life*, 5 January 1953, p. 16.

7. Galbraith, p. 190.

8. John Kenneth Galbraith, *The New Industrial Society* (Houghton-Mifflin, 1967), p. 229.

9. Vatter, pp. 6-7.

10. Vatter, pp. 166-167.

11. Galbraith, *New Industrial Society*, p. 311.
12. Seymour Melman, excerpt from "Our Depleted Society" in *The Economic Impact of the Cold War*, James J. Clayton, editor (Harcourt, Brace, 1970), p. 82.
13. Galbraith, *Affluent Society*, p. 255.
14. *New York Times*, 11, 12 April 1979.
15. Vance Packard, *The Hidden Persuaders* (McKay, 1957), p. 20.
16. Paul Baran and Paul Sweezy, *Monopoly Capital* (Monthly Review Press, 1966), p. 115.
17. Daniel Boorstin, *The Democratic Experience* (Random House, 1973), p. 426.
18. Galbraith, *Affluent Society*, p. 201.
19. *Fortune*, March 1956, p. 100.
20. William S. Dutton, *Adventures in Big Business* (Winston, 1958), p. 50.
21. Galbraith, *Affluent Society*, p. 158.
22. *Fortune*, May 1956, p. 134.
23. *Fortune*, September 1956, p. 40.
24. C. Wright Mills, "Two Styles of Social Science Research," in *Power, Politics and People*, Irving Louis Horowitz, editor (Ballentine 1953), p. 556.
25. Packard, pp. 36, 37, 59, 90.
26. Martin Mayer, *Madison Avenue U.S.A.* (Harper, 1956), pp. 238-240.
27. G. Allen Foster, *Advertising: Ancient Marketplace to Television* (Criterion, 1967), p. 195.
28. Galbraith, *New Industrial Society*, p. 208.
29. *The New Yorker* 10 October 1949, p. 91.
30. Irving Settel and William Lass, *A Pictorial History of Television* (Grosset & Dunlap, 1969).
31. Packard, p. 165.
32. Joseph Klapper, *The Effects of Mass Media* (The Free Press, 1960).
33. Packard, pp. 158-159.
34. Packard, p. 158.
35. Boorstin, p. 90.

Chapter Six
1. For a more thorough study of the monopoly trend in American capitalism, see Baran and Sweezy, *Monopoly Capital*, and Douglas F. Dowd, *The Twisted Dream* (Winthrop, 1974).
2. W. Lloyd Warner, *The Emergent American Society* (Yale University Press, 1967), p. 92.
3. A.A. Berle, *The American Economic Republic* (Harcourt, Brace, 1963), p. 149.
4. *Fortune*, April 1950, p. 99. For a history of the beer industry, see Stanley Baron, *Brewed in America* (Little Brown, 1962).
5. *Harvard Business Review*, March 1961, pp. 137-139.
6. *Business Week*, 3 July 1954, pp. 68-69.
7. *Business Week*, 27 February 1954, pp. 48-52; *Fortune*, November 1972, p. 103; Pete Hamill, "Beer Crisis," *New York Post*, 21 February

1973, p. 35.

8. Helen Leavitt, *Superhighway—Super Hoax* (Doubleday, 1970), p. 26.

9. Robert Snell, "Report on American Ground Transport," Subcommittee on Antitrust and Monopoly, Senate Judiciary Committee, 26 February 1974.

10. Snell, p. 38.

11. Snell, pp. 28-32.

12. Snell, p. 37.

13. Snell, p. 39.

14. Leavitt, p. 34.

15. George W. Hilton and John F. Dues, *The Electric Interurban Railways in America* (Stanford University Press, 1964); Mitchell Gordon, *Sick Cities* (Macmillan, 1963), pp. 14-15.

16. *New York Times*, 12 June 1973, p. 1.

17. Snell, pp. 40-41.

18. *New York Times, Sunday Week in Review*, 3 June 1973.

19. Lewis Mumford, *Interpretations and Forecasts* (Harcourt, Brace, 1973), p. 370.

20. *Time*, 13 May 1974, p. 47.

21. James J. Flink, *The Car Culture* (MIT Press, 1975), p. 176.

22. Packard, p. 129.

23. Quoted by General Leslie R. Groves in his report to Secretary of War Stimson concerning the Alamogorgo bomb test, 18 July 1945, Sherwin, p. 312.

24. Sherwin, pp. 298-299.

25. Nuel Pharr Davis, *Lawrence and Oppenheimer* (Simon and Schuster, 1968), p. 296.

26. Quoted by Ben Bradlee in "The Plight of Fallout City," *Boston Globe*, 14 June 1979, p. 2.

27. Tod Ensign and Michael Uhl, *G.I. Guinea Pigs* (Playboy Press, 1980), part I.

28. For an historical and analytical overview of the nuclear energy program, see Anna Gyorgy and friends, *No Nukes, Everyone's Guide to Nuclear Power* (South End Press, 1979).

29. *Life*, 18 March 1957, p. 65.

30. Wayne Andrews, *Architecture in America* (Atheneum, 1960), p. 157.

31. Cranston Jones, *Architecture Today and Tomorrow* (McGraw-Hill, 1961), p. 64.

32. Jones, pp. 121-123.

33. Lewis Mumford, "The Case Against Modern Architecture," *The Highway and the City* (Harcourt, Brace, 1963), p. 169.

Chapter Seven

1. *A New Life in the Country*, Report of the President's Task Force on Rural Development, March 1970, p. 29.

2. *New York Times, Sunday Business Section*, 25 November 1973.

3. Michael Harrington, *The Other America* (Macmillan, 1962), p. 135.

4. Lee Fryer, *The American Farmer* (Harper & Row), 1947), pp. 141-143; *Farmworkers in Rural America, 1971-1972*, Hearings Before the Sub-

committee on Migratory Labor, Committee on Labor and Public Welfare, U.S. Senate, pp. 786-1096.

5. Fryer, p. 2.
6. Frank Norris' novel *The Octopus* (1901) is the classic treatment of this situation.
7. Peter Barnes, "The Great Land Grab," *New Republic*, 5 June 1971.
8. *Life*, 5 February 1954, p. 27.
9. Fryer, pp. 6-7.
10. Fryer, p. 106.
11. Edward Higbee, *Farm and Farmers in the Urban Age* (Twentieth Century Fund, 1963), p. 14.
12. Higbee, pp. 105-106, 115-116.
13. Ezra Taft Benson, *Freedom to Farm* (Doubleday, 1960), pp. 199-200.
14. Vatter, p. 256.
15. *Fortune*, May 1956, p. 124.
16. C. Wright Mills, *White Collar* (Oxford University Press, 1956), p. 19.
17. Jim Hightower, *Hard Tomatoes, Hard Times* (Agribusiness Accountability Project, 1972), pp. 2-3.
18. Hightower, p. 85.
19. Hightower, p. 84-86.
20. Beatrice Trum Hunter, *Consumer Beware* (Simon and Schuster, 1971), pp. 115-116.
21. David Pimental, "Realities of the Pesticide Ban," *Environment Magazine*, March 1973.
22. *Encyclopedia Britannica Yearbook, 1948.*
23. Rachel Carson, *Silent Spring* (Little Brown). Excerpts from this best selling book were also serialized in *The New Yorker*.
24. Hunter, p. 19.
25. Towards the New, USDA Agriculture Information Bulletin, N341, 1970, pp. 7-8.
26. Perelman in *Farmworkers in Rural America*, p. 1110.
27. Frances Moore Lappe, *Diet for a Small Planet* (Ballentine, 1971), p. 18.
28. Michael Perelman in *Farmworkers in Rural America*, p. 1110; Lappe. 14-15.
29. Hunter, p. 304.
30. *New York Times*, 24 October 1974, p. 1.
31. Dick Simmons and Lee Fryer, *Earth Foods* (Follett, 1972), p. 38.
32. Simmons and Fryer, p. 39.
33. Hunter, pp. 34, 37; Simmons and Fryer, p. 41.

Chapter Eight
1. *Life*, 17 December 1945, p. 27.
2. *Fortune*, August 1947. p. 61.
3. *Life*, 21 October 1946, p. 126.
4. James Q. Wilson, *The Metropolitan Enigma* (Harvard University Press, 1968), pp. 165-167.
5. Harrington, p. 65.

6. Wilson, p. 139.
7. Tanzer, *Sick Society*, pp. 99-100.
8. Nathan Strauss, *Two-Thirds of a Nation* (Knopf, 1952), p. 195.
9. Stanley Aronowitz, *False Promises*, (McGraw-Hill, 1973), p. 274.
10. Martin Pawley, *Architecture vs. Housing* (Praeger, 1971), p. 78.
11. Martin Anderson, *The Federal Bulldozer* (MIT Press, 1964), pp. 16-19.
12. Jane Jacobs, *The Death and Life of Great American Cities* (Random House, 1961), p. 310.
13. Jacobs, p. 83.
14. Lewis Mumford, *The Urban Prospect* (Harcourt, Brace, 1962), p. 184.
15. Jacobs, p. 211.
16. Paul Goodman, *Growing Up Absurd* (Vintage, 1960), p. 74.
17. Jacobs, pp. 34-37.
18. Jacobs, p. 113.
19. Anderson, pp. 68-69.
20. Jacobs, p. 307.
21. Oscar Handlin, *The Newcomers* (Harvard University Press, 1959), pp. 86-94.
22. Anderson, pp. 7-8.
23. Strauss, p. 153.
24. Jacobs, pp. 277-278.
25. Jacobs, p. 309.
26. Jacobs, pp. 8-11, 295-297.
27. *The Village Voice Reader*, Daniel Wolf and Edwin Fancher, editors (Grove Press, 1963), p. 185.
28. John Gunther, *Inside U.S.A.* (Harper, 1947), p. 542.
29. *Life*, 21 October 1946, p. 126.
30. *Life*, 6 May 1946, p. 83.
31. Martin Meyerson, Barbara Terrett and William L.C. Wheaton, *Housing, People and Cities* (McGraw-Hill, 1962), p. 34.
32. *Wall Street Journal* 16 August 1973, p. 1.
33. *Life*, 19 December 1955, p. 7.
34. William M. Dobriner, *Class in Suburbia* (Prentice-Hall, 1963), pp. 106-107.
35. William H. Whyte, *The Organization Man* (Anchor, 1957), p. 3.
36. Whyte, p. 10.
37. Whyte, p. 331.
38. Dobriner, p. 6.
39. *New York Times*, 25 March 1955, p. 32.
40. *New York Times*, 25 March 1955, p. 32.

Chapter Nine
1. Vatter, p. 69.
2. Robert Lekachman, *The Age of Keynes* (Random House, 1966), p. 190.
3. Harrington, pp. 2-6.
4. Richard Parker, *The Myth of the Middle Class* (Harper Colophone, p. 68.
5. Parker, p. x.

6. *Fortune*, December 1956, p. 130.

7. Aronowitz, pp. 193-196.

8. Lynn Goldfarb with Julie Brody and Nancy Wiegerman (The Woman's Project), *Separated and Unequal: Discrimination Against Women After World War II* (New England Free Press, 1972), pp. 2, 12.

9. Joel Seidman, *American Labor From Defense to Reconversion* (University of Chicago Press, 1953), pp. 154-155.

10. William H. Chafe, *The American Woman* (Oxford University Press, p. 178.

11. Chafe, p. 176.

12. Woman's Work Project, p. 21; Rosalyn Baxendall, Linda Gordon and Susan Reverby, *America's Working Women* (Vintage, 1976), p. 309.

13. Vatter, pp. 229-231.

14. Seidman, p. 220.

15. Daniel Bell, "The Subversion of Collective Bargaining," *Commentary*, March 1960, pp. 699-701, (reprinted by New England Free Press).

16. Bell, p. 701.

17. Parker, p. 13.

18. *Fortune*, November 1946, pp. 135-139.

19. Murray Kempton, *America Comes of Middle Age* (Viking, 1962), pp. 39-40.

20. *Fortune*, November 1946, p. 165.

21. The discussion of the degradation of work and the appropriation by management of the workers' knowledge and skill follows that of Harry Braverman, *Labor and Monopoly Capital* (Monthly Review Press, 1975); discussion on the engineering profession follows that of David Noble, *America by Design* (Knopf, 1977).

22. Aronowitz, p. 248.

23. Aronowitz, p. 131.

Chapter Ten

1. Robin M. Williams, *American Society: A Sociological Interpretation* (Knopf, 1960), p. 39.

2. Williams, p. 52.

3. *McCalls Magazine*, May 1954.

4. Betty Friedan, *The Feminine Mystique* (Norton, 1963), p. 41.

5. Norman Podhoretz, "The Father on the Hearth," in *Commentary*, December 1953, pp. 534-540.

6. Marynia F. Farnham and Ferdinand Lundberg, *Modern Women: The Lost Sex* (Harper, 1947), pp. 237, 245, 166.

7. *Atlantic Monthly*, April 1953, p. 450; *Nation*, 21 February 1953, p. 155.

8. *Saturday Review*, 21 February 1953, p. 27.

9. Frank Buxton and Bill Owen, *The Big Broadcast, 1920-1950* (Viking Press, 1966-1972).

10. Friedan, pp. 31-33, 45, 47.

11. Friedan, p. 12.

12. Friedan, p. 143.

13. *Life*, 24 December 1956, p. 23.

14. *Life*, 24 December 1956, p. 49.
15. Friedan, p. 53.
16. Friedan, p. 69.
17. Frank Goble, *The Third Force* (Grossman, 1970), Pocket Book edition, p. 4.
18. Goble, p. 6.
19. Abraham Maslow, *Toward A Psychology of Being* (D. Van Nostrend, 1962, 1968), Insight edition, chapter one.
20. Friedan, p. 7.
21. *Newsweek*, 7 March 1960, pp. 57-58.
22. Friedan, p. 59.

Chapter Eleven

1. *Life*, 11 November 1945, p. 29.
2. Benjamin Fine, *1,000,000 Delinquents* (World, 1955), p. 26; *Nation*, 5 June 1954, pp. 482-484.
3. Harrison Salisbury, *The Shook-Up Generation* (Harper & Row, 1958), pp. 15-19.
4. Fine, p. 27.
5. Fine, pp. 19-25.
6. *Readers Digest*, May 1954, pp. 24-93.
7. *U.S. News and World Report*, 17 September 1954, pp.80-84.
8. *New York Times Sunday Magazine*, 12 September 1954, p. 11.
9. Salisbury, p. 21.
10. Paul Goodman, *Growing Up Absurd* (Vintage, 1960), p. xvi.
11. Claude Brown, *Manchild in the Promised Land* (Macmillan, 1965), p. 147.
12. Brown, pp. 179-180.
13. Andrew Dowdy, *Movies Are Better Than Ever* (Morrow, 1973), p. 68.
14. Enid A. Haupt, *The Seventeen Book of Young Living* (Popular Library, 1957), p. 142.
15. Evelyn Millis Duvall, *Family Living* (Macmillan, 1955), p. 32.
16. Haupt, pp. 13, 41, 50.
17. Gay Head, *Boy Dates Girl* (Scholastic, 1955), p. 26.

Part Three-Prologue

1. Ann Charters, *Kerouac: A Biography* (Straight Arrow, 1973), pp. 38-63.
2. Charters, p.53.
3. Arnold Shaw, *The Street That Never Slept* (Coward, McCann, 1971), pp. 267-268.
4. For the bopster's attitudes towards the Second World War, see: Ross Russell, *The Low Life and Hard Times of Charlie Parker* (Charterhouse, 1973), p. 139; Dizzy Gillespie with Al Fraser, *To Be, or not...to Bop* (Doubleday, 1979), pp. 119-120; also Babs Gonsalves, *I Paid My Dues* (Lancer paperback, 1967). Harry "the hipster" Gibson, the jester of the bop scene during the war years, noted for his song "Who Put the

Benzedrine in Mrs. Murphy's Ovaltine?" also sang "Frantic Ferdinand the 4-F Freak," an approving ditty about a hipster draft dodger.
5. Wolf and Fancher, p. 49; Mailer, "The White Negro," in *Advertisements for Myself* (Putnam, 1959), pp. 337-358. Quote cited by Norman Podhoretz, "Know Nothing Bohemians," *Partisan Review*, Spring 1958, reprinted in *Doings and Undoings* (Noonday Press, 1964), p. 156.
6. Cassady is the hero of Kerouac's *On the Road* (Viking, 1957); John Clellon Holmes also captures his charismatic intensity and his impact on Kerouac's circle in the novel *GO*, first published in 1952 and reprinted in 1977 by Paul P. Appel. Tom Wolfe's *The Electric Kool-Aid Test* (Farrar, Straud & Giroux, 1968) captures Cassady in 1966 and 1967 with Ken Kesey as a Merrie Prankster.
7. Kurt Vonnegut, Jr,. *Cat's Cradle* (Holt, Rinehart & Winston, 1963), Dell paperback, pp. 12-14.
8. The best studies of the beats are: Bruce Cook, *The Beat Generation* (Scribner, 1971) and Dennie McNally, *Jack Kerouac, the Beat Generation, and America* (Random House, 1979).

Chapter Twelve
1. Gordon Ball, editor, *Allen Verbatim* (McGraw-Hill, 1974), p. 144.
2. Donald M. Allen, editor, *The New American Poetry* (Grove, 1060), p. 387.
3. Ball, p. 152.
4. Kenneth Rexroth, *American Poetry in the Twentieth Century* (Herder & Herder, 1971), p. 170.
5. Allen, p. 414.
6. Michael Harrington, *Fragments of a Century* (Saturday Review Press, 1974), p. 33.
7. Harrington, *Fragments*, p. 47.
8. Rexroth, p. 141.
9. Charters, p. 229.
10. Jack Kerouac, *The Dharma Bums* (Viking, 1958) NAL edition, p. 10.
11. Kerouac's description in *Dharma Bums*, p. 13; Rexroth's comment in Bruce Cook, pp. 63-65.
12. *Life*, 30 November 1959, pp. 115-116.
13. Kerouac, *On the Road*, p. 21.
14. Gary Snyder, *Earth Household* (New Directions, 1969), p. 111.
15. *Life*, 30 November 1959, pp. 115-116.
16. John F. Bridge, "Keats and the Beats," *Wall Street Journal*, 2 October 1958.
17. *Saturday Review of Literature*, 6 February 1960, p. 42.
18. Kenneth Rexroth, "The Art of the Beat Generation," in *The Alternative Society* (Herder, Herder, 1970), p. 2.

Chapter Thirteen
1. Alex Wilder, *American Popular Song: The Great Innovators* (Oxford University Press, 1972) is the definitive study of the music of the great pop composers. No one has yet celebrated, in book form, the delicacy and

beauty of the great pop lyrics. Nor has anyone tackled the politics of popular music and its sexism.

2. Charlie Gillet, *The Sound of the City* (Dell paperback, 1972), p. 15.
3. Bill C. Malone, *Country Music USA* (Texas Press, 1975), pp. 213, 216, 231-234.
4. *Encyclopedia Brittanica Book of the Year, 1956*, p. 470.
5. Arnold Passman, *The Deejays* (Macmillan, 1971), p. 190.
6. Mike Jahn, *Rock* (Quadrangle, 1973), p. 40.
7. Gillett, p. 52.
8. Henry Pleasants, *The Great American Popular Singers* (Simon & Schuster, 1977), p. 209.
9. *Life*, 27 August 1956, p. 101.
10. *Life*, 27 August 1956, p. 108.
11. Passman, p. 237.
12. *Time*, 1 October 1956, p. 71.
13. *Inside MAD* (Ballentine paperback, 1953), pp. 47-48.
14. *Time*, 13 July 1959, p. 42.
15. Maslow, pp. 7-8.

Chapter Fourteen

1. Marty Jezer, "50 Years of Nonviolent Resistance," text of War Resisters League 1973 peace calendar, reprinted in *The Power of the People: Active Nonviolence in the United States*, Robert Cooney and Helen Michaelowski, editors (Peace Press, 1977), p. 108.
2. *Life*, 20 August 1945, p. 32.
3. Wittner, p. 132.
4. Wittner, p. 177.
5. Niccolo Tucci, "Common Sense," in *Politics*, July 1945, p. 196.
6. Dwight Macdonald, *Memoirs of a Revolutionist* (Farrar, Straus and Cudahy, 1957) is a collection of the author's essays from *Politics*.
7. *Politics*, June 1945, p. 165.
8. Macdonald, *Politics*, April 1946, p. 100.
9. Macdonald, *Politics*, March 1945, p. 95.
10. *Politics*, December 1946, p. 401.
11. Mills, *White Collar*, p. 147.
12. *Partisan Review*, September-October 1952, p. 582.
13. David Tyack, *Nobody Knows: Black Americans in the Twentieth Century* (Macmillan, 1969), pp. 69-70.
14. *August Meier and Elliot Rudwick, CORE: A Study in the Civil Rights Movement, 1942-1968* (Oxford University Press, 1973), pp. 33-40, 54, 61.
15. Louis Lomax, *The Negro Revolt* (Harper & Row, 1962), p. 75.
16. Tyack, p. 76.
17. Commager, *Documents*, p. 663.
18. John Hope Franklin, *Black Americans* (Time-Life, 1970), p. 146.
19. Martin Luther King, *Stride Towards Freedom* (Harper & Row, 1958), p. 54.
20. King, p. 102.
21. Meier and Rudwick, p. 97.

22. *Liberation*, March 1956 (Volume 1, Number 1), pp. 3-6.

23. For the story of the Ban-the Bomb Movement see Jezer, Wittner, and Nat Hentoff, *Peace Agitator, The Story of A.J. Muste* (Macmillan, 1963).

24. Harrington, *Fragments*, pp. 60-61.

25. *Nation*, 9 March 1957, pp. 199-206.

26. *Nation*, 16 May 1959, p. 444.

27. Lomax, pp. 122-123; Meier and Rudwick, p. 101; Howard Zinn, *The New Abolitionists* (Beacon, 1964), pp. 16-23.

28. Howard Zinn, *Postwar America, 1945-1971* (Bobbs-Merrill, 1973), p. 204.

29. Zinn, *New Abolitionists*, p. 17.

30. A good account of the civil rights movement is Howell Raines, *My Soul is Rested* (Putnam, 1977).

31. Chorus of popular civil rights song, sung during the early 1960s at civil rights rallies and demonstrations throughout the country.